Broken Trust

ROSE MARIE YOUNG

BROKEN TRUST - Empowering Stories of Healing for Relationships, Finances & Wellness

Compiled by Rose Marie Young

LWL PUBLISHING HOUSE
16 Rutherford Road South,
Brampton, ON L6W 3J1
Email: lwlclienthelp@gmail.com
Website: www.lwlpublishinghouse.com

Book Layout © 2020 LWL PUBLISHING HOUSE

BROKEN TRUST - Empowering Stories of Healing for Relationships, Finances & Wellness

Anita Sechesky – Living Without Limitations Inc.
ISBN 978-1-988867-66-3

Book Cover Design: N. Sechesky
Inside Layout: LWL PUBLISHING HOUSE Editorial Team

Table of Contents

Section One

RELATIONSHIPS

Section Two

FINANCES

Section Three

WELLNESS

Legal Disclaimer

BROKEN TRUST - Empowering Stories of Healing for Relationships, Finances & Wellness does not substitute any form of professional counsel such as a Psychologist, Physician, Life Coach, Counselor or Holistic Practitioner. The contents and information provided does not constitute professional or legal advice in any way, shape, or form.

All chapters and co-author bios are written at the discretion of and with the full accountability of each author. The Publisher, Anita Sechesky, LWL PUBLISHING HOUSE, or Anita Sechesky – Living Without Limitations Inc. is not liable or responsible for any of the specific details, descriptions of people, places or things, personal interpretations, stories and experiences contained within. The Publisher is not liable for any misrepresentations, false or unknown statements, actions, or judgments made by each author in this book, who are responsible for their own material and have shared their information in good faith to encourage others.

Any decisions you make, and the outcomes thereof are entirely your own doing. Under no circumstances can you hold the Publisher, Anita Sechesky, LWL PUBLISHING HOUSE, or Anita Sechesky – Living Without Limitations Inc. liable for any actions that you take.

You agree not to hold the Publisher, Anita Sechesky, LWL PUBLISHING HOUSE, or Anita Sechesky – Living Without Limitations Inc. liable for any loss or expense incurred by you, as a result of materials, advice, coaching or mentoring offered within.

The information offered in this book is intended to be general information with respect to general life issues. Information is offered in good faith; however, you are under no obligation to use this information.

Nothing contained in this book shall be considered legal, financial, or actuarial advice.

The Publisher or LWL PUBLISHING HOUSE assumes no liability or responsibility to actual events or stories contained within.

The advice contained herein is not meant to replace the Professional role of a Certified Professional Coach, Psychologist, Counselor, Holistic Practitioner, or any medical advice. Please consult with a doctor or family physician.

Dedication

I would like to dedicate this book to everyone dealing with brokenness, especially with what's going on in our world today. There is always hope and healing for you. I trust that you will find inspiration within these pages to encourage and strengthen you.

Rose Marie Young

Foreword

BROKEN TRUST – Empowering Stories of Healing for Relationship, Finance & Wellness was birthed out of the vision of complete healing for Rose Marie Young. As her Publisher, I have been working with Rose to develop the structure of this incredible book. Inside these pages, you will find a variety of experiences from individuals from all walks of life, ages, and backgrounds. Rose has managed to connect with some of the most incredible people who have been to the brink of emotional limitations only to find their strength and willpower to reset their lives into a place of empowerment.

I can say that this leadership experience for Rose has also empowered her and her beliefs in the fact that despite whatever one may walk through they can also be healed.

Speaking from a place of someone who is in healthcare for over twenty-five years coaching and mentoring individuals who are searching for ways to become more confident in themselves, I strongly believe this book will bring the needed inspiration.

From my experiences, I can honestly say that not everyone you meet in life will admit they have felt broken or destroyed emotionally. It is a very sensitive topic and one that is tread upon with caution in new relations or sometimes it can be the very thing that draws people closer together. Rose has carefully chosen her co-authors based on their life experiences and how she wanted the impact of this book to shape and inspire others. The stories inside this book will give you a hope to continue on your journey knowing that just because things have happened, it does not mean you do not deserve another chance at happiness. Congratulations to the Compiler, Rose Marie Young, and her team of co-authors! I am so proud of you for sharing your stories to inspire, motivate, and encourage others.

This book should be recommended for anyone seeking solutions to coping with their stresses of daily living, anyone diagnosed with a challenging illness, confusion of where they fit into this huge and sometimes overwhelming world of lost trust and brokenness.

Thank you, Rose and co-authors. It has been a pleasure to work with you on this anthology and to see your vision come to life.

To your writing success!

Anita Sechesky

RN, ICF-Certified Professional Coach, Founder, Owner, CEO, Publisher & E.I.C. at LWL PUBLISHING HOUSE, #1 Best-Selling Author, Book Writing Coach, Ghost Writer, Keynote Speaker, Workshop & Conference Host, and the INSPIRED TO WRITE Podcast Host.

Anita is the author of multiple Best-Selling books in the Faith, Inspirational Self-Healing, and positive psychology genres. She has successfully published over 580 authors, and also writes and publishes children's literature as well. Anita is a Motivational Keynote Speaker and Mentor, enjoys hosting INSPIRED TO WRITE workshops, facilitates Masterclasses on Emotional Healing, and speaks at events that focus on living your best life possible. She has worked in many Emergency Rooms and health care facilities all over Ontario and has witnessed how one's emotional well-being can impact the human spirit, health and wellness, relationships, and overall potential. It is Anita's greatest desire to promote healing of not only the body, but also the mind and spirit of each man, woman, and child through her vision.

Email: **lwlclienthelp@gmail.com**

Website: **www.lwlpublishinghouse.com**

Facebook Business Page: **LWL PUBLISHING HOUSE**

Facebook Business Page: **Living Without Limitations in Print**

Facebook Private Group: **2020 INSPIRED ACTION - PLAN TO SUCCEED!**

YouTube: **Anita Sechesky - Living Without Limitations Inc.**

Soundcloud: **INSPIRED TO WRITE Podcast**

Acknowledgments

I would like to acknowledge my mother, Daphne James, who catapulted me to believe in myself and to never give up on my dreams. Mom, you instilled in me that the meaning of failure is not trying. You have also taught me that experience will always be the best teacher and through these experiences, I will always be able to learn and have great values. Through your own brokenness, you demonstrated to me about forgiveness, and most of all, you have shown me how to love. Thank you for teaching me manners and respect. Thank you for all your encouragement and inspiration for me to establish and maintain a meaningful life.

Many thanks to my children, JJ, Nikkila, and Sherika, for standing by me and believing in my dreams. To you, I say I will always love and appreciate you. You are my world. You bring me great joy and give purpose and meaning to my life.

I would like to recognize Anita Sechesky, Steve Sechesky, and the entire LWL Publishing House company and Media Support Team for their exceptionally professional work and their continuous support during the process of this project. Thank you, Nathaniel, for putting the effort and time into creating such a beautiful cover design for this book. Thanks, everyone for a job well done.

I am especially thankful to Anita for her great enhancement of this anthology. Her compassion and encouragement during the process of bringing my vision to life are very much appreciated. Anita, I see you not only as my publisher but also as my soul sister and my friend. Thank you for all your kindness, patience, and guidance.

Many thanks to all my other soul sisters in *Soul Sister Letters*, Koreen, Dominique, and Pastor Pat. Thank you for your inspirational words and letters of encouragement, as well as all your prayers.

To my amazing friend, Ronna Ebanks. Thank you for the extra ears and for giving me a shoulder to lean on when I needed it the most. Thank you for standing by me during the bad times and for cheering me on during the good times and in all my success. You are a beautiful soul with a beauty that radiates inside out. You are what a true friend looks like.

I would also like to thank my friend and my lovely soul sister, Althea Karen Brown, for her kindness and all her encouragement. I will always remember our trip to the Big Apple. Thank you for helping me to break out of my shell and for helping me to regain my self-confidence when I was struggling to find myself and all the "ways" to continue pushing forward.

To my beautiful friend, Miss T. Thank you for being the wonderful and awesome person you are. Thank you for encouraging me to write my story. I feel extremely blessed to have met you. You have always helped me to see the brighter side of things. Thank you for introducing my publisher to me and thank you for introducing my chiropractor. You are a wonderful person who will always be a part of my becoming and healing story.

To all the doctors and specialists who have spent many hours, days, and years helping me to recover from the brokenness of my injuries. I thank you for everything you have done contributing to my physical healing as well as my emotional healing. Special thanks especially to my chiropractor. I will be forever grateful to you for being so patient and kind. Thank you for taking the time to not only assisting me with my wellness but also listening and for giving me good medical advice.

Thank you to all my co-authors for your support and respect. I have formed a beautiful and warm connection with each of you which I appreciate and will cherish for a lifetime.

I am also very thankful to everyone else who stood by me and have supported me on this journey. Your kindness will never be forgotten.

And to all my readers, I acknowledge you. and I hope that the words on these following pages will help you in your becoming as you emerge into your own fundamentally unique self. May they bring you hope and peace in your hearts.

Above all, my greatest gratitude I give to GOD, my heavenly father who has given me wisdom, instilled this vision within me, and has blessed me with His guidance to see it become born. I am overwhelmed with gratitude because He has also answered my prayers by blessing this anthology project with the right, qualified, and selfless co-authors who were willing to pay it forward by sharing their testimonies of becoming. I am very blessed to have them join me in sharing so many different perspectives of how we can all help others who are dealing with brokenness around the world. To God, I give all the praise and all the honor and glory.

Rose Marie Young is a #1 Best-Selling Author in the KINDLE version of her anthology BROKEN TRUST: Stories on Relationships, Finances & Wellness. She is also a Best-Selling co-author in Soul Sister Letters – Let's Talk About Love, Faith, Abundance & Divine Purpose. Additionally, Rose Marie is an Entrepreneur, a Mindfulness and Life Empowerment Coach, a Registered Cardiology Tech., and a Personal Support Worker. She has been featured in the inaugural edition of LWL Lifestyle magazine as an upcoming Compiler. Rose is also writing her solo book along with three new anthologies on Happiness, Money, and Wellness and desires to help others feel and become empowered in all areas of their lives.

Facebook: Rose Young

Instagram: rose.marie.young

Email: rmarie1695@gmail.com

LinkedIn: Rose Young

Email: BTConsultant.123@gmail.com

Broken Trust

Introduction

This one-of-a-kind self-healing anthology is a celebration of the testimonies from many different amazing authors who have shared in collaboration to help empower others.

> I would like to express my gratification to all of those wonderful co-authors who have shown great dedication and commitment to the completion of this book. Most importantly, I am very appreciative of their vulnerability and courage to write the stories which they have willingly shared on these pages in hopes of enlightening others. To each of them, I say thank you for believing in my vision. Thank you for respecting my leadership as your compiler and for also respecting the guidance from LWL PUBLISHING HOUSE's publisher and staff, who have greatly contributed to having this project to come together successfully. Thank you everyone for such a great team. It was amazing working with each of you. Thank you for your insights and for being yourselves. You are awesome!!

God has blessed us and positioned each of us to release our stories so that we can help others to be blessed.

It is with great pleasure that I introduce this wonderful self-healing anthology of real-life stories. Although each chapter is unique and different, they were purposely written to encourage, inspire, and bring healing to those who have been affected by mistrust. These stories will not only help those who are searching for inner strength and inner peace, but they will also help others who have been struggling to find their inner voice and to restore and overcome their brokenness in this world.

Broken trust can affect anyone regardless of who we are and where we are from. It can alter our personalities and change our focus. It can cause us to enter a state of lowliness and unhappiness within ourselves. It can also cause us to restrain ourselves from connecting with others. Overall, it can cause significant damage to our health and our well-being. As you begin your healing journey from being a victim of illness, betrayal, disappointment, and other unjustified distrust to a place of consciousness and awareness, you can keep in mind that there is hope for having a great come back from all those disappointments. This book can be the bridge that mends the trust between yourselves and others. It will be the companion that you can reference for support and draw strength from all the amazing heartfelt stories that live inside its pages.

There are three main categories comprising this book: Relationship, Financial, and Wellness. Each of the chapters covers different mistrust stories along these three themes. Within each chapter, you will also find different applications to empower you. One might have at some point been able to trust, but somehow for reasons beyond his or her control became a victim who has been scarred from severe brokenness. Letting go can be extremely hard. Reliving the regression and hurt of that brokenness can have many damaging effects on one's health and can cause major complications. By revisiting the past over and over, the scars left behind can get progressively deeper causing one to become increasingly lost within self-neglect and unavailability.

For each person, the healing process will most likely be different. The key is to have the right mindset. Attitude is very important as well as persistence. It's all about taking action. Give yourself permission and time to heal and remember that not everything and everyone is going to be the same. It's okay to ask for help. Everyone goes through something – don't be ashamed. Although you may be feeling overwhelmed and isolated while facing the challenges and trials, remember that you are never alone.

There are many different ways by which lives can be affected, and even destroyed, by broken trust – from an experience of personal or business relationship breakdown to an emotional or personal loss and loss of self-valve. It can also be through an experience of neglect, online or personal bullying, physical, spiritual, sexual, mental, or financial abuse. Broken trust can even result from misunderstandings or miscommunications (a disability or illness in which case one may not be fully educated, for example). I believe that trust is the strongest link we have between ourselves, the universe, and each other. Once that link has been broken, everything else fails to connect. For that reason, it can be very difficult to learn to trust again.

Based on my personal life experiences and from my many years working in the health field as a Cardiology Technologist and as a healthcare worker, I have witnessed different aspects of broken trust. Some of the many results from its effects include anxiety, hopelessness, PTSD, loss of confidence, guilt, fear, and many more. When someone has lost the ability to trust, it can be very crippling. Not only does it affect us emotionally, but also psychologically as well as spiritually. As I have witnessed numerous types and levels of mistrust, I can honestly say that there is an immediate awareness of healing that is needed in those lives affected. Self-healing from broken trust means that one's primary focus should be on self-care and self-improvement. Without healing, an individual can become lost subconsciously within oneself. Over time, it can lead to more serious problems through self-neglect, unavailability, and total depression. Without proper healing, one will be living and walking constantly in total darkness of distrust.

As this anthology's compiler, I felt it was necessary to create this book with an expression of different aspects of broken trust from a diverse collection of voices. I also felt that it was my responsibility as a survivor to help others who are going through such turmoil and clinging on to the pain and suffering they have endured. Additionally, this book will help others who like me have experienced a hard time reaching out for help when it feels as if no one can be trusted. At times, one might feel uncomfortable talking about their issues and not knowing who to confide in can be hard. Having a book with different voices of encouragement would have helped my healing faster when I was going through my share of turmoil. As the compiler and as mentioned, a survivor, it is also my main intention to help you shift your focus to a place of love and healing. As you love yourself, you will also realize that trust is very important in your life. Learning to trust ourselves and others can make a big difference in how we see ourselves and how we view the world around us. Despite all the negativity you may have faced, never leave yourself behind. The chapters within this book will help support you not only on your physical self-healing, but also on your spiritual, emotional, and social healing.

With the proper tools, knowledge, and help from my co-authors and me, you will be able to begin letting go of the pain and the hurt. It is a wonderful feeling to be able to bring this vision of self -healing to life and to share it with you.

Many people have trust issues based on the unknown fear of the "What ifs." They become anxious about losing control and becoming vulnerable. Yes, broken trust can cause spiritual, physical, mental, and emotional damages to our lives. However, there is healing. All of my co-authors and I have contributed our personal stories to help encourage you and to help you understand that we too have been where you are. We understand. We had all committed ourselves to bring this vision of self-healing to everyone who needs support.

This book was written with respect and love to honor you for all you have endured. Its purpose is to enlighten you and to bring awareness, knowledge, and different tools of inspiration to help you heal and to find your voice. Both my Coauthors and I have had to overcome the darker side of misunderstanding, and the darker side of mistrust. We have written these stories to help you raise your vibration to a more positive and higher level. It's our hope for you to step out of the darkness and move forward into a place of light and toward a brighter future.

This anthology has also been created to help mend and restore all those broken relationships, restore financial stability, and security as well as restore self-esteem and independence. Through my personal experience and the experiences of all the other co-authors, I trust that each of these chapters will bring hope and comfort to you and anyone who has ever endured such experiences. I also believe that you will be encouraged and empowered with a mindset by which you can become stronger and more confident to restore and regain your value with a refreshed new and positive energy. As the compiler of these wonderful stories, It is also my wish that after reading this book, you will be able to find the beauty in your uniqueness as you also become empowered and become unbroken by growing from your own experiences. Your stories, like others, carry a great value that can help others lift their spirits and their vibrations to a much lighter level. Your aspirations don't have to be what others want them to be. You are you. Your illness, your losses, nor your disability doesn't define who you are. It is also my desire that you will find peace and become enriched from each story. TRUST that you are worth it to be Blessed, to be Happy, and to be Empowered.

Love, Light, and Peace to you

Rose Marie Young

Section One

RELATIONSHIPS

Our strength lies within our ability to move beyond our pain.

Rose Marie Young

Evolution Through Broken Relationships

WRITTEN BY: ROSE MARIE YOUNG

*I*t is always in our best interest to first know ourselves in order to formulate a healthy and well meaningful relationship with others, especially those who are not within our immediate family dynamics. However, too often we are drawn to unhealthy relationships in which we become entangled and webbed. We become attracted to the wrong type of people who intentionally or unintentionally cause us unnecessary stress and pain.

Broken trust in any relationship can affect our minds, our bodies, as well as our souls. It can be very damaging to our self-esteem and our overall health and well-being.

Thinking back in time, I realize that my brokenness in my relationships was simply because of my lack of understanding and unawareness of "my true self" and what I truly wanted for me. The problem was that I always tried to please everyone and was always striving to make sure everyone was happy regardless of how I was feeling. I was definitely not living my life to please myself. Like most of us do to some extent, I tried to mimic what society wanted, what others expected of me, and what they considered to be a GOOD relationship. However, I really needed to examine my intuition of what my inner soul was trying to tell me.

I needed new perspectives in my life. Needless to say, I was unable to become unbroken until I was able to make that realization.

I have no idea of the exact time when it happened but after several years of being broken, I woke up! I then began to realize that some people can be double-minded and, because of that, also unstable. I also realized that the relationship I was involved in was one-sided and unbalanced – I was in the relationship by myself. I felt disappointed, ashamed, and overwhelmingly depressed. However, I did not want to sacrifice my happiness nor my health. It was hard for me to believe that someone who I considered to be very close and one of my best friends, or so I thought, could have broken my trust so badly. To my disappointment, my friendship was taken for granted and all my kindness was taken for weakness. Not only that but after years of investing my time and positive energy, how could someone discard such an amazing relationship and our friendship? In my opinion, it seemed as if, to this person, everything that we had been through was rather meaningless and our relationship meant absolutely nothing. This was not what I expected. So, I decided to walk away. However, when I did, I took some things with me that I was unable to shake for a while: the Hate, the Shame, and the Brokenness. Even though I left that relationship behind, I was incapable of moving on. I was stressed and unhappy because of the heavy burden I was carrying around from all of that brokenness. It was very challenging for me to explore other positive adventures or even express my feelings to anyone. My soul needed healing before I could venture into any new directions. With my knees to the floor at my bedside, I turned to the only being I knew I could trust in that moment and time of my life. I turned to God. Yes, at some point I realized that everything was out of my control and only God was able to take control of the situation. And so, I prayed to Him to forgive me for being so unfair to myself and for being so blinded by such an unfamiliar spirit. I prayed because I was drowning in self-pity and could not help myself. I knew that building complete trust with God was extremely important for my survival and that deep down, He would not blame me for allowing myself to be in the situation in which I was broken. I also knew in my heart that He would answer my prayers if I asked Him sincerely. His answer to me was that although He forgave me, I needed to forgive myself, and most of all I needed to forgive that particular person as well as everyone else who had wronged me. And so,

I did. Now, here I am in a place where I can finally laugh again, and my mind feels content because I choose to forgive. I forgave to have peace in my mind and my spirit. I forgave because I needed healing for me to learn to trust again. Yes, it is a good thing to forgive, but because we are all human, we will at times remember. Do not be distracted by the negative feelings or memories of what once was. Focus on your becoming. Center your attention on a brighter future that lies ahead. The past is no longer relevant. Know what you want and what's important to you, and as you move forward, navigate your mind to a feeling of success and happiness.

Every day, each of us is faced with many different challenges in our lives and our relationships with others. However, we have to learn that we are as important as the next person. It is essential to know that you have a voice and you have choices. It is also vital to be mindful of the choices that you make because everything that we do will, at some point, affect someone else's life. Stay true to yourselves.

Whatever you are going through during your time of brokenness, just know that you are not alone. With our ever-changing world and these times of uncertainty, so many relationships have been challenged. Your relationships will most likely be tested at times. Regardless if it is a working relationship or a personal connection, be strong and focus on the positive. It is extremely important to connect and align yourself with people who you can trust. As mentioned, stay true to yourself always. Do something that makes you happy and connect with others that brings you joy. Never let anyone steal your joy. Don't ever give up on yourself.

Learn to forgive. Before I was able to do that, I was weighted down from the stress and pain caused by culprits of the darker side of my yesterdays. Now I can move forward, focusing on a more positive future.

Although you have been hurt, you do not have to base your entire life on the heartache and the bad experiences. Instead, apply the lessons from these events to learn, grow, and strengthen your mind. Use them as tools to become motivated and empowered. Remember that God has a Divine purpose for each of us and I do believe that as you are faced with all the uncertainty in your relationships and your life, you will one day discover your purpose. Not only will you find purpose, but you will be able to connect in relationships that are aligned with your true self, discover happiness, and eventually you'll be able to live a more meaningful life doing what you love while relating to and working with others who love, respect, and appreciate you for you.

By positioning yourself to become empowered from your brokenness, you will be able to make a significant difference in someone else's life. I know from experience that there can be many distractions from the external environment which can sometimes interfere with our peace and spirit which is our inner environment. However, if you focus on new and positive insights and enable yourself to direct your attention on new directions, you will be able to overcome those distractions, free your mind, and become unbroken from toxic relationships.

As I write this chapter, I can only imagine the overwhelming increase of all the broken relationships between so many families, employees and employers, and friends. There is so much brokenness because of Covid-19. Emotions as well as health and well-being are affected. However, in times like these, we need to be strong for each other. Remember that we are all stronger together. Be encouraging and trust in God because, with Him, all things are possible. Think passionately about the future in a positive way.

In light of everything, whether you choose to stay in a relationship or not, be sure that the choice you are making is wise and, most importantly, a responsible one. It should not only make sense for you, but it should also be of your own free will. Overall and most importantly, it should be safe and toxic-free for everyone involved. You are a phenomenal person. You are unique and an awesome being, and you should be treated as such. Love yourself and never let anyone make you feel guilty for it. You deserve the very best. You deserve respect and you, my friend, deserved nonjudgmental and unconditional love.

"He healeth the broken in heart, and bindeth up their wounds"
Psalm 147:3 KJV

Chapter One

Purpose Through Pain

WRITTEN BY: DEBRA WRIGHT

When you walk through some tough times, you begin to wonder what the purpose of all the pain is. I know that many of us can identify with this because we have each been there at some point in our lives.

I have thought about this for so long and wondered many times why God allowed me to go through the fire time after time. As a teenager growing up in a strict Christian home, sometimes I felt like I was missing out on life because I could not do quite a few things that other young people my age could do. This was a big issue for me because I wanted to go out with my friends to some of the places they would go to and stay out later than 7 p.m. Yes, I know that seems like nothing looking back now but for an eighteen-year-old, it feels like your whole world is going to fall apart.

In retrospect, this was not so bad. The protectiveness of my parents was just really because they loved me and wanted what was best for me. However, in the middle of my eighteenth year, I decided to take a chance, and in the end, I ended up in pain. I grew up in a small village in the Caribbean and some of my girlfriends and I always fantasized about meeting our Prince Charming. We would meet, fall in love, get married, and live happily ever after. One day in late September of 1985, I was out with my mom and I met a young man. After getting to know one another for a short time, I fell madly in love and had a time of my life. I could only focus on my relationship and nothing else.

Being in love, made me ignore all the warning bells that were going off. I wanted to be in his company constantly, even against my parents' wishes. Unlike North America, an eighteen-year-old is not considered an *adult* in the Caribbean. Parents are still in control, and there is no government assistance if you decide to leave home.

During this relationship, I endured some real pain and heartache, but I was in love. I was willing to still go the distance because I thought this was the love that I wanted. When the relationship eventually came to an end, I never closed the door.

The person who comes into your life is not necessarily a bad person, but it may be that they are not good for you at a certain time, or not at all. I enjoyed a lot of good times over a couple of years, but it also came with heartaches along the way. My trust was broken because of lies and in the end, I had to leave home to make a new life for myself in a different country. While I carried the pain from the breakup in my heart, I still yearned for this man, but I had to keep it moving. There was no closure because we just stopped communicating.

> **Key Fact:** *When you are in a relationship that ends, make sure to close all doors because they have a way of coming back to haunt you.*

I was about to graduate from college in the fall of 1987 when an old friend from back home came to visit. We started talking and became better friends. We eventually realized we had feelings for each other and after six months of dating we got married. We were together for twenty-five years and raised a family. However, life began to change, and I could not understand what was happening to us. My idea of family was based on what I saw as a child and as a young woman.

Growing up, life was great. Besides getting into trouble and wanting to have more freedom as a young person, life was indeed fine. I watched my parents navigate life's ups and downs with prayer, love, and understanding.

These examples of what family life should be are what I based my hopes and dreams upon for our own family. The relationships I found myself in did not match up with my expectations. I had children and I tried to align my family that way. It worked for a while but when a couple is not working together in harmony as a family, there are bound to be major problems. The bible says that *two cannot walk together unless they agree*. Some basic things caused challenges that I had to work through. No matter what I tried, we could not make it come together. Whether it was the finances, the kids, and eventually even religion, nothing worked.

As a mother, your children always come first. I remember a time when my children were relatively young and became sick at the same time. I did not have my driver's license and I could not find anyone to drive me to the hospital. There and then, I vowed never to let that happen to me again and this propelled me to finally get my driver's license. Situations force you to evaluate where you are and take necessary actions.

Even though my children were thriving, I felt like I was dying inside. I had a marriage that drained me of my essence. There was lots of criticism, but there was no communication. My life as it was made me feel less than a woman. A woman likes to be complimented and feel she is beautiful. However, when these things are not communicated by her spouse, she somewhat begins to lose her self-esteem and self-confidence. That was me; I became withdrawn and sometimes unsure about how to keep it moving. One thing that kept me going was the beautiful thought that my children would grow up and I would be able to do the things I wanted to do with my life.

Key: *Communication is key in a relationship.*

In any relationship, communication is key. Between a husband and wife, communication is important to keep the marriage going. Likewise, at work, with siblings, parents and children, friends, we all need to be able to communicate to move our relationships forward. It does not matter the nature of our relationship; we need to have good communication. I tried everything that I could to change the communication in my family. I suggested counseling and even overnight trips to see what would help to make the relationship work. All to no avail.

How can you live in a home and not say a word to one another, or when you speak, no one answers you? This was my situation and it went on year after year.

One day I laid on my bed and I just cried out to God. I said, "Lord! I need you right now. Please speak to me." I heard an audible voice say to me,

"Read Judges 5:12." That bible scripture says *Wake up, wake up, Deborah!... sing a song!* (MSG).

I was floored. The God of heaven called me by name. I fell on my face and cried out to Him. You see, during this season, I was drowning in the depths of loneliness and my blood pressure was through the roof. So, for the Lord to hear and answer gave me such a lift in my spirit.

The situation at home did not change, but there were some good days where we enjoyed ourselves and had a measure of peace. I looked forward to those days. It was as if one was alone in the desert and desperately in need of water.

As the years passed by, many rough patches crept up constantly and I felt that as much as I tried, I could not catch a break. My health was very challenged. On a vacation trip with the family to Pennsylvania in July 2001, I felt very tired and lethargic, and I could not understand what was happening to me.

When we arrived at our destination, I got on the phone with one of my cousins and happened to look up and into the mirror. At first, I thought maybe it was just because I was speaking that my mouth seemed twisted. I checked again and realized that there was a definite problem. We had just driven eight hours in the heat, and I was scared. I was taken to the hospital and because I was hypertensive, the physicians thought maybe I was having a stroke but thank God it was not that. I was diagnosed with Bell's Palsy.

With a diagnosis, I was able to get some medicine to help the swelling of the nerve go down. My upcoming testimony though was what I cherish the most. This happened on the weekend and we returned home on Monday evening. I was given an appointment to see a specialist the next day and he gave me six months for it to go away. For some people it never does. I was scared but that night we had a church service and I asked for prayer. The man of God prophesied that although the doctors said six months to see healing, in just six days I would return and sing for the Lord. I accepted it and went home. On Sunday morning, I was able to sing and testify of the goodness of God. If you see me today you could never tell that for a short time in my life, my entire face was twisted to the left.

Relationships can be incredibly challenging, and many times we go into them with unrealistic expectations. For me, I had the mindset of happily ever after, but from that fairy-tale perspective. I was an avid romance novel fan. I devoured them with veracity. The books would take me away from my reality even just for that time and space. I was hungry to feel loved and during one of my vacation trips, I was reconnected with my first love. Remember I said previously you need to close doors when you go through a breakup? It is especially important to do so. Some doors that we do not close leave room for some big surprises. This meeting was not premeditated because I had lost contact for about thirteen years. This chance meeting brought to the forefront all the hurt of the past and the present.

I was enduring a relationship where I did not feel worthy and appreciated. I was harboring hurt and now I was reconnected with someone from my past. How do I now navigate my new reality? My heart was torn, and I was not thinking straight. I decided to keep in contact and throw caution to the wind. As you can probably guess, it was disastrous. I had just made a terrible situation worse and I did not know how to get myself freed from the emotions. I felt loved and cherished, I had someone that I could talk to and felt like they connected with me too. Many people talk about soulmates, but do you understand what it means? The dictionary states "a person ideally suited to another as a close friend or romantic partner." So, when we have soulmates and become intimate, we acquire soul ties.

You may ask "What are you talking about?"

According to the Urban dictionary, a soul tie is "a spiritual/emotional connection you have to someone after being intimate with them, usually engaging in sexual intercourse. The feeling that you can't be rid of them from your mind and your life, even when you are far away, you still feel as if you are apart of each other as if you've given up some intangible part of yourself, that cannot be easily possessed again." [1]

So here I am, losing myself to this overwhelming feeling and my relationship is getting more complicated without knowing how to pull it back. Eventually, I was able to end it. The guilt and shame I felt from reconnecting with my old flame had me in a dark place. I wanted to be a good partner, but I felt I let myself and my family down.

I began reading Christian romance novels and I started noticing a theme throughout the novels that I was reading. In one book, there was one scripture that became a mantra. At first, I did not think much of the words I was reading. I knew the scripture but at this point, I was just reading to take my mind off my current predicament, not really paying attention.

One day I saw the scripture again. *"For I know the plans I think towards you,"* said the Lord. *"They are plans for good and not disaster, to give you a future and a hope."* Jerimiah 29:11 NLT.

I also began hearing it on the radio and at church. One day while sitting in my family room reading, I said, "Lord I am listening. I know you are trying to tell me something." I prayed after that and I felt that something was going to change, not sure what and how but I knew for sure it would.

Most of my life, I believed in romance and happily ever after. As a matter of fact, I still do.

My marriage ended in divorce and even though it was wrought with pain, I still mourned the loss of what could have been. The lessons I have learned is that through the pain and hurt that I endured, they brought me to my purpose in life.

Though my trust was broken many times in the two serious relationships I had, it did not keep me down totally; I would not allow it. I made sure to fight my way back to the top. I started a business when I was told that I would never be good at it. I went back to school and made sure my children were well-grounded and successful in life.

Through the pains I have suffered, I have been able to help other people who are hurting by listening to them and giving them some strategies to help them navigate the obstacles they are facing.

While I was experiencing the pain, I had no idea that God allowed those situations for me to know the purpose he had for my life. These failed and painful relationships did not cause me to lose faith in humanity. I still believe in happily ever after. I was able to trust again and remarried a few years later.

[1] https://www.urbandictionary.com/define.php?term=soul+ties

Debra Wright is a wife and mother first, but as a Forgiveness Coach, Speaker, and an Author, her passion is to help people who have been broken, hurt, and may be struggling to find their way to recovery. She helps to bring restorative empowerment through goal setting and execution plans as required. Debra is the author of her memoir and has two more books in the works. Look out for her anthology Your Pain Has a Purpose through LWL PUBLISHING HOUSE. When she is not writing or coaching, you can find Debra enjoying her family including her grandbabies who she adores.

Twitter: https://twitter.com/Debramwright

Instagram: https://www.instagram.com/debramwright/

Facebook: https://www.facebook.com/Debrawright21/

Email: debra@debramwright.com

Broken Trust

Chapter Two

Feathered Signs

WRITTEN BY: ANNA PEREIRA

I never thought I was strong enough to leave. There I was driving away with tears that covered my entire face. I couldn't wipe them away quickly enough before they blurred my vision. I was in so much shock I felt like I was dying on the inside. My whole life, as I knew it, was being left behind as I looked back through the rearview mirror. I was not thinking clearly. I was hurt, angry, sad, numb, and I most certainly felt lost. All my dreams of being a wife and mother came crashing down. I was already at an age I mentally decided in my head that being a mom was fast escaping me. I knew that at my age it would be hard to get pregnant, never mind the medical implications that could jeopardize me or the child I so desperately wanted to have. We were trying to get pregnant but were unsuccessful, not realizing this was, I believe, God's divine intervention which later on became a blessing in disguise.

I knew I had no choice but to be strong and persevere, but my mind was on overdrive and an emotional wreck. There was no time for logical thinking; I was a mess. I sobbed like a baby for days on end I cried at everything, or anyone having a disagreement with me. Even though they were not being hurtful, just the thought that they were disagreeing with me set my waterworks on overdrive. Like I said earlier, I was a mess and I felt like I was at my end. I wasn't given a chance to mourn the loss of my relationship. I had to be strong on the outside, but on the inside, I was dying 1000 deaths. Depression was soon to follow as a sidekick to my already broken life. This was fantastic as I was not only sad and alone, I was now fighting depression to boot. The perfect storm was brewing, and I was so busy trying to survive my ordeal that I was the very reason I became entrenched in sadness and hopelessness. I was beyond broken. I had a gaping scar that left deep wounds no one to this day ever knew was once taking up space hidden deep within the walls of my heart. I was scared, alone, and just wanted to run far and never look back. I thought of moving to another province at one point. The pain was too much at times; I couldn't even breathe. I tried for a few days after to find a way to just make it minute to minute, then hour to hour, and eventually, I was able to make it through day to day. I cried a lot. I would cry myself to sleep thinking that if God so loved me, He would just take me home in my sleep. Can I tell you I prayed to go home daily? I always asked God to take me home in my sleep so I wouldn't feel anything. How pathetic was it that I wanted to die? I was that broken, that's how pathetic. What was going to happen to me? Was I ever going to get through this?

I spent the next year trying to secure a new real estate brokerage as I was a recently licensed real estate agent. I got my license pretty quickly and if that isn't perseverance, I don't know what is. I remember spending my whole day at a local coffee shop with a laptop and a cup of coffee and I would study all day long. I would buy two coffees and a donut or cookie so I wouldn't get kicked out for using their restaurant. I spent many months there until one day the owner spoke to me and said I couldn't take up a booth for the whole day unless I was buying more than a coffee and that I was welcome to use a smaller table for two instead. I was so embarrassed I didn't return the following day or ever again while I was studying. I just changed locations as I needed to be able to study with no interruptions and no judgments by anyone, including coffee shop owners. You see, I was locked out of the place I was living in every day, so I didn't have a choice but to find a coffee shop that would allow me to study all day without buying a lot of food. I was soon going to figure out that my inner strength was not all me and my own doing. There was a greater force, far stronger than myself, that was driving this. I had my entourage of close friends, what I call my village of people, who came together to get me through what I felt at that moment was the hardest earth-shattering time of my life.

As I drove off that particular day, those feelings that I was experiencing would later haunt me for weeks and months to come. Quite frankly, it took me years to come through to the other side. I was always guarding my heart, never trusting anyone or anything, faith was running on empty, and I had no time to digest the details of what was happening. I had a life to continue with. I had to make it...or I was doomed.

What started as a plan to be married and have children soon became a distant dream. Today I realize it was a good but limiting dream of a girl who was so broken and not even ready to take on the role without fixing herself. How could I be prepared to be a mother of a child if I was so broken inside? Let me be clear, I was 100% in love, wanted to be married, and so desperately desired to be a mother.

So, as I was leaving that relationship behind, I started a new career as a real estate agent. I decided to move back to my parents' home. Well, it wasn't a decision that I made freely, it was made for me. I was not ready to do more than scream and vent and yell at God as to why me. What did I do so wrong in my life that I was being given the short end of the stick? I was running on empty with my so-called faith fuel tank. It seemed for the following couple of years, I was always trying to fill my faith tank with fuel, however, it seemed to dissipate faster than I could fill it.

I soon settled into my new normal life being an inexperienced real estate agent, which had many of its challenges. Leave it to me to pick the best time to change careers. I had little money in my bank account, a credit card maxed out, a failed relationship, and a car that was breaking down. If it wasn't raining, it was surely pouring in my world as I knew it in 2012.

"So, what next?" was a question I asked God all the time. I remember working for a Brokerage early on in my career and there was this spiritual mortgage agent we'll say. She would tell me that it was okay to yell at God because He had big shoulders. He knew my heart and understood that I was hurting. This conversation went on for a few minutes and it was like a light bulb went off in my head. I was having a moment of enlightenment, right then and there. I was shaken to my core in my spiritual beliefs. I was so hurt about my past that I blamed God and wanted Him to know that I was mad and angry with Him. The whole time He knew what was going on. He was God, of course. He knew my heart and what I was feeling. I didn't want to stay mad at Him. I needed to talk to Him and understand why this happened, where did I go wrong, or wait...was I wrong? Maybe this was God's way of showing me to take the fork in the road. Maybe I wasn't listening to the inner voice to do it sooner and maybe God decided to take over the steering wheel and guide me down His destined path for me. Was I just aimlessly living life to be safe? Okay, hold on...I had so many questions, God. Let's start with this one: Why now, at forty-two years of age? Shouldn't I be further ahead with my life? I am exhausted here. I don't want to play this game anymore. I am counting to ten and then opening my eyes and this better be a bad dream.

...8...9...10...

God wasn't done with me. He was trying to show me the love He had for me, only I couldn't hear Him. You see, sometimes we ask for our prayers to be answered and sometimes He's trying to answer them but we're too busy to hear Him talking to us. This is where I was in my life. I was having prayers answered but I was missing the signs. Instead of allowing, I was resisting, and resisting is never the way to live. You'll miss all kinds of blessings along the way. Fast forward a few months later. I ended up working for my current brokerage where I have been for the past eight years of my current nine-year career. Needless to say, it's a place that I have grown many lifelong solid friendships along the way, and it's definitely where I had the most profound growing pains.

"Now what, God?" So, I was looking to challenge God because I was trying once again to take full control over every situation, every encounter, every relationship, every experience, you name it. I was never going to allow anyone or anything to hurt me ever again. I began sabotaging everything I could that came to me – good, bad, or indifferent. I found a way to discount it and remove it from my life. See, that's what we do when we are scared and hurting. We toughen up and erect walls all around us to protect what we think needs to be protected. I'm here to tell you that you don't need to be strong all the time, you don't need to be perfect, you are enough...just as you are. You are enough. When I was trying to control things, I was asking God for signs to prove He was real and that I was on the right path in life because, frankly, I was feeling forgotten by Him. Everyone else was moving on in life but I seemed to be stuck. I figured He hated me and that I must have done something so wrong in my life that I was to bear this pain and suffering as my punishment. Boy, was I so wrong, still looking to prove there was no God. I started to ask for a sign from Him that He was working through my life, something that had meaning to me. The first thing that came to my heart was feathers. Yes, you read that right. I wanted to see feathers. I was so sure that I had this thing figured out to prove to myself that God was not listening to me and that He wasn't real. It didn't take long before I started seeing feathers everywhere – on my car, on my keyboard (that was freaking me out, to be honest). The word feather would appear in books or commercials on TV and people started saying the word feather randomly. I found feathers in my shoes, on my hallway floor outside my bathroom, just about everywhere. So now I was like "Ok God, it's game on now. So, here's what I want. I want to see a blue feather! I want to know if I am where I need to be and if you are going to help me through this and if I am going to be okay. I want to see a blue feather before the end of the day!" I, being stubborn and yes, I do have a very stubborn streak, figured I had this all figured out on how I was about to prove God isn't real and if He is, He doesn't hear me. I was about to prove there is no God or at least He didn't appear to be working through my life.

I was scheduled to take a client of mine out to see a home this one particular day, and after showing the property to her and her husband, we came back to my office to discuss the property in further detail. I had forgotten about my battle with God earlier. As I sat down with them to turn on my computer, my client stated, "I have something I need to give you. I am not sure why, but I know that I have to give this to you." My client handed me a Bermuda $2 bill. It was from the hometown she loved so much. Do you have any idea what is on the $2 Bermuda bill? I know what a Bermuda $2 bill looks like only because of the shock on my face when I received it. I had to excuse myself and made a mad dash to the washroom. I got on my knees and cried in the office bathroom that day. I devoted myself to God 100% that day. I made a vow to honor Him and never doubt Him – I am still working on the latter. I am, after all, only human. The $2 Bermuda bill has a bluebird on it. Not only did He give me the blue feather, but He also gave me lots and lots, and I still have that bill to this day as a reminder God is not dead – He is alive and present, working through our lives daily. Let him in and hear Him talk to you. That small voice of reason that you hear, the one that tugs away at your heartstrings, the one that makes you second guess, the one that asks you to forgive someone, the one that tells you it will be okay and this will pass...trust that voice. God is trying to talk to you.

So, the next time you feel broken or maybe hurting from a lost relationship, let me tell you God is bigger than all your problems. He can move mountains. I went on to become a top producer with my brokerage and have been a six-figure earner ever since, bringing home one of the highest awards in the company this past year. If you let Him, He will be your greatest fan and cheer you on. Believe in yourself and ask for the signs. They are all over the place. You just have to be still, listen, and hear Him.

Anna Pereira is a successful Real Estate Agent in the Greater Toronto Area. Anna settled in the GTA in 1990 where she furthered her education, via Sheridan College, George Brown College, University of Waterloo, and the Ontario Real Estate Association. She became a Counselor for Abused Women and Children in 1997, subsequently taking on many paths, from Social Services, Supervisor, Operations Manager, Outside Sales, and now being a Top Producer in Real Estate. She is a choir member with her church and continues her dedication through volunteering in the community. Anna enjoys music, singing, writing, and all things Real Estate.

Facebook: https://www.facebook.com/@annapereiraipro

Email: listwithanna@gmail.com

Instagram: https://www.instagram.com/annapereirarealtor

Twitter: @Anna Pereira

Linkedin: https://www.linkedin.com/in/anna-pereira-realtor%C2%AE

Chapter Three

Blindsided

WRITTEN BY: KADIAN MAYNE

I remember this day vividly like it was yesterday. It was one summer morning. My fingers hit the snooze button on my alarm clock every five minutes while I tossed and turned in bed. Waking up before dawn every morning for work was surely not something I looked forward to, but I was grateful, nonetheless. As I scrambled to throw on any clothes I could find, I rushed out the door with only four minutes left to catch the bus. My day was not off to a good start. As I approached to cross the street, the bus quickly drove right past me. I sighed as I missed it by only two seconds, knowing I'd have to wait for a half-hour for the next bus to arrive. I shouted, "Urgh...this day can't get any worse!" I guess I spoke too soon.

I finally made it to work with hurried steps. The look on my manager's face was disappointment as she told me this would be my last warning for tardiness. Anyways, it was now lunch and as I sat to eat in the crowded food court, this would be the very moment my day got worse. I was informed by a little birdie that the guy I had been dating for the past few months was cheating on me and to make matters worse, the girl was carrying his child. I was in complete disbelief. I had never felt my heart beat so fast. I was enraged and distraught. I didn't know what to think, or feel, or how to even react. At this point, I was causing a lot of attention to myself and was receiving strange looks from everyone around me. All I could think about was my face being pictured on the latest news report for committing a crime, but I knew I was better than that. I was immensely devastated to no end. What awful timing – my lunch was over and I had to carry on for the rest of the day, smiling and servicing customers as if I wasn't hurting and holding back tears on the inside. As shocked as I was, a part of me was suspicious for a while that he was seeing someone else, but I had no real proof. Now, I didn't want to accuse someone of something based on hearsay, so later that day, I confronted him. As expected, he denied it at first, but eventually confessed and of course, I ended that relationship. I left and never looked back. I was not about to lose my dignity over someone who couldn't even respect me. Leaving was painful, but I knew staying would hurt more.

Looking back at this, now years later, it's crazy what we consider to be love. The word is used so loosely that it often lacks real meaning. Love doesn't hurt you. A person who doesn't know how to love hurts you and I had to learn this rather quickly. Is that the only time my trust has ever been broken? No, it wasn't the first and it surely wasn't the last. The deceit did not end there. I once had a best friend. We were inseparable. We did everything together and told each other everything. We were like sisters. A friendship that would last forever...or so I thought. My world came crashing down the day I found out that she was sneaking around with another guy I began dating, behind my back. Heartbroken yet again. I was in utter and complete shock. I've heard about things like this happening to other people, but never in a million years would I think this would be my reality. It felt like I was living in a soap opera, but instead, this was real life, my life. Anger and anguish took over me. How could someone who you hold so dear to your heart, betray you in that way? I had to cut her out of my life right then and there. All those years of friendship down the drain. I found it so hard to trust anybody else after that.

No wonder they say, "Trust takes years to build, seconds to break, and forever to repair." This statement resonates with me so much. Once that trust is gone, it's gone for good. There's no coming back after that. The wound cuts very deep, and no amount of stitching can heal it fast enough. At the time, I was young, insecure, and didn't know how to be alone. I thought that being in a relationship would make me happy. Yet, ironically, I wasn't. I later discovered that true happiness comes from within. It's internal, not external and I had to create it on my own. My need to be in a relationship blocked my judgment. I ignored the red flags, but the little things that you ignore now, come creeping up later, and they did. I had gone from one toxic and unhealthy relationship to another, being treated poorly and verbally abused. We hope that they will change, but many never do. The first straw should have been the last. Life has taught me that you need to set the tone on how you want to be treated. People treat you based on what you allow. If I had stayed with my ex-boyfriend who constantly insulted me and called me names, even after expressing to him numerous times how hurtful it was, that would have been equivalent to saying that I am not worthy of respect. I had to demand it, even if that meant walking away. I reminded myself that I don't need another person to validate me. Only I validate myself.

Taking everything into account, I had to take some time out to focus on myself and to find my purpose. I was lost, confused, and didn't really know who I was or who I wanted to be. I went on a soul-searching journey and I'm glad that I did. During this time, I applied for college and studied nursing. I didn't complete the program, as it wasn't quite for me, however, the knowledge I gained will last a lifetime. I then went on to pursue a career as a personal support worker. I have the attention span of a squirrel, so school wasn't exactly a walk in the park, not to mention that I also struggle with procrastination. Either way, I worked hard and remained focused. I also found my passion for singing, which led to my interest in writing music as well. I later released my first song, something that I've always wanted to do for a long time. I fell in love with nature and became whole again. This journey was refreshing, but also an eye-opener. Aside from my former best friend, I had to let go of a few other friends who didn't mean me well and I felt I couldn't trust, for various reasons. When you grow into yourself, you begin to drift apart from those you've known your whole life. Childhood friends and I no longer had anything in common anymore. This was depressing and a bit difficult to accept, however, it's inevitable. Some people just aren't meant to be in our lives forever and that's okay. A new chapter can't unfold if you're still flipping through the old pages. The ones that are destined to be in your life will find a home in you and you in them.

I look at everything as learning experiences. Each person that I met has taught me valuable lessons, which has helped shape me into the person that I am today. Whether good or bad, a lesson is a lesson and I am grateful for all the people who walked into my life, even those that turned it upside down. If I learned anything, it was to not be too trusting of other people (which was one of my biggest downfalls) and partially why I kept getting myself into certain situations. I had to hold myself accountable. I didn't see people for who they were. I saw them for who I wanted them to be. Looking at life through rose-colored glasses only did more harm than good. I had to remove those glasses and toss them aside. Sometimes we want to be in control for the fear of losing control. Life is only a lucid dream until we wake up. I needed to develop a balance between trusting too much and trusting too little. People will reveal their true selves sooner or later; you just have to pay close attention. Forgiving was the hardest part. Growing up I was the most unforgiving person ever. If anyone dared to do me wrong, I would hold a grudge against them for a lifetime. This was very detrimental and a troubled mindset to have. I had to learn how to forgive. Convincing myself I had forgiven was easy, but actually forgiving, well that was the hard part. I didn't know exactly how to do that. This is where I developed a stronger relationship with God. I found the church, got baptized, and started living a prayerful life. I spent years searching for my purpose and all along, my one true purpose was serving the Lord. I found myself in Christ. It was then I learned the power in forgiveness. One day while standing in church, the priests read this scripture: *"Be kind to one another, tenderhearted, forgiving one another, as God in Christ forgave you"* (Ephesians 4:32) and just like that, it hit me. I'd been holding in so much anger and hurt for far too long. I had to find a way to forgive my former best friend, my ex-partners, and all those who had done me wrong. Fasting and praying became a huge part of my life. And I had to realize that I am also not perfect. I've made mistakes as well and I would want my loved ones to forgive me. Forgiveness is a two-way street. You need to give it in order to receive it and I can now happily say that time healed everything for me. My faith in God is what kept me going and is what also made me a better person. As the scripture says, *"It is better to take refuge in the LORD than to trust in man."* (Psalm 118:8)

People will hurt you, use you and abuse you, but God will never let you down. Believe me when I say that there are plenty of trustworthy people out there with good intentions, but sometimes you can't be certain of who will have your back or who will talk behind it. At the end of the day, you have no control over the actions of others. People are going to do what they want regardless, but with God, you can't go wrong. At times when I felt like the world was against me, He was my only comfort.

Even after all that I went through, I was still open to love. Although a part of me wanted to give up on it, I remained hopeful, but I certainly wasn't looking for it. True love comes knocking on your door when you least expect it. I was so focused on my life and on my goals that the last thing on my mind was a relationship. I reached a stage where I was finally content in being alone and discovered true happiness within myself. I had done the inner work and was at peace. Who would have thought that a spontaneous trip back home would lead me to finding the one? If anybody had told me prior, I wouldn't have believed it. Now five years later and engaged, everything really does happen for a reason. Due to my past relationships, I knew what was right for me because I've been wronged. I knew what respect was because I've been disrespected, and I knew what being loved correctly was because I loved myself.

I have expressed all this to say, as humans we all experience hardships. In fact, we are facing one of the most difficult ones right now with COVID-19. This is a global pandemic that's impacting the whole world, currently, as we speak. This has been going on for months now and doesn't look like it's about to end anytime soon. No one could have prepared for this, yet hundreds of thousands of people have been infected by this virus and countless people have died. I personally know people who have lost loved ones and friends from it. It is such a tragedy and we all have been affected by it, in one way or another, but the only way we can get through this is by prayer and by trusting the Lord to guide and protect us all through this difficult time that we are facing. This shows you how fragile life is, but regardless of what we go through, we must rise above it and not let anything, or anyone, keep us down. Your mind is the strongest tool that you have. Your thoughts are so powerful, and a healthy mindset is everything. Throughout all that you go through in life, you have to stay positive and uplift yourself. No one is going to do it for you. Therefore, take it upon yourself to be your own motivator and cheerleader. Having a positive mindset can take one so far. You can achieve wonders by just believing in yourself and also trusting yourself, above all else. Sometimes people betray us, and we want to take revenge, but you have to remember, how people treat you is their karma, but how you react is also yours. You have to just move on, leave in good grace, and let the universe take care of it, while also wishing them the best. On the other hand, sometimes people do deserve second chances; it all depends on what you are willing to tolerate, as long as you don't lose yourself in the process. Sometimes it's not about what you've been through, but about what you've learned from it.

Forgive others and live to love another day. In the midst of it all, don't forget to also forgive yourself. The key is to treat people how you want to be treated. Do good to others and good shall follow you. The best thing you can do is to love yourself and to be yourself – wholeheartedly. Once you accomplish that in life, you are unbeatable and unstoppable. Find what makes you happy, what makes you excited, what breathes life into you, and be the best version of yourself that you can be. Wake up each day with a purpose and if you don't know what that is, then take the time out to find it. Each of our footprints tells such a different story. What is your story going to be?

Kadian Mayne is an enterprising young woman. She has a PSW Certificate, Travel Counselor Certificate, years of customer service, a published song, and several budding business ventures under her belt. Born in Spanish Town, Jamaica, and raised in Toronto, she is on a mission to pursue her goals, uplift her community, and live for God using her creative talents and entrepreneurial mindset to glorify Him. Kadian is a co-author in this anthology and has been featured in the first edition of *LWL Lifestyle* magazine. She hopes to illuminate lessons learned along the way and to provide encouragement and inspiration for others to live life to its fullest potential.

Instagram: www.instagram.com/god_bless23/?hl=en

Soundcloud: https://m.soundcloud.com/user-344490683/loveable-luvnsou

Chapter Four

Discovering A Beautiful Soul

Written By: Monifa Wilson

To quote Bob Marley, *"Truth is, everyone is gonna hurt you. You just gotta find the ones worth suffering for."*

In my life, I've learned that despite it feeling like we're suffering, we're actually growing. And the two are often mistakenly and interchangeably used, due to the pain that they both inevitably produce. So, to reword: *Truth is, everyone is trying to find themselves. You just gotta find the ones worth being patient with.*

These words resonate so deeply with me because I constantly find myself grappling with hurt – or "suffering" – as Bob so eloquently put it... and most of us do. It took me a long time to learn that other's mistakes are not your burdens to bear, even if they do end up hurting you directly. A series of relationships in my life were the main teachers in this ongoing lesson. I must admit, however, that learning this lesson and applying it are two completely separate tasks, and I am currently chipping away at the latter.

Now, while growing pains may be something that we are typically not interested in, we must bear in mind that the fruit it bears is so sweet. With this in mind, I am always reminded of Romans 8:18. Paul *"reckon[s] that the sufferings of this present time are not worthy to be compared with the glory which shall be revealed in us,"* essentially reinforcing the fact that our reward is far greater than our pain, should we persevere. Because of this acknowledgment, I am now able to move forward with so much more clarity and understanding. And it's all because my trust had to be broken a few times.

My eyes are now opened to see that one of the most amazing aspects of life is connecting with the many souls that have been intricately placed in our lives by the Creator. It is through these connections that we discover our truest selves and begin to unravel the truths in life that we would have, otherwise, not been able to unlock; and while uncovering these truths, life becomes more meaningful each time. In no way is it ever easy to navigate these connections, however, whether we decide to stick with the souls we've been granted, whether we don't, or whether we hang on for dear life to those not meant for us, we can always accept the lessons we've gained, which is rewarding every single time if you allow them to be. These connections eventually form relationships, and these relationships ultimately shape the entire course of our lives. Who knew that something we've grown so accustomed to could be so critical to our growth and advancement as an individual? I would even go as far as to say that every relationship you form adds sustenance to your life...again if you allow it to. So after being broken, and renewed, and fed, and drained, and taught, and stretched, and watered, I've finally learned that these were actually lessons that those relationships were handing to me, and I was then able to embrace and receive them in order to fulfill whatever purpose they had for me in my life.

It didn't start off so simply, however...

I would say that I have experienced several character-defining relationships, but I assure you that we would be able to spend years that it would take to recount them all, in more productive ways. So, I can briefly recall, however, two relationships that affected me very profoundly in more recent timing.

I had bonded with a remarkable soul that sparked a five-year-long friendship that I was so sure would last this lifetime. It was an unconventional connection that somehow worked. We clicked for reasons that were beyond us. I helped her to fight her battles, and she taught me the meaning of loyalty and confidence – the things I was most unfamiliar with in my life at that time. We not only complemented each other, but we needed one another. After some time, we eventually fulfilled each other's roles in our lives. Think of a mentor serving the purpose of guiding you, a teacher teaching you, a bus driver driving you…and then finally arriving at your destination. A strain, unbeknownst of its origin, appeared in our friendship like a plague. We began to struggle to maintain something that once flowed so naturally. And as you could imagine, the shift not only confused the hell out of me, but it angered me. I'm sure that it confused both of us because we began to avoid the obvious. But, like the soldiers we are, we pushed through it, commendably. What is not so commendable, however, is how we stretched a generally healthy friendship for about two and a half years into a bumpy one for half a decade, and then severed it brutally with bitterness.

I began to resent our friendship. It was originally beautiful, so I refused to accept anything less. Many factors took a toll on our friendship, as most relationships tend to endure after a while. But ours seemed to deteriorate so steadily, almost as quickly as it began, so I fought. I expressed my concerns repeatedly, and it seemed to improve ever so slightly at some points, thus creating an illusion of overall rectification that we so willingly ran with each time…until we could no longer run. It's impossible to run from the glaring truth for too long without awful consequences. And there it was: the end of the road. Or so we thought. We both grew weary, and evidently evolved in ways that no longer suited each other's lives; something that was clear to happen from the start, in all honesty. Out of emotional distress, it seemed as if she discarded me like a full piece of paper. All of the notes, lessons, and memories that I filled her page with were no longer valuable to her. So, she turned a new one.

And out of emotional distress, I burned on the inside.

As fate had it, we were not able to end our friendship amicably. As if that were not enough, we were also unable to conclude it easily. The end of the road revealed another path full of anger, revenge, bitterness, and overall, the opposite of how it began. In short, her owing me money dragged the weight of our now failed friendship even further in the mud. We underwent a small claim, unnecessary back and forth, and self-induced emotional turmoil. We allowed our impulsive feelings to dictate our actions. It's funny how humans never seem to remember the good times while we're going through the bad. Because if we were to set our forgetful and prideful nature aside to do so, her and I would have probably parted ways peacefully. Months later, after resolving the money issue by her repaying me in full, we no longer speak. It felt very hollow in the space she once resided, considering how close we were. We have no contact with one another anymore, aside from the mutual friends we've gained along the way. I was hurt at first, to say the least. Stunned, and for a long while, actually. But God allowed me to exercise and experience the free gift of reflection. After careful examination and mediation, I was finally able to confirm the beginning statements of this story to be true. Essentially, our friendship was only for a season and a specific reason. So why be troubled that the Summer has ended? Only upon this conclusion was I then able to admire the beautiful Autumn. The leaves around me were not a sign of death, but rather rebirth. I am now able to appreciate the color it has added to my life.

So, to Sister Friend, I thank you. Thanks for a beautiful summer. I hope I see you in heaven someday.

And to God, Thank You. Always.

To further recount (like sheep, before I head to bed), I discovered another beautiful soul. One who now reminds me of Sister Friend, but different. It's the kind of attraction that catches you by surprise. The first thing I noticed was not his vibrant smile, or the pain beneath his eyes, nor his quirky sense of humor, but rather his spirit. It radiated more than any of the aforementioned qualities. I thought nothing of it, until an uncanny circumstance brought us together, which allowed us to roam each other's auras even more. It tackled me, this connection. I was very comfortable at the time with my singleness for once in my life, so I suppose it had to, in order to work its predestined purpose. As unexpectedly as it came, is as much as it unexpectedly intensified. He became the object of my affection and forethoughts rather quickly. I became attached without permission. As it turned out, my passion soon began to surpass his. A connection I never planned for began to consume me. After noticing that the effect of the relationship was not the same on him as it was on me, I acted like I always do when presented with hurt in any of my relationships, I fought. "Well, I'll give him time," I thought. "We have an amazing connection. What is there not to get on board with?" "I'm worth his time and attention, am I not?"

Eventually I somehow, and subconsciously, convinced myself that I wasn't. I set my self-worth based on his actions. It is exactly this destructive thinking that plunged me into a constant tug of war with him. It was confusing because I could tell that he cared for me deeply, but I didn't understand the distant behavior. I failed to realize that he was also undergoing his own battles. He had his giants to face that had nothing to do with me. I couldn't see what he was hiding, despite my desperate search to understand. And still, I was understanding. I approached him calmly with my concerns (sound familiar?). It yielded nothing but toxic fruit. He never meant to hurt me. In fact, he remains to be one of the sweetest people I know. But the truth of the matter is, he captured me and then neglected me. He caused me to fly into a frenzy of self-doubt and self-worth issues.

We went at this rollercoaster ride for a year and a half until I finally waved the white flag. I called off this "not a relationship" relationship, freeing myself from the coma I put myself in. Once I made room for myself, I was finally able to receive new blessings into my life. New energy, almost like a fresh start. To be honest, it was a long ending, but one that satisfied me. After the hurt settled of course. He so willingly agreed, it was as if he gave me my wings I needed and then took off – like a hawk. Thankfully, the situationship ended amicably.

The loss of Sister Friend and Hawk gave me the space to finally gain understanding and freedom to understand what I deserve, pray for, and go after instead of holding on to dead weight.

While I must admit that it was extremely painful to deal with the loss of these relationships, it would be so foolish of me not to acknowledge the lessons I've learned throughout these losses. I have come to realize a couple of things:

> The ability to form loving, healthy relationships is a mutual effort that comes with hard work. Stable relationships do not evolve overnight; they are intentional efforts of commitment and dedication. Relationships should involve relentless support for each other and building each other up. I found that the other party in my failed relationships did not see it this way, or at least they didn't act that way at some point. I was struggling to hang on to something that was not mutually beneficial.

> I must also mention that even though losing these relationships brought much anguish in some cases, it also brought about immense

relief and freedom. This caused me to learn that hanging on to relationships based on broken trust can be more detrimental than helpful. I was fighting to hang on to a one-sided relationship that was seemingly of no value to the other person.

I have been able to cope with the devastation of having my relationships destroyed by finding comfort in the fact, and I reiterate, the fact that the Spirit of God can bring peace when I am hurting and feeling as if the walls of this frigid world are closing in on me. Proverbs 3:5-6 became very real to me: *"Trust in the LORD with all thine heart; and lean not unto thine own understanding. [6] In all thy ways acknowledge him, and he shall direct thy paths."* I have been able to glean strength from this verse and chose to trust Him although I was not able to fully grasp the true reason for it all at the time. And parts of this truth are still being revealed to me day by day.

That's the beauty of being limiting creatures, serving a limitless God.

If it were up to me, I would have gone into and come out of every experience scratch-free, void of any of the hurt and pain that came with my broken relationships. But how else would I have been gold, without the fire? And just like Shadrach, Meshach, and Abednego, the Angel of the Lord remains with me through it all.

I've noticed within myself that I carry grudges and resentment unintentionally and subconsciously. Well today, I am actively working on this trait, as my conscious and higher self wants nothing to do with those things. Further association will only slow down the beautiful and divine process. I can genuinely say that I do not regret having experienced those relationships. They've beautified me in ways I could have never even thought to do to myself.

Let me ask you a question? *"We all want love but we're so afraid to fall first. But tell me what's worse...never loving at all or possibly getting hurt?"* (Skye Townsend, 2020)

I say love for the win. And God is love. God always wins.

I invite you to do the same by letting go of what weighing you down while blasting the song "Gold" by Joseph Solomon with me, any chance that you get.

Blessings.

Monifa Wilson is an upcoming entrepreneur who enjoys singing and writing. She was born in Toronto, Ontario and is pursuing her passions to live creatively, contributing as a healthy member of society, and spreading the light of Christ. Monifa is currently attending Marca College for hairstyling, writing, and recording music, making the first step in her writing career as a coauthor in this very inspiring anthology. She hopes will have a positive impact on her life, as well as the lives of others, her community, and the world at large.

Broken Trust

$\mathcal{C}$hapter $\mathcal{F}$ive

The Loss of My Flow of Joy

WRITTEN BY: AMANDA BROWN

$\mathcal{D}$eceit and Dishonesty. Have you ever felt like you were trapped in a deep, dark vortex that was just spinning and spinning out of control in a downward spiral with no way out? Kind of like that feeling when you take one step forward and two steps back. How did you feel? Well, everything that I loved and worked so hard for was stripped from me through deceit and dishonesty, which left me feeling powerless.

You see, life did not turn out as I had planned, and like many young women, I had big dreams with a bright future ahead of me. The fairytale life of one day being a bride, a mother, and having a family of my own was all an illusion because that is not how life unfolded for me. As strong as I was, I had been conquered by the devil and I am here to tell you that if you're feeling like I did with your life spinning out of control, you are not alone. My hope for you in reading this story will be to help awaken your awareness to be more open to the signs that I somehow managed to miss or avoid altogether. The old cliché saying "If I only knew then what I know now" could have saved me a world of hurt on so many levels.

My story starts out like so many others. It was not until I started to open and share that I realized how important it was that my story is told. The hope of sharing my story with you is to save at least one if not many women from falling into the same pitfalls that I did. I want to gently remind you to be kind to yourself (we are not perfect) and to pay attention to the signs that could potentially lead you down a very dark path.

Lack of Self-Love

Self-love can be very destructive when we lack it, or very empowering when we honor it. Our life path can be hugely altered if we do not learn to love ourselves and live in our truth. In the beginning, when we are young adults trying to navigate through life and trying to figure things out, we do not recognize what lack of self-love looks like. It is not until we have some life experiences to help awaken our awareness to the signals we often overlook and shrug off like it is no big deal or insignificant. I know I did that very thing and ignored the signs. As I reflect on my own life, I recognize now if I had loved myself more, I would have not allowed my life to take the path it did, and my life would have taken a very different direction. You see, we are all born as sweet innocent beings, oblivious to the evil forces that linger among us, and the predators that are looking to steal our confidence, our self-worth, and our dreams. If your awareness is lacking, it is difficult to recognize your patterns that typically become more apparent through your behaviors. The cliché, "You can't judge a book by its cover," is so true. Often, how we see someone show up in life from the outside, is not always a true reflection of what is happening on the inside.

Have you ever felt like you were crumbling on the inside and that people did not see the real you, and they could not see you suffering because you were such a good actress? Were you feeling isolated, confused, and alone? Where do you turn, who do you talk to?

Most people who know me, see me from the outside looking in as a strong, vibrant, confident woman who went after life and lived every moment to the fullest. Not a care in the world.

At a noticeably young age, I became a professional woman in a career with the promise of a full and happy life with a lot of potential for growth and prestige…the world was my oyster. I worked extremely hard in my career to become the best version of myself and to perfect my skills so that I could offer my clients the best of what I had. Some would even say I was intimidating.

What people did not see, was how unhappy and lonely I was. Inside I was craving to be loved and to be accepted. I was looking for that perfect mate to help complete me and create the dream...that fairytale life I spoke of earlier. After all, isn't that what we all want and hope for?

One day, I woke up and realized that I did not know who I was anymore. It was like I was living someone else's life – almost like an out of body experience. Have you ever stopped and thought about where you are in your life and had an AHA moment where you did not know where the last five years had gone? That was me. I remember feeling completely displaced and for a moment, a sense of sheer terror came over me. For the first time in my life, I felt scared and wondered what the heck happened. How did I end up in this life that I felt so far removed from? I could not identify with who I was anymore. Have you ever done that? Woke up and thought, "Where am I, who's house is this, why am I here?" I wished so many times that I could close my eyes and open them again to find myself back in my old life that I missed so much and that this was all just a very bad dream, but instead, when I opened my eyes, I was still in this place I didn't recognize. Somewhere along the line, I did not love myself enough to genuinely believe that I could have it all...that I deserved to be happy. I had settled. I thought in my mind that I was not deserving enough and that I would never find the right person to create the life that I truly deserved, so I would have conversations in my head justifying all of the good I would see in these mates that were so wrong for me and try to find the good while overlooking the not so good qualities. I wanted to save these what I call "broken" partners because it made me feel worthy or valued knowing that I could show them a better life. In the end, it was always ME who suffered, not them. Because I was not true to myself and I did not love myself enough to feel that I deserved to have it all, I was the one who paid the ultimate price! When looking for a mate to spend the rest of your life with, do your due diligence. Spend time with them and try not to get caught up in the euphoria of false love. If something does not feel right, it probably is not. That tiny little voice we all have in the pit of our gut will guide you through the right paths, but we need to listen to it and not push it away, as I did so many times.

Shame

I am sure you can relate to what I am saying, and it is for this reason I am here to tell you that shame is a common emotion when we feel like we have failed. The embarrassment and shame of feeling like I had failed were so strong in my core emotions, that my pride would not allow the outside world to see how miserable I truly was. Suddenly, I realized I was living a lie and that my life was not one made from love and support, it was all based on greed and deceit. I had been lied to for the betterment of another. I would avoid social situations so that people could not see how unhappy I was. I started to find love through food which made me feel better behind closed doors, but I was gaining weight and did not feel secure outside of closed doors and would bury myself in self- loathing. I was starting to self-isolate in fear that the outside world will see my unhappiness. True love has no judgment. It has compassion, grace, and forgiveness. True love is selfless, supportive, and encourages us to grow and feel safe, I had none of that. I was in a relationship that did not allow me to grow and tried to control me every step of the way. It was more like a dictatorship and I was told what to do and how to do it and who I could do it with. Does that sound like love to you? If any of these words such as fearful, shameful, guilty, embarrassed, selfishness, narcissistic reflect in your world, beware, you might be someone's project. You might be under a wicked spell into believing that this is love, the real deal, but sadly like me, I was being conquered by the devil. You see, the devil has many faces and he walks among us daily, we just need to be mindful of his trickery so he cannot defeat us!

When you feel so alone and do not know which way to turn, what do you do? There were times I wanted to drive off the side of a cliff to find peace and end this horrible nightmare I had found myself so deeply entwined in. I felt stuck with nowhere to turn. You might be asking yourself, "How does a fun-loving, charismatic person go from being on top of the world to the bottom of a dark vortex?" I know I did. How could I not see the signs all along? The answer now looking back is easy for me to see. It was simply because my lack of self-love was so deep, that I was willing to accept any and all bad behavior thinking it would get better in time, just so it looked like I had it all from the outside looking in. You cannot judge a book by its cover. I was completely isolated, feeling so alone, missing all my relationships from my previous workplace. I was in a toxic relationship, a toxic environment and at my core, I was so lonely and miserable. I had been coerced into leaving my beautiful life in the city I loved, with the people I loved. I was made promises that were never kept, the hope to return to the city I loved but was sadly disappointed and found myself in a dark cellar waiting to rot. I had to start believing in myself if I was going to get out of this alive.

Low Self-Esteem

When unhappiness brings us to an unhealthy place in life it can lead to so many natural health disasters. I had such low self-esteem. I knew I had to make changes, but I did not know where to start in terms of making an exit strategy. I had become physically unhealthy, gained a lot of weight while comforting my stuffed emotions, and I physically looked different. The twinkle in my eye had disappeared, my laugh became faint, my smile became weak and my heart was heavy, but I knew I had to get out of there if I was going to have the life I deserved. My body was talking to me and if I did not start listening, something terrible would happen and then one day, something did happen. I found myself in a life-threatening situation with a DVT (deep vein thrombosis). The doctors told me if I did not take this seriously, I could possibly lose the most valued possession we have, MY LIFE! My heart sank as I listened to the doctor's words and I can remember feeling scared yet again. What was happening to me? Where did I go wrong? Here I was, in a miserable situation, trying to suck it up and make the most of it but my body had a different idea. You see, I was so unhappy, that spiritually and emotionally, I was looking for a way out. So, guess what? My body was giving me an out. I was about to pay the ultimate price if I did not make some major changes. In that very moment, I made the decision to fight for my life, get well, lost weight, and get out of that situation. I would learn to love myself more and feel good about who I am as a person. I made the decision that I was worth it and I would make the most out of my life moving forward.

There is a huge connection between the mind and the body and when they are out of balance where one is unhealthy, the other naturally follows suit. We must remember to keep our minds healthy through positive affirmations and reaffirming that it is okay to make mistakes and to remember that we are human. We develop our character by the experiences we have had and without failures, we cannot possibly grow. I like to say that we are all spiritual beings having a human experience. Healthy thoughts lead to a healthy body and vice versa. If I only knew that back then, my life today would have had a vastly different outcome. I would have loved myself more, been kind to myself, and cut myself some slack and I would not have made the decisions I did. Looking back now, I had put so much pressure on myself to be the perfect child, the perfect role model, and to be a good person.

Today, I practice meditation and find myself in a much calmer space, I love myself more, and I now understand that I am just as deserving as others. It is still a challenge at times because we are not perfect, and I am a constant work in progress, but I have found happiness and the freedom that I so desired and I am living my life well. I learned to believe in myself more and I took back my power. This can also be your story too! Once I found my inner strength, I became unstoppable and there is nothing or anyone who will take away my light again!

If I can shed a glimmer of hope to any of you, I will share with you that no person is better than you. We are all created equally, and we are all entitled to have it all. If another human in your life is trying to take away your power or put out your flame because you are shining too bright, stand firm, and be strong enough to be who you are without shame or guilt and ask for what you want. Hold on to your power. Life is too short, and we are not on this planet for long, so live it well, and be happy and remember, the best revenge is a life well-lived. Sometimes when things happen in your life, your brokenness can be the start of your healing and a new beginning.

Amanda Brown is a dental Hygienist and an entrepreneur. She graduated from Cambrian College in 1990 and completed her Dental Hygiene certificate. She then moved out west to Vancouver and advanced her education through UBC and leveled up with the Local Anesthetic course. Amanda also has an interest in health and wellness and is a manager at Isagenix International. She has a strong interest in helping others and maintaining a healthy lifestyle. Amanda also has a diverse accolade of talents. Amanda is creative in the kitchen and garden. Reiki and auricular therapy are a few of her other loves and she enjoys writing.

Chapter Six

A Broken Society

WRITTEN BY: MICHAEL J AMBROSE

I moved to Canada at the age of seven from England, United Kingdom. We lived with my auntie and her family for the first couple of years. She had already established herself in Canada and this allowed my family to start our new lives. Our blended families did struggle at first, but eventually, we did come together as blood should. One of my earliest memories is my first day of school. I remember waking up in Toronto and feeling excited and nervous. On this day I remember I prepared myself. I choose my clothes, packed my backpack, what shoes to wear, all these were to get me ready for this big day. I ate my breakfast; my lunch was packed, and I was off to catch the bus. As the big yellow school bus stopped in front of me, I remember getting on and looking around at all these faces I did not know. I sat at the very back of the bus by myself, looked out the window, and wondering how my day would unfold. I remember feeling every bump that bus went over, the constant chatter and laughter of the children around me, while I sat in my thoughts of uncertainty. This was the first time I was outside of my element that I could remember. Looking back, of course, I survived my first day, but I do remember thinking it was never going to be over. Getting back on that big yellow school bus at the end of the day was a victory.

After six months, my family decided it was time to find our own home, so we moved to Scarborough, Ontario, and were fortunate enough to purchase a house in a predominately established white neighborhood. Settling into this community I felt the pressures of being the only black family in the neighborhood. My childhood was strict – everyone in my family was expected to work harder as a black man which I internalized and identified as episodes of anxiety and suppressed depression. My older family members did their best to triumph over these obstacles and adversities but unfortunately, their perceptions and apprehensions were put on me and further enflamed my internal adolescent battles. I was young and impressionable at this age, so these emotions strongly attached themselves to my personal development.

During my elementary school years, I knew I wanted to be validated, but I unintentionally developed behavioral issues that clouded my creativity. I felt I never fit in. Coming home each day from school to a strict household, I felt I was unable to open up about my inner emotions, so I was always struggling inside. I learned quickly how to mask my emotions and silence myself and avoid bringing any more unnecessary attention my way. I am grateful for what my family gave me because they tried to remain consistent always. As I started to become comfortable with my new surroundings, I realized I had allies across the street with an older boy who had introduced me to his family. This family welcomed me, and I watched as this particular family lifted each other up with effortless positivity, love, and encouragement. Our families were completely different. These parents believed in their children and cultivated their creativity by outwardly showing the support. They showed acceptance to one another always.

It was during my teenage years that I started to see more love around me, and I grew deeper into who I was becoming as a young man. I was learning about my culture, my beliefs, and the strength I had as a black man. In high school, my culture was throughout the halls. I was grateful for the interactions I had with all races but especially mine because it was my identity. My voice was finally being heard; I was starting to understand myself.

I developed both fits of anger and anxiousness because I was a shy child by nature. I had no confidence and I became a follower. Many times, I felt more comfortable alone, even around others, and I felt the emptiness. I was learning this at such a young age. I had no one to talk to, no one to open up to, and I became unsure of myself. I suppressed my emotions every day. It was as though I was not myself, I learned my triggers and saw how they were tied to my lack of confidence and fear. I was afraid to let my real self be seen. I did not know how to embrace my uniqueness; I was in a war within myself. I learned how to live internally and that I would continue to suppress my unstable and volatile energy. I truly felt I never fit in. There were only two black children in the school, and I was one of them. I was constantly teased because of my skin color and my accent, I was called the derogative "N word" more times then I can count, and let me tell you that it does something to a child. Coming home each day from school to a strict household, you just did not express your feelings. My inner emotions were just that, mine. Silencing myself was my protection. I am grateful for what my family gave me, they tried to remain consistent always. Eventually, I do remember becoming comfortable with my surroundings. I started to make a few friends on our street, and it was then I realized I had allies across the street – an older boy who became a close friend but who also introduced me to his family. This family welcomed me into their home, and I saw a family lift each other with effortless positivity. Our families were different. These parents believed in their children and cultivated their creativity. They showed acceptance always. I know they changed me.

I made new friends, and I started to build my confidence and believed in myself. It was in these years I found my passion for music and performing. I harnessed my power through beatboxing and dancing. I had many beatboxing influences growing up who performed. I would watch these artists perform on Friday nights. This was my first exposure to Hip Hop. Beatboxing allowed me to be comfortable to be alone and in my thoughts. I worked on my drum noises with my mouth, harnessing my vocal percussion. Through trial and error, I became consistent with my art, and I wanted to keep the hip hop rap influences with me. I would create a rap inside of my head and through that, I would visualize in my mind and then open my mouth and lace the beat with vocal percussion. I would then break it down and bring it back, boom-bap, boom-bap. I kept this steady throughout my growing years. It became a form of meditation for me.

After graduation, I enrolled in a community college studying Law Enforcement. I thought I wanted a career in this field, but as life evolved as it sometimes does, I went in a different direction. I finally decided to go back to school and learn a new trade and enrolled in driving school to become a transport driver. I was able to work for myself for a few years, but my creative side was something I still wanted to pursue. It was always around me from my younger years, I then realized it was the time to start something new, and this time I had nothing to lose. At the age of twenty-nine, I launched my own company, specializing in promotions and event planning. Through this experience, I was able to collaborate with a local organization and a radio station to help promote all these events. It was a social event showcasing local artists to promote their talents. I knew what the performing arts brought me in high school and now I was watching many young men and women work on themselves through their skilled performances. I am proud of the success of each event that was organized and the local talents that were promoted. I'm sure these opportunities made a positive impact on these young people in some way.

In 1995, I became a father. The day my daughter was born changed my life forever. When I saw her for the first time, I fell in love immediately. There was so much love to give this child, my child. I was young, twenty-three years old, and I did not know what this type of responsibility meant. My relationship with the mother of my child struggled and unfortunately, our relationship hit a path that I was not yet mature enough to lead. As our relationship grew further apart, I had to learn to love my daughter from a distance. I did not have the tools needed to be a responsible father. I was torn – should I run or should I stay? Ultimately, I chose to stay, but unfortunately, my family dynamic became less and less. I did the best I could with my limited experience. I have discovered that life is a matter of choices, but with every choice you make, it will not only affect you but those around you. A hard lesson to learn as a young father.

In November 2007, my second daughter was born. She brought me new love, and I knew I was more than capable of expanding my love as a father. I learned that love just expands naturally and automatically. I am blessed to have my daughter in my life; our relationship grows every day. I ensure that I'm spending time with her giving her the tools to empower herself and become stronger every day. She is my little warrior. My beautiful daughters are my greatest blessings in this life and I wouldn't have it any other way. This is a blessing that I have never regretted to this day.

Today as a single father, a son, a brother, an uncle, and a friend, I will never be silent again. I think of myself as a "Real One." Yes, I have made mistakes, but I have learned many lessons from each one of them. I am humbled by all my experiences, and at forty-seven years of age, I will continue to work to achieve the best version of myself. It's something I work on every day. I concentrate on my energy; I work on the inside which allows me to protect myself. We all face challenges daily, there are good days and then there are better days, but what is important are the lessons. I keep my life positive. I have had my heartbroken, I have witnessed sorrow, but those moments have brought me to where I am today. I know if we all do the work on ourselves, we would raise the vibrations and balance our lives better. I want to make each day count. Self-love is not selfish. I do believe in myself and if I do not fit in everywhere, I am okay with that. The "Real Ones" never do.

I have struggled in my past and I may still struggle again, but I know if my tears fall it's because I did the best I could with what I had. I am on a journey of self-love and in doing so, I am finding my power. My social media platform is a community of like-minded spiritual gangsters, providing positive vibes, self-love, social consciousness, and spiritual awareness. Everyone needs a place to heal. In a time of social injustice, silence is not the answer. We need to come together and create solutions. One thing I do know is all we have is the present. Our full power is in today. Do not concentrate on the mistake; have good intentions. If you are separating yourself to continue your positive growth, if you are stepping out of your comfort zone, this is positive. I have come to understand and learn that at the end of the day, you came into the world by yourself and you will leave by yourself. What you do in between is what matters. Money can be replaced but time can not. Time is the real riches.

We have all been there, we are face to face with adversity, the choice is always in front of us. If we concentrate on the pain, and all the negativity that goes with it, we will continue to suffer. By reaching deep within and pulling out your positivity, we can acknowledge the lesson, and when you catch the lesson, like a seed planted in the dark earth, you begin to grow and nurture yourself with love.

Think about this;

What is fear but your shadow that you were afraid to confront, not just to look at but to see, what holds you back, what makes you step back, what makes you second guess as you collect more and more stress. Perceived by society's unwavering torment, psychologically having me tripping and believing when I fall, I have made a mistake. These mistakes are hesitations. Believe in yourself, and don't underestimate. You are great, you scrape the plate and are never late. Always on time, when I rhyme as I combine my design made available by the divine, as I intertwine.

Love and fear, half the time I say who cares, but I know its just the fear, you want to keep it real, best believe you have to burn and be reborn, drop the mask, it's not an easy task but this will allow you to last, think fast, we are in the aftermath.

So why do we clash, it's because injustice is harsh. It is not equal, there will be many sequels until we get it right. This is a time to get it right. Believing in yourself can only make it right. So, what do you do, sleep all day or seize the day it's all up to you.

Michael J Ambrose was born in England, UK, is of Trinidad and St. Vincent descent, and moved to Canada at a young age. He studied at Seneca College where he received his Law Enforcement Diploma for a career as a police officer. In 1999, Michael became a transport professional which allowed him to work for himself. In 2017, he worked for the City of Toronto as a Heavy Equipment Operator. As a child, Michael also showed a love for music and used that talent to become a musical artist. He has performed in many venues throughout Toronto, providing an outlet for other young artists.

Chapter Seven

Rooted in You

WRITTEN BY: NIKKILA YOUNG-HENDERSON

*T*hings started to fall apart in every area of my life. I then became stuck as life continued to move forward; I felt left behind yet, stagnant in the present time.

"Everything is just fine! Nothing to worry about. I'll just go back bigger and better than I ever was before! I will be untouchable!"

I know. Motivating, right? Only that didn't work out the way I thought it would. I kept telling myself, "I'll do better," and "I'll be better" when there was one vital detail I was not realizing at the time and had just completely forgotten about. A very simple detail that held so much meaning. One that changed my life forever.

It all started when I landed a great job at what I thought to be one of the best places that anyone could work at. I was happy and excited to have the opportunity to be apart of a career like that. I knew it was going to take a lot of hard work and dedication to get to where I wanted to be in my career. So, that's exactly what I did. I got to work!

It was a little under a year later. I had gone through a lot of ups and downs during my training, but I had finally met the qualifications to officially work at my new job! Everyone was so excited for me and congratulated me; I was ecstatic! "This is it! I finally did it! This is exactly what I needed!" I was so ready to work even harder now to be on top of my game and to climb to the top of the corporate ladder. My main goal was to become very successful and wealthy, and now there was nothing in the way that could stop me from achieving that!

That burst of excitement was very short-lived when I find out my husband and I were expecting, and I had no choice but to stay home from becoming very ill. I felt defeated and broken. That whole time being locked away at home, I went into a depression because I felt that all I ever wanted to achieve in life was right there in front of me and it had slipped away from me in just a single moment. I felt that I was going to be left behind; everyone would achieve big things and I would need to start from square one...again.

During that long time of being locked away from the busy moving world, I realized in my space of stillness that it wasn't over; I could still return to work and achieve all that I had originally intended to. I was also at peace when I realized that my absence was for a good reason and that there was no real loss. Instead, an incredible blessing was about to come into my life.

After my time away, I finally went back to work. I was very excited and happy to see the faces I had missed so much and haven't seen in such a long time. I was expecting to be welcomed with open arms, but that wasn't the case. Things weren't the same way as they were before. Something was different. I felt it and it didn't take me long to figure out what that was.

I was seen as a threat – and was treated as such. I had a better understanding of what it would take to be successful at work because I had already been through many mistakes in the past that I had learned a whole lot from. Everyone saw a new and improved me. The way that I walked, talked, and even dressed was different. Instead of seeing me as an asset, there was a fear that I would steal the spotlight. You see, I believe whatever is meant for you, you will have, and no one can come in the way of that...unless you let them. A candle does not lose its flame in the process of lighting another candle. "I shine, you shine, we all shine together." In this case, "I support you, you support me, and we all grow together." But that isn't the way most people think. If everyone saw it the same way, I'm quite certain I would have been just fine returning to work, but things had gone from bad to worse.

I kept trying my best to show that I had what it takes to be there; that I was an asset rather than a liability, but I found myself disappointed time and time again. The more I improved my performance, the worse the animosity towards me was. I could not believe what was happening to me. I started to question myself. "Was I doing something wrong? Is there something wrong with me?" I stopped believing my goals were attainable. All that I wanted felt so much further away than it did before. "Will I really make it to where I want to be in life? Will I ever be happy?" I was growing completely numb inside.

And this is where everything in my life started to fall apart.

My relationships at work were affected because I felt uncomfortable with the environment I was in. I didn't know who I could talk to or trust. I felt like I was fighting a silent battle all alone. I started to close off and distance myself; not only at work but now in my personal life, from my family and friends. I didn't know how to explain to anyone what I was going through because it just seemed like saying the words out loud would sound ridiculous or irrational, so I kept my feelings and emotions to myself.

My financial growth had been stunted because I wasn't working to the best of my ability anymore. Physically, my body was there but I was living in my head all the time. I was so deep in my thoughts that in a way, I wasn't even in the room. Most of the day would pass and all that I was hearing would go right over my head. My performance was lacking and my income was not growing.

My physical wellness took a plunge as well. The emotions in my head began to manifest themselves into my body and I started feeling very drained. My body would feel weak all the time. I wasn't getting much sleep and sometimes I would even forget to eat. Being stressed out can take a huge toll on your body and at that point, my personal health was depleted because I didn't know how to take care of myself the right way anymore.

Things were spiraling out of control until I couldn't manage to work anymore. They got so bad that it was suggested I stay at home until I figured my life out. So now I was back at home again, the second time around. There was a feeling of defeat that surrounded me; a familiar feeling I once experienced before. I was right back where I started. I laid there in a pool of shame. How did I get here? How did I end up right back in the same place I was in not long before? I felt like my life was over, like I had lost everything, and somehow my soul felt as if it would be for good this time.

I was laid up for months in a state of depression, similar to the one I felt when I had left the first time. I cried and questioned my life and my worth. If I could never return, where else would I go? What was I going to do? I grieved so much that I felt nothing was worth living for anymore. In that moment, I felt like a complete failure.

To compensate for how I was feeling, I kept telling myself, "Everything is just fine! Nothing to worry about. I'll just go back bigger and better than I was ever before! I will be untouchable!" I would tell myself this over and over. And then it hit me. What was I even saying? Who was I kidding? So, I continued each day waking up to the dark unknown. I had no idea what I was going to do with my life.

But it wasn't over. This is where I had a pivotal moment in my life.

One day, I came across a movie where the main character worked at a corporate job that she loved, and this woman had a very trendy chic look. She gave off boss lady vibes. Throughout the movie, she went through many changes with her appearance. Over and over she would change the way she looked because she was no longer happy with her previous style. This was her going through a state of growth. At the end of the movie she had found self-love and was able to appreciate herself for who she was. She stopped trying to change the way she looked just to impress others. She quit the job she once loved so much because they did not respect her and could not see her true worth.

Just like the girl in the movie, I constantly tried changing myself so that I would be accepted. "Maybe if I wear this blazer today, they might take me more seriously. Maybe if I change my hair, they'll notice me." And then it hit me – I finally remembered that simple detail I had forgotten about.

I was perfect, exactly the way I was – every flaw and all. I am fearfully and wonderfully made, and God made us perfectly in his image.

That is when everything became clear to me. I just wasn't meant to be there any longer. I know I was placed there to go through pain and adversity regarding my personal growth. I know my trust was meant to be broken so that I could regain trust within myself. God has allowed me to grow so much because of this experience but the truth was, it was time to move on.

I kept finding myself in a continuous painful cycle of feeling like I needed to change and forcefully push myself to transform into someone I just was not meant to be. At that moment, it was decided that I would break that vicious cycle and I made one of the biggest decisions I have ever made in my life – I threw in the towel and quit!

Finally making that decision to quit was a bittersweet moment – both a huge relief and the feeling of grief because I was letting go of something I once dearly loved. A heavy weight that laid on me had been lifted. I felt like for the first time in a long while, I could actually breathe and finally move forward in my life.

If you keep pushing yourself in something that is not meant for you, God will find a way to keep steering you away from that path until you finally redirect towards the direction of your purpose.

You can't fulfill your life's purpose in a place that does not serve you.

It's okay if you don't have everything figured out. Life is meant to have challenges. As long as you make the decision to keep pushing yourself forward, and not let anything keep you down, you will be on your way to achieving a fulfilled life's journey.

Finally, that old chapter is officially closed and I'm now embracing a new chapter in life. Closing that door has allowed other doors to open and continue to open up ever since: new opportunities, new ideas, new people, and fresh experiences.

Several amazing things started to happen, and my life was beginning to flourish.

I've met new people and began to attract like-minded people into my life; people who could relate with me, understand me, and support me. The connections I made were with those of class, kindness, and respect. I opened myself up again and was capable of better communicating with my fellow peers. I could finally enjoy spending precious quality time with family and friends again.

With meeting awesome new people came many new opportunities that made way for obtaining the manifestation of financial abundance into my life. I had ideas locked away in the back of my brain that were coming to the surface. I finally had the courage to work on personal projects and not be afraid to bring many of these ideas to life. The various skills that I had built over time are being utilized in many of my recent and current projects. The time I thought had been wasted was not futile at all. God knew exactly what He was doing to prepare me for the next season in my life.

I also started a wellness journey where I am now more conscious of what I'm doing with my body and what I am putting into it. I wanted to make sure that my well-being was one of my top priorities and my personal health had drastically improved. I started taking better care of myself by making healthier eating choices like going on a gluten-free diet, working out more, using non-toxic products in my home, etc. All the conscious choices I made helped with sleeping better and made me feel much more energetic. I could sleep through the whole night. No more restless late nights. Life was good.

All that I've gone through was my blessing in disguise. Everything happens for a reason and God had (and still has) better plans for my life. I was meant to grow from this experience. The pain and heartache I've been through is now a vessel of hope and inspiration for others. No matter what life throws at you, believe in yourself. Never settle for something that makes you unhappy because you're apprehensive to start over. Don't be afraid to lose something you have in your life because God will bring about greater things that are better suited for us. From our view, we can't always see the big picture of what God is doing in our lives and where He's leading us. Don't ever fret. Know that God is going to lead you to that place of healing. God has an omniscient view of our lives and knows exactly where He wants us to go, even when we can't see it ourselves. So, take it easy, don't be too hard on yourself, and always trust in the Lord.

I want you to stand firm and proud of who you are. You're beautiful and you're amazing just the way you are. There's no need to search and have others validate you to feel complete as an individual. Search no more because the happiness you're looking for is already rooted in you.

Nikkila Young-Henderson, born in Toronto, Ontario, currently resides in Brampton, Ontario. She is an entrepreneur with a passion for the Arts and graduated from several colleges, including Niagara College, Humber College, and Body Pro Institution. At Niagara College, she graduated from General Arts and Science: Pre-Media and Design. At Humber College, she received a diploma in Fashion Arts. Nikkila presently specializes in nail technician and is also an ambassador for health and wellness, working as a Marketing Executive, educating and advertising for a wellness company. Her passion is to help inspire others to become the best version of themselves.

Facebook: Nikkila Young

LinkedIn: Nikkila Young

Instagram: nikkilayoung

Email: nikkila.young@hotmail.ca

Chapter Eight

Faith and Freedom

WRITTEN BY: ROXANNE PASHNIAK

*I*f you are going through any kind of brokenness or hardship, I encourage you that there is hope. Brokenness always leads to a breakthrough; do not be afraid to try again, to trust again because when you put your trust in the right place, you find faith and freedom. All things broken can be mended not with time but with intention. I hope you find the courage to move forward with a renewed strength and increased faith knowing that you were created on purpose for a purpose. I feel now more than ever before that my story needs to be shared because we live in a broken world full of darkness and we need to shine our light for others. I hope you are blessed.

For a child, it is difficult to comprehend why someone who was entrusted to take care of them and protect them would instead harm them. My brokenness began at a very early age. We lost my dad in a workplace accident and it was just my mom, my older brother, and I for the first eight years of my life. I have a lot of happy memories from back then; many wonderful times spent with family as we had a very close bond. I am grateful for the memories that were shared with me of my dad. I think I always felt that there was a missing piece of my heart. When I was nine years old, a man came into our lives and our hearts. It wasn't long after that he began to abuse me. He was someone I was supposed to be able to trust, yet for four years I didn't say anything as the abuse continued. I felt very confused, violated, ashamed, and afraid. Each time, I hoped it would be the last and wished he would go away. I did not feel secure to be alone and often I would be very disconnected from what was going on around me. This is when I believe I learned to cope with stress, fear, anxiety, and trauma. I could escape to a place in my mind – a safe place. I don't recall a lot of good memories from that period of my life except for the summers when my brother and I would go and stay with my grandparents. I spent a lot of time imagining a different life. I always wonder what it would have been like if my dad were still alive. I even remember a dream I had once. He seemed so real to me like he was there – it was wonderful. When I told my mom about what was happening to me, that man went away, and he could no longer hurt me. I started getting counseling, but it was very difficult. I felt sick talking about what I experienced, however, in time it seemed to get easier. My emotions and confusion about the abuse left a feeling of emptiness in my heart. No matter how much counseling I received, locked away in my mind, imprinted deep within, were the memories of the abuse I experienced. I always felt the need to be surrounded by other people; I never liked being alone. For a long time, I convinced myself that I was okay, that I had dealt with it, and I could put it out of my mind. But I know it affected my ability to focus and learn in school and as I got older, it affected every relationship I had.

Throughout my teenage years, I had a lot of friends, but I found it difficult to belong. I realized it hard to trust and I was really confused about who I was. I didn't understand it then, but I was searching to fill the emptiness in my heart. I was looking for love, affection, attention, validation, and belonging in unhealthy relationships which would only result in having my heart and trust broken even more. I am grateful for what I call the divine appointment when my life would change amazingly. I had been going through a very difficult time and a friend invited me to visit for the weekend. I decided at the last minute to leave from work and take the trip because I needed to get away. In the summer of 1997, he walked into my life. He was different from all the others. He cared for me, respected me from the beginning, and he loved me more then I think I loved myself back then. He was gentle and patient, funny, and handsome. He was kind and I knew there was something special about him. In 1999, I married the man of my dreams. With him I felt safe and secure; I felt loved and respected. I was happier than I had ever been. I was so excited to build a life with him and this was the first time I found myself dreaming of a future. We were married for about a year when I became a mom for the first time. As I held our son for the first time, I felt a love hadn't experienced before. I never imagined loving someone so much as I did at that moment. He was perfect. My heart seemed a little fuller. I remember when we found out that I was pregnant, I felt like everything that was ever wrong in my life faded away a little more. I was so happy to have my mom with us that first week but when it was time for her to go, all I felt was fear and doubt. I wasn't ready for her to leave. I think this was the first time I felt the weight and responsibility of motherhood, of keeping this little person safe. I was a mom, but would I be a good mom? As time went on, my confidence grew and so did the overwhelming need to keep him close and safe, probably natural for a new mom, right?

Our family would soon grow again when we welcomed our daughter two years later, but it wasn't long after she was born that the feelings of security, happiness, and confidence turned to worry and fear when my husband was diagnosed with cancer. Those all too familiar feelings of fear and anxiety returned, and I felt the weight of the world on my shoulders. I wanted to wake up from this bad dream. I dealt with depression and I can recall one day in particular at the health unit when I had taken my daughter for her two-month check-up and immunization. The health nurse asked me how we were doing, and I had a complete breakdown right there in her office. Everything wonderful in my life seemed to be falling apart; I was falling apart. She referred me to someone in the mental health, but that experience brought me back to that traumatic period of my life, receiving counsel from someone who had no idea what I was going through. There was so much that I wasn't prepared to deal with. I was angry and afraid; I did not understand. I spent a long time being angry with God for everything that happened in my life. Everything I learned from my mom and church when I was growing up didn't make sense. She taught me to pray and have faith in God. I believed He was in control of everything, so why? Why would God bless me with this wonderful man and our beautiful children...and then take him away? Why would He take their dad like He took mine? I put all my focus towards working, trying to provide for my family and I found that was all I could control, all I could do to stay strong.

It would be the faith and strength of my mom that would see me through this time because I was broken and weak. In the year that passed, throughout my husband's treatments and recovery, I found strength in him and our babies. It was my purpose to be strong and to care for them. My faith grew and our prayers were answered: the cancer was in remission and I learned that we could and we would overcome many things together. Financially, we were broke. I wasn't capable to provide for my family while my husband wasn't able to work but somehow, some way, I worked three jobs and with support from our family, friends, and community, we found a way through, by grace. I believe it was the strength I gained and the lessons I learned through the battle with cancer that would give me the strength and courage to face the healing journey to come. My kids would begin school and it brought me back to my past. It was almost as if I was reliving my childhood through them. Every decision I made came from a place of fear and worry and an overwhelming need to protect them. When I reflect on how I never really allowed them to do anything or go anywhere unless they were together stemmed from my fears of someone hurting them because when I was with my brother, I always felt safe. As they got older and I began to realize that certain stages, events, and situations would trigger memories from my childhood, it began to significantly affect my relationship with my family. It became clear to me that I was not okay. I was always trying to control everything and everyone and I was tired and exhausted most of the time. I wasn't happy and I didn't understand why. What I had become wasn't the wife and mom my family needed me to be, and I was not happy with myself. I did not like who I had become.

Through all the stress and two pregnancies, I gained a lot of weight and I thought if I could lose weight, I would feel better. I wanted our family to be healthy and I never wanted to go through another illness, so wellness and weight loss became my focus. I was searching for peace, happiness, and freedom but I still wasn't quite ready to face it as I continued to search for happiness in others and from the outside. I always prayed for answers, but I wasn't ready to trust. I struggled to understand how to heal the pain, anger, and resentment I was holding on to. I wasn't open to receiving what I really needed. It would take my wellness journey before I would be open to making the changes I needed to find my way back to find healing and forgiveness. I found a community of people and a premium nutrition program that would begin a transformation in me. I began sleeping better, the brain fog lifted, my stress was managed, I was losing weight, my aches and discomforts were calmed, and I was happy. The overall physical and mental wellness was a blessing. I learned then how important it was to take care of yourself. What is happening to you emotionally and mentally will manifest into physical illness. I began sharing my wellness journey helping others to feel better, become well, and live a better, healthier lifestyle. I was working with an amazing group of individuals and through this network of people, I found an incredible mentor who encouraged me to build my faith and believe in myself. About this same time, my kids had started attending a local youth group, so I decided to go to the Community Church...and I found my way back to God. I think back at how God used so many people and blessed me so much with my children. Something I learned was how important it is to surround yourself with people who help you grow and uplift you – people you can learn from. I joined a warrior women's ministry and began to learn who I was and that I was created for a great purpose. I learned about forgiveness and that the hardest person to forgive was myself. I learned that if I wanted forgiveness, I also needed to forgive. Then I forgave the man who broke my trust and caused me pain, anxiety, fear, and trauma... and it set me free from the self-imposed prison in my mind and the brokenness in my heart. It was through surrender and letting go that I was finally broke free! I found my worth, I learned to love myself, and I found an incredible peace. I found my passion for servant leadership and empowerment. I began to love fully, and I learned that the pain from my past no longer had a hold on me. I became a better mom, wife, daughter, sister, and friend.

Believing I had a greater purpose in life empowered me to go to that place inside my heart and mind that I feared to go – where the memories and pain kept me trapped, angry, ashamed, and afraid. The weight of the burden I carried with me for so long that affected me in all areas of my life and every relationship I had was not my burden to carry. All I had to do was let go. I believe God restored me and gave me a new heart when I surrendered and handed Him the broken pieces. One of the most important things I learned was that I could not control circumstances. I could not control anyone else. I could not control what goes on outside of me. I could only control myself, heal and change what was going on within me. I finally learned what it meant to let go and let God. I am amazed how God can take the worst of pain and circumstance and turn it into something wonderful and beautiful when you let go and let Him lead. In the chaos I found my calm, through the fear I found faith, in the brokenness I found forgiveness, in the healing I found peace, and on my journey, I found *Freedom*. As I think about this pandemic and I reflect on times in my life when I didn't know how I would get through the most difficult times, when we had to close our business, when we were drowning in debt, when we faced fear and uncertainty, I learned that when nothing is certain, anything is possible. The more I grow in self-awareness and understanding, the more I realize I've now experienced a few divine appointments, much like the one when I met my husband and I can see many times where God was working in my life.

As I continue through this journey, as I grow and stretch, I have made a deeper connection to the spirit within me. I have learned to let go and let God. I discovered the gifts and talents that exist in each one of us. Through study and application of who I was created to be, I understand that I was never defined by my circumstances or what happened to me – I am who I choose to become. There is a plan for your life. Along the way, you will experience pain and brokenness, heartache and disappointment, failure, defeat, and betrayal, but you are an overcomer and you are never alone. Ask for guidance, and practice love and gratitude daily. When you shift, you become aware and when you pay attention, trust and follow your intuition for your divine appointment is awaiting you. Remember, all things broken can be mended not with time, but by intention.

Roxanne Pashniak is an inspirational entrepreneur who currently resides in Ardmore, Alberta, Canada with her beautiful family. She enjoys motivational writing in her spare time and is a Best-Selling co-author in this anthology. Roxanne studied Human Potential and Success at the Proctor Gallagher Institute and Beauty Culture at Est-elle Academy of Hair Design. She is passionate about health, wellness, and healing. Roxanne is an Empowerment Coach and a Transformational Speaker by which she encourages others to discover their gifts and talents and uncover their infinite potential. You can connect with Roxanne through the following links:

Website: www.inspiringpashion.ca

Instagram: www.instagram.com/inspirepashion/

Facebook: www.facebook.com/roxanne.pashniak

Broken Trust

Chapter Nine

Enough is Enough

WRITTEN BY: CRYSTAL MCRAE

"I give in!" I looked up to the sky and shouted out. "I give in, I am done," I repeated.

Looking back, I was handing my frustration and hurt over to something else. I could not keep it in anymore. I could not ignore it anymore. I could not pretend anymore. I was done, I gave it over to something else not knowing what I was doing. I just knew that something had to change.

Over a dead cat. My life the way it was then was coming to an end. But my life truly started that evening. All because of a dead cat.

That evening, the air was still, the sun was an hour from setting beyond the horizon, and the trees, garden, and pasture were purely abundant this time of year. I was in my happy place comfortably stationed on the riding mower cutting the grass around the yard. I always found such serenity in my thoughts with the numbing sound of the engine surrounding me and this beautiful place we called home. The barns, the barbwire fence, the hills and dugouts, it was our little piece of paradise and a little more.

I noticed something, like a lump, something that did not belong in the middle of the grass, ten feet from the barn. My mind started to quickly come up with a possible explanation for something that out of the ordinary.

As I approached this strange object, disbelief started to sink in. "Oh no, it couldn't be..."

Up in the loft of the barn were half a dozen rambunctious furry and funny kittens born that spring. Their mom I had picked up in town as the residents were complaining of this stray cat hanging around our town building. Always an animal lover and willing to rescue anything that needed help, I scooped up this cat and brought her to the farm.

Not long after, I noticed that her tummy was getting a little too big and a short time later she had delivered a handful of babies in the loft, tucked tight in the corner and protected by square bales. She loved our visits, always running up to us full of pride with her responsibilities as a new mom.

Approaching this strange object, no matter my disbelief, I was faced with the disheartening fact that this lump was "Momma." She was so close to the barn but was not going to get back up to her kittens who were now orphans.

I walked back to the house and entered the kitchen. My heart was hurting, the sadness and reality started to set in.

"Something killed momma cat," I whispered.

The reply hurt my heart even more.

That was it. It was nothing but that was it. The straw that broke the camel's back. The end of my ignorance that this part of my life was nothing but a façade and I was simply not happy. No more. I was done.

I remember walking back outside with a towel in hand so that I could pick up Momma and move her. I did not get halfway to the barn when I just fell to my knees and let out a cry.

I did not leave because of abuse, violence, fighting, cheating, or anything like that. I left purely because of the lack of fulfillment I was feeling. It really had nothing to do with my relationship, Momma cat, or the fact that things weren't even that bad. To the outside world, I had gone crazy to walk away from our dream farm, happy family, and what appeared to be "a normal life."

Some people questioned why I decided to take the "hard road" and did

80

not just stay in this not too terrible marriage. Some people thought I was a bad mom for breaking up my family with two small children. I did not think that I felt in my heart there was more to life than pretending everything was okay. Yes, from the outside, it sure looked rather good – the "perfect family." But inside of me, a whole other story was written.

If it were not for a dead cat, I would not be living the story that was within me today. I would not have discovered my true potential, my purpose, my dreams, and who I was. If there was a "hard road," it was learning and discovering who I really was and am and what I was put on this earth to do; growing into that person every day determined to become the greatest version of myself. The "hard road" was discovering my strength and courage within.

I refused to live by the boundaries of other people's beliefs. In hindsight, their beliefs about me, what I could and couldn't do, what I should and shouldn't do, was a reflection of what they thought of themselves and it had nothing to do with me at all.

It was the beliefs and ideas that their parents had instilled in them, and in the generations before them. The word "divorce" is often synonymous with some catastrophic event, bad circumstance, and discouraged among many. But why? Why is choosing fulfillment and happiness frowned upon when two people are not fulfilled or happy together?

I think about that day now and then. It has been almost seven years. Seven years of conquering the demons within, beginning to unlearn many ideas that were passed down to me that did not belong to me nor true to begin with that were limiting my potential and the life I really wanted to create.

I too had this preconceived idea of what a "single mom's" life looked like. I decided I was not going to depend on anyone or anything and that I would make my own way and succeed very well at it. Ideas of poverty, lack, and limitation were all around me in various forms, but I refused to accept them as my own reality or future.

Often, we worry about the "how." How will I earn enough money on my own? How will I live? How will this work out? How about my family? How will this affect my parents' perception of me? How will people talk about me?

The truth is, yes, some people will talk about you and then they will talk about someone else five minutes later. And that is truly none of your business.

I was so fearful of what other people would think, but looking back, it did not matter. I remember one morning when the kids went back to school. I walked with them and dropped them off at the playground, turned around, and was walking home. It was the strangest feeling. I was the mom that dropped them off in the drop off zone for vehicles and drove back to the farm. That day, I was walking to my new home in town just minutes away. I was so paranoid that every car that passed me by was judging me, staring at me, questioning why I was walking in town...I felt so ashamed. I was torn inside because even though I knew my decision was right and necessary, other people would have a different opinion. This is how much we let the opinions of other people control our thinking, decisions, and ultimately our lives. It must stop for you too.

I also felt that others would think I was a disappointment, a big failure, and that I was selfish for "breaking up" my family and "hurting" my kids when really, now looking back, not making the decision to live my life fully was going to hurt my kids and I would be disappointing myself. That is what truly matters, isn't it?

We so often seek the approval of others more than our integrity and truth. We base our decisions on the opinions and beliefs of the people around us and it's crippling to your calling and the potential within you. You know that you are here to do something special, and if the circumstance or situation you are in is not giving you space to grow and dream, then you must do something about it. It's up to you and only you. If I can do it, so can you.

Not everyone is going to understand you, your decisions, and the way you want to live and that has to be okay with you. It's your job to understand yourself, to love yourself, to forgive yourself; not your family's, not your friend's – this is your job. Your family and friends want to make sure you're safe, secure, protected, and ultimately want you to be happy but what makes them happy may not be what makes you happy – and again, that is okay!

When you get to the end of your road, you don't want to be thinking "I wish I had..., I should have..., if I could go back..." But you can't. You cannot go back; we don't get a do-over or second chance. We get one shot at this thing called life, one shot and nobody knows how much time we have.

I do not buy into the "broken home" story and idea. My home now is no more broken than a home with two parents that do not even like each other to begin with. My life was not awful or horrible by any means, but I could not ignore the knowing within that this was not all there was to it.

Was moving to a small town on my own as a stay-at-home mom with two little beautiful baby boys easy?

Was staying on the farm as a stay-at-home mom, unfulfilled, with two little beautiful baby boys easy?

I do not think there is an easy or hard way. It is just the road you are on. It was just the road I was on. It was my road. You have your road.

I had to learn how to let go of the limiting beliefs society has conditioned us with as a "single mom" or "divorced parents." I had to learn how to abandon and let go of the disapproval of others and make peace with my decision. I had to recreate the person I thought I was and what I could do with my life. I went against the status quo. I refused to settle. I said enough was enough.

I went out on my own, full of hopes and dreams despite feeling insecure sometimes and I was ignorance on fire! I devoted myself to my career as an entrepreneur, business owner, and success coach and gave it everything I had. I heard the whispers and snickers of family and friends. I heard the whispers and snickers of my limited belief system. I heard the words "you're not good enough" in my head far too many times to count. I refused to surrender to mediocrity. I refused to settle for "just good enough." I decided that I was better off being a dreamer than being "safe than sorry."

Did I mess up from time to time? Yes. Did I get it right all the time? No. Did I have to develop wings along the way? Yes. Did I have it all figured out every day? No.

We are not here to tiptoe through life hoping to get to the end safely. We are here to live! Stretch our imaginations as to what is possible! To challenge what we believe and learn to think for ourselves. We spend too much time trying to fit in when we are meant to stand out! To discover our purpose, our potential, and most importantly who we really are.

Just think, really think.

Who are you? Why are you here? What do you want?

I ask myself and others these questions. It is my firm belief that these three questions are far more important than "What do you do for a living?" What do I do for a living? I live! I create! I explore! I expand! I grow!

We all have this strong innate desire to become more, do more, and have more. That is the essence of life and our being. Do not get stuck in your everyday life and forget why you are here and how you truly want to live. Who told you that you cannot live your life on your terms? What dream did you give up on? Do your goals belong to you or are they someone else's? Who do you want to become? What contribution do you dream of making to society? Why are you here?

When life throws a dead cat in your path, you must stop and think. If today was my last day, would I be doing what I am about to do today? Is this the life I want to live? If the answer is no for too many days in a row, then you know something needs to change. And that change begins with you.

If I can do it, so can you.

I am not an expert in relationships, but I am an expert in creating a life you love by design. If you know deep down inside that there is more to you, more than you are here to do, trust it. Your infinite potential and intuition are guiding you. Do not let other people's opinions and beliefs make decisions for you. You are responsible for your thoughts, your feelings, and every result in your life.

This chapter is dedicated to those who are feeling uncertain or afraid to do what they know in their hearts needs to be done, whether that is leaving a job that you are not happy in or a relationship that you know is not going work for you. There is no such thing as a "failed marriage" or a "failed attempt" at anything. Everything is an experience that you can learn and grow from if you choose to take that point of view. It is what it is: harvest the good and forgive the rest.

If you know something must change, that change must start with you. Listen to your inner knowing and heart. It knows. Be brave enough to go against the status quo or the opinions of other people and what society says. Stop settling and go after what you want.

"In order to be me, I've got to be free. To be free, I've got to be me. Not the me I think my parents think I should be. Not the me I think my spouse thinks I should be. Not the me I think my kids think I should be. In order to be free, I've got to be me. So, I better figure out who "me" is." – Bill Gove.

Blessed be. Create the life you love.

Crystal McRae, CPGC, is an Entrepreneur, a Certified Proctor Gallagher Consultant, and a Success & Results Coach. She is a contributing co-author in this anthology and had a feature article in the 1st edition of LWL Lifestyle magazine published in the spring of 2020. Crystal turned her own personal experience into a duplicatable system to help people reach their infinite potential in health, wealth, and relationships.

Chapter Ten

Tenacity and Resilience

WRITTEN BY: MARLENE MAE HENRY

$\mathcal{A}$s a person of faith, I appreciate the value of Spirituality especially in troubling times when prayer, meditation, and reflection are pillows of healing and comfort for the soul. However, there are times when these indispensable tools, although meaningful to the individual battling with personal life challenges in the healing process, require more than just the words "Get over it," "Pray harder," or "You must have done something wrong." This can plunge one into further feelings of hopelessness and despair. The need for counseling and community support are best served to aid the individual to transition from helplessness towards a place of healing and wellness. However, when life happens unexpectedly with facing the reality of emotional health and well-being, that is another story!

I wrote this chapter to encourage others that when life takes an unexpected turn, and a disappointing turn leaves you feeling distressed, disappointed, and disoriented, don't give up! Use your experience to fuel your passion, turn your failure into success, and most of all, never give up on your dreams.

Years ago, I qualified as a second career recipient and enrolled in a two-year college course which would start in the fall of the same year. The previous year, after having waited four years for a sponsorship application to be approved, it finally happened, and the feeling of accomplishment and relief was overwhelming. Those moments of joy compensated for all the time and effort I invested over the years along with the financial cost of airline tickets and long-distance calls. I felt a sense of relief and hope for a brighter future, the reality that this long-distance relationship was now a reality and we were finally together in real-time. My family, friends, and faith community (a small nucleus) was happy for me, having provided emotional, social, and spiritual support through the process. Things were going very well for me emotionally, mentally, and financially for that first semester. I became a sponge at school and was fascinated with my program, learning, and soaking up everything. The ability to align the concepts and terminologies and reflect the contents to my everyday experiences was a fluid process for me. For example, I was co-experiencing in the "honeymoon stage" where there is a sense of awe with dreams and aspirations to be captured, seized, and accomplished. It was not until my first semester that I noticed a change in my relationship and my whole world came crashing down leaving me in a state of shock and bewilderment. I felt like a deer caught in headlights. I became confused, emotionally distressed, and ultimately depressed. The "honeymoon" was over. I wondered what the hell had happened!

When the enormity of my situation hit me, a mixture of feelings overwhelmed me, including sorry, anguished, distress, and defeat, and I retreated into an introverted state of existence of silence. This was not my normal character of an outgoing and active personality. As a means of self-rescue, when the enormity of my situation hit me, I felt foolish for having believed that my life was worth fighting for; that the odds were too much against me now that I was alone. The thought of giving us appeared more reasonable than to fight. Moreover, I felt mentally, emotionally, and psychologically tired. Persistent thoughts plagued my mind, having to explain to those around me. What would people say? In desperation, I prayed and cried for days, while wrestling with the state of mental confusion. I asked God why and sought answers, but none came. I made up my mind that when I returned to school the following January, I would inform my program supervisor that I was quitting school. I scheduled a meeting and after relating my sorrowful story, I was advised to see the school counselor. I reluctantly agreed and was guided to the counselor's office. After the meeting, I left the office a changed person. The counseling session morphed into a dialogue and the conversation became so stimulating that I found myself responding and engaging in a way that surprised even myself. Not only did I receive and benefit from a compelling, emotional, and mentally stimulating conversation, the meeting fueled and renewed my passion. I was told by the counselor, "You are counseling me, not the other way around."

To minimize my financial situation, I gave away the entire contents of my three-bedroom apartment to family and friends, and a friend took me in for the balance of the semester. During my last year, I couch surfed and on one occasion, I was sleeping on someone's floor.

During that time, my private life was a mess but my study life, though challenging, felt rewarding. I poured myself into my studies. The library became my place of study and the school caput a place of solace and solicitude. Commuting to campus was a challenge as it often took over two hours back and forth. I remember in preparation for exams, sleeping on campus many times to minimize time and commuting costs. But through all of this, I began to realize that with everything I was going through, somehow, I knew there was purpose in my pain.

During my study experience, I signed up as a Student Ambassador and represented the "matured student" intake cohort. I became Vice-President of the campus club, I also signed up as a mentor volunteer assuming five students, and I employed creative ways and channels in mentoring students assigned to me. For example, we would meet one-to-one during class breaks, during lunch, or while waiting in the cafeteria line, via e-mail or by telephonic means. In addition, I was able to garner enough financial sponsorship to participate in a cross-border practicum experience attached to my program study during my final semester.

It was also during this turbulent time in my life that I started a nonprofit organization that collaborates with other organizations in providing awareness, information, training, and facilitation to support individuals, groups, and communities in maximization of their full potential.

Coupled with my personal life's challenges, I participated in the hands-on experiences and new pedagogy of learning interacting with individuals, groups, and the community. Because of all the stress I was going through, I had developed health issues and was diagnosed with hypotension and type 2 pre-diabetes. To understand more about my situation and to help others, I signed up and got trained as a Community Diabetes Awareness Ambassador. What I learned, I was able to take it to my community and raise awareness in the possible detection and treatment when dealing with type 2 diabetes. I facilitated various information sessions through church groups, the local community and college, and at University I raised the subject through group work project and advocacy among other social burdens. This included the increased financial cost as the health factors for students upon graduation in developing diabetes from precarious diet and eating habits. I was living with both of these experiences myself.

Having personally experience vulnerability, I connected with those who are also vulnerable. I remembered during my last semester, the professor placed four power-point pictures on the screen and then asked us to identify which of the slides resonated with us. We were to place ourselves in a group. The picture I chose depicted a row of trees on each side of along a narrow stretch of road. Wow! This did me in. I started to cry when my turn came to share why I chose to be in the group. I tried to speak but the tears turned into uncontrollable sobbing. Without a word said, the group all huddled together and gave me a group hug. This gesture provided comfort, understanding, and connection for me. That day, I learn what empathy and compassion to an individual from a group or a community felt like. I am more aware, I pay more attention, and I'm learning to listen more in my interaction with people. These experiences have also fueled my passion with my work in support of individual capacity-building using the tool of education.

At the end of my college study, I graduated successfully but I did not stop there. I was encouraged by my program coordinator to pursue an undergrad degree. I remember her telling me, "What you do is not only important but why you do what you do." So, I chose a particular stream of study that would provide further pedagogical insights for me. Needless to say, I had to move to another city and the personal challenge did not end; it became more bearable as I was not alone. Two other students accepted the transfer degree offer and we lived and studied together. My room was without furniture but because of my past experience finding creative solutions, sleeping was not so bad, and living off the school pantry was a blessing. I was also active in campus life and volunteered in various activities to maximize learning opportunities.

In the end, my academic exploration and advancement gained me my

BA. in Community Development (ComDev) Cum Lade on the Dean's list which and was published in the local newspaper. Because of my positive learning experience, I decided at the end of my studies to stay and I became an import making this city my new home. I was successful in gaining employment, I became an active member of a local church, and I also give back to the community through volunteerism with local organizations and community groups. Having moved from an urban smaller rural city, the social and cultural integrations for me were the most challenging but from personal experiences, I found the twin value of tenacity and resilience compatible for my personal self-development and confidence building in any given situation.

I felt more ready, more informed, and most equipped for the next level as now I understood what systems needed to be challenged through advocacy for laws to be put in place that seek to promote inclusion and equity so that everyone can benefit.

I continue to press on and am presently pursuing my masters with a proposed 2021 graduation.

I found out through my personal experience that culture plays a part in how we approach personal challenges. For me, it was the culture of silence and the stigma associated with having to expose personal weakness and failure. From my experience, when I was experiencing my personal breakdown and dealing with the trauma that precipitated, my mental health and wellness were extremely compromised, and because many persons did not understand, I received many critiques suggesting demonization in my situation, and I was further isolated and stigmatized. I had to make a deliberate effort to stay focused on my faith in God, that although I did not understand, I would continue to persevere. The more I pressed on to pursue my goals, the more I felt a sense of accomplishment and my self-confidence was beginning to be rebuilt. I learned it is a process. I seek to encourage those reading my story that you do not have to be ashamed of personal failure or be timid in seeking professional help and counseling. Life happens where we are helpless to do anything about it, but how we respond can either make or break you. The choice is yours and mine. I believe in order to navigate physical, emotional, social, mental, moral, and spiritual spaces, counseling is a vital component not to be ignored. I was counseled to refocus my sense of self-defeat to one of possibility and passion by using what I presently had to empower myself.

At that time, it was the study opportunity that I was given through the Second Chance Career program. I had to make the conscious choice of not looking at my present situation as the end of life. What was happening to me did not define who I was; I am valuable and an overcomer. I often had to resist "self-fulling prophecies" with fear of failure by talking to myself many times and I was able to hear my inner voice inner to reclaim my self-confidence and dignity. Through the process and experience, I discovered my life's purpose. As a visionary and trained Community Chaplain, I recognized the invaluable benefit of counseling for individuals, groups, and the community as part of the self-care process. I am now an advocate of the holistic approach to individual mental wellness and care with equal merit and validity of Spirituality, Social support, and Counseling that can be useful in assisting individuals to address, manage, and overcome personal challenges.

When the COVID-19 pandemic struck, I must admit that I was disoriented and taken off guard with having to switch to the online platform. I felt uncomfortable for days and feelings of anxiety and confusion overwhelmed me. Since I purposely opted for all campus in-class learning, I was not mentally or psychologically prepared for the sudden change. In addition, I was overly concerned about my inability to remain focused, hearing the negative news from the media, and managing my personal health. To compound the issue, the environment I was staying in was temporary and transitional, and not conducive for private and seclusive study. I was using both the nearby and campus libraries to study and complete assignments. Once again, a friend came to my aid and accommodated me for a couple of weeks. I was able to finish the semester successfully and traveled home safely and appropriately.

Having the confidence with an online platform, I kept busy by partnering with other organizations to execute a virtual fundraiser to help international students, visitors, and vulnerable individuals affected by COVID-19. Through this experience, I met so many great individuals and we have now become a new family with common goals and purpose, not to mention that I am more prepared for my final year using the online learning platform.

Looking back over this and other experiences, I have learned some valuable lessons:

One – courage to disclose deactivates pride and open doors for transparency, support, and healing.

Two – forgiveness of self, and others, bring enrichment to life, and allows positive steps to the next level.

Three – don't discount your failures; learn from them. Remember, we are all imperfect people.

Four – look for opportunities to influence change in your sphere of influence and create a path for others to follow. It will outlive you.

Hence, I am humbled to say, I survived the pain, I thrived in the challenge, I am flourishing with the experience, and having fun living in purpose. My journey continues!

Marlene Mae Henry is the President of Helping Hands International. She promotes a holistic approach to self-care through awareness, information, training, and counseling. Marlene holds a Bachelor of Arts (B.A.), Community Development (ComDev) cum laude, Algoma University, and a Social Service work diploma, Honors, Seneca College. She received the Seneca College "Leading by Example" and "Student Mentoring in Life and Education" (SMILE) Awards, was featured in the Alumni 2013 Red Magazine, and was the poster child for "Because it Matters" Ad Campaign (2014). Presently, Marlene is pursuing a Master's Theological Studies (MTS) from Tyndale University, is the 2020-202 Student Counsel Seminary VP of Operations, and received the Baraca Philathea Scholarship for Christian Education.

Instagram: #marlene9127

Twitter: Marlene #@mmaehenry

LinkedIn: #mmaehenry

Facebook: #Marlene Mae Henry

Broken Trust

Section Two

FINANCES

Sometimes the best things are gained by losing everything.

Rose Marie Young

You Are Bigger
Than Your Presence

WRITTEN BY: ROSE MARIE YOUNG

*H*ave you ever been taken for a financial ride? In my opinion, everyone should be financially educated and be made aware of how the financial world can affect each of us either positively or negatively. This is a real and serious issue. Educate yourself.

Over the years, as many others do, I have experienced and have witnessed the struggles of financial hardships. In this chapter, I am only giving you just a glimpse of one such experience. It was a very difficult time for me as I was extremely stressed. I was already going through so much anxiety and depression caused by the losses from two major life-changing car accidents when these individuals were introduced and interjected themselves into my life. These perpetrators seemed so very sympathetic to my situation. Sadly, during that specific time, I was already in so much pain, not only physical but also emotional pain and anxiety from the stress of losing my self-esteem as well as my jobs.

In my mind, they wanted to help. The pitch they gave was fantastic, but it was rather a very false presentation. Perhaps they had made this same presentation to many others who like me, believed them. Looking back now, it seems so rehearsed. I was even misled by the impression that one of them was a church minister. They told me they could help me make some financial investments that would protect me from losing even more. However, they did not. It took me a while to realize that they only wanted to capitalize on what they could get for themselves. They intentionally went out of their ways to sabotage me instead of helping with any of my financial affairs. In the end, they stole it all. My bank account was left empty...and so was my life. This left me completely shattered. I lost all my assets as well as my house and home.

My heart was bruised by their dishonesty as I struggled to comprehend what had taken place. How could I be so wrong? I trusted them. However, as mentioned, to my surprise they did not have my best interest in mind. They were dishonest from the very start, but I could not see it because they gave me a false representation of themselves. They lied with shameless smiles on their faces each time we met. Now I questioned why and how did I attract those people into my life? The answer is simple: I was not my best self, and in those moments, I was only attracting the negative I was feeling within me. I became quite depressed and blamed myself for a while, but because of my strong faith in God and months and months of prayers, I was able to overcome. If it was not for my faith, I could not have made it to where I am today. Although it took a while, this experience has helped me to grow and has taught me a lot. It has truly changed my life for the better.

Now, as I watch and see what's going on in our world today, I realized that there are so many individuals who need emotional healing. So many people struggle with financial brokenness by default, lack of financial knowledge, or even because of unfortunate circumstances like that of the worldwide pandemic. Some people have lost their businesses, others have lost their jobs, their homes, and even worst, the lives of their soul providers. It can be a hard battle to be strong, but it can be much harder when one's financial brokenness comes from the people in whom you trust. It is very disturbing to see people taking disadvantage of others just because they feel they can. No one should be put in a position where he or she is left to feel financially helpless or hopeless. No one should ever be forced to become homeless or have to wonder where their next meal will be coming from. It is just wrong for all humanity (but as we know, life happens).

You might be feeling completely frustrated and overwhelmed by the brokenness of your financial affairs, but with the right mindset and knowledge, you can and will rise back up from the ashes. From my experience, I strongly believe that we should not only take time to educate ourselves, but we should also take time to investigate those we are entrusting with any fiscal investments. It is important to get a second opinion before signing and making any financial exchanges as well. Regardless, brokenness in your business or any of your monetary affairs does not have to be a lifetime sentence. Money and otherworldly material things are simply just that. The number of zeros in your bank account, or the number of dollars in your wallet, do not define who you are as a person and most definitely are not representative of your true worth nor your self-value.

Bottom line is, in my situation, like many, I had to start over. Always remember, it is not the fall, but the climb. Don't give up. Keep climbing. It may take many steps, but eventually, you will be at the level where you need to be again. Not to make light of any situation, but I have been where you are. I understand why you are upset. I have felt the disappointment of being blindsided and not knowing where nor how to get the support I needed to rebuild. Once there is life, there is hope. Be persistent, be optimistic, and have faith. Equip yourself with materials that contain information designed to give you answers and will educate you in your financial situations. As the saying goes, "Knowledge is power." Harness that power and use it to catapult and elevate yourself to a higher level. Ask for help. Pray for help. Never loses sight of the person you are. You always have a voice and you always have a choice. Don't let your financial brokenness keep you down. Try not to provoke your spiritual being with anger and hate for those who have wronged you. With a positive abundance mindset, you will be able to keep your focus on rebuilding and renewing a positive transformation of your entire life.

No need to hold on to grudges as they can cause severe mental damage. Forgive and release the negative energy of everyone who has taken from you what was not given. Forgive those who have deliberately caused you harm and those who have despised you during and before your brokenness. Even if it takes some time, you will need to forgive everyone including yourself. Without forgiveness, you can never be healed. Without forgiveness, you will always feel broken. Libertate yourself. It's time to take back control by allowing and permitting yourself to be. Also, by allowing yourself to forgive and having a clean heart, you will able to open up a mind of creativity and a mind of possibilities for your new future. You can be stronger than you have ever been with a clear and much better understanding of what your intentions are for new adventures as you walk away from the past. No longer will you feel the oppressions of the limitations and the imprisonment of your oppressors. Instead, you will feel freed and empowered.

I do believe that sometimes the universe purposely allows us to go through brokenness to prepare us for deeper understanding, patience, and growth. It grooms us for better things to come. At times when certain things happened, we cannot accept responsibility nor can we take care of ourselves at that moment, but you can use your brokenness and mishaps to build your courage and strength. I understand that sometimes the emotions and frustrations can become an obstacle as you may have tried hard for your voice to be heard. Focus on the positive. You will overcome. Nothing lasts forever. This too, whatever it is, will pass. Take control of your emotional state of mind. Free yourself from emotional damages. Yes, you have been hurt, but forgive and allow yourself to open up your inner space and let others in. By letting go of all the anger, you are allowing your heart to heal, which enables you to grow and helps you to gain access to an abundant life. It can be a challenge to get back up but allow yourself to reconnect with your true authentic self.

Yes, the world can be unkind at times, but by overcoming and growing from your brokenness, you can influence others who might be facing the same challenges as you have. You can be the change that makes the difference in so many lives affected by financial brokenness. Although you might not able to see it now, your story has a purpose. Believe that you are capable of doing greater work in this vast universe even within your brokenness. You Are Stronger Than Your Present Circumstance. You will rebound and you will be well. Remember, you have a God who is always in control. He is bigger than your situation and He is standing with you. Deuteronomy 20:4 says, *"For the Lord your God is he that goeth with you, to fight for you against your enemies to save you."* Although you have been wronged, be honest, and be your truth. Not to worry; have faith that God will align you with the right people in your life who are trustworthy. Speak financial abundance back into your present as you move into your future. God will restore your losses – and more. He will build a fence around you while he allows you to rebuild and grow.

Do not stay a victim of your financial circumstances. Reclaim your power. It will take your determination, great expectations, and action to regain what you have lost, but do not give the culprits control over your life. The financial struggles that you are experiencing right now will eventually create a foundation for your future. Find and develop the positives from all the negatives, and like a camera, take another shot. You will find your strength in your brokenness.

"For where your treasure is, there will your heart be also"
Matthew 6:21 KJV

Broken Trust

Chapter Eleven

Building a Money Mindset

WRITTEN BY: BRIAN HENRY

*T*his chapter will help you understand the culture shock of immigration and how credit drives and complements your finances and your success in the building of wealth and all other relationships in your life.

I grew up in my birth country Jamaica, where I lived for the first nineteen years of my life. That's where I received all my primary and secondary education. I attended Spanish Town Primary School in Spanish Town, St. Catherine's, Jamaica. In 1980, I completed Grade 6 and was transferred to Bog Walk Secondary School where I started in Grade 7. We had to move to this new city because we were living on Squatters Land and one day, a group of hooligans raided our home and robbed us of the little we had.

New School: Bog Walk Secondary

I was just in time to catch the beginning of the school year. The three years I spent at Bog Walk Secondary School taught me how to trade for a living. I was of the "have nots" community, and a place where, deep in my heart, I knew would not be my home for long, so I really never settled in mentally. In my fourth and final year at Bog walk Secondary School, I checked out and checked myself into the famous and upscale Dinthill Technical High School. This was where the kids who lived in the "haves" community went to school...and so should I.

Entering Dinthill on Scholarship that I Gave Myself

On Monday, September 3, 1984, I got dressed for what was the first day of my final year at Bog Walk Secondary School. After the normal thirty minutes walk to the taxi stand to get a taxi for school, I decided right then and there that I was going to Dinthill, which was located in the opposite direction. And so, I did.

Upon reaching the new student registration office at Dinthill, I saw some students who actually received scholarships because of their athletic or academic abilities. Anyway, to make a long story short, I convinced the registrar office I belonged here and I was admitted.

After I was accepted, I was placed in the special scholarship class with all the others who had received genuine scholarships in class 2H.

Dinthill became my life for the next three years where my friends and classmate were my world until I graduated in the summer of 1987 with five subjects.

Migrating to Canada and The Biggest Disappointment of My Life

On Monday, November 2, 1987, I landed at Pearson International Airport. I was nineteen years and ten months old, ready for my riches, and to live the life of the "haves." I was sponsored to live in Canada by my dad, whom I had no relationship with or ever spoken to until July 1986. I grew up living with my mom. To be frank, all my life I had waited for this day to move and live in Canada. I was under the impression that once I migrated, I would become one of the "haves" because only where I was coming from had the "have nots." No one ever told me they were here too. So, I made the big crossover by migrating to Canada. In late October, after receiving my permanent visa and my travel ticket, I wasted no time in giving away all my belongings because I was going to Canada where I would be rich once I get off the jet plane. I could not have been more wrong in my life! I was very wrong!

Everything that I was told that Canada would be was nowhere in sight. The night went on fine. I delivered the bag of goodies I brought. I was taken to a small room overnight, which was the size of the interior of my special truck – a Hummer H2 (I have owned a few of them over the years) and was picked up the following morning. I was given a long, silky trench coat because it was autumn and the temperature was about three degrees. My address on my landed document was in the St. Clair Avenue West area of Toronto, an area that may be familiar to some readers. It was a seedy rundown part of the city with funny looking metal boxes on wheels attached to the overhead electrical wiring in the middle of the road. I was told they were streetcars. Remember, I was under the impression that Canada was golden, and all the "have nots" were back in Jamaica, not in Canada. After being in Canada, I understood Jamaica was actually paradise. By this time, I realized the fallacy and deception were clear and real. I felt I was tricked by the media, the people who had come before me, and the images on TV. I was upset – with the world and myself.

My first real job was at a button factory the second day I was in Canada. I was on the night shift, working from 11 p.m. to 7 a.m. I was the only black man, or should I say boy, because I was not a man yet working there. This was my first exposure to white people. I started my shift at my station making buttons. About two hours in, we got a fifteen-minute break, signaled by an alarm. After a few minutes I went back to my station, but I was late so the machine was already going because it stopped and started with the alarm, so it already had started, causing the buttons to be backed up. The supervisor had to run and shut it off. For the next hour, I stood in the same spot. I was getting tired, so I called the supervisor and I told him I was really tired and wanted to sleep. I wanted to know where I could go lie down. At this point in my life, I really did not know people could work all night and not be expected to sleep. I wanted to know who would be taking over or should I shut off the machine. The supervisor laughed and walked away. I called him back and said, "Sir, I am falling asleep. I am not joking." He realized that I was serious, and he then called the other supervisor and they both had a good laugh. I was fired and sent home at 3 a.m. in the streets of Toronto on my second day in Canada. All I had was 50 cents (35 cents was my fare to get home) which was 50 cents more than I had bought with me to Canada a day earlier. Over the next few months, culture shock and the fact that I now really missed my friends and family started to take a toll on me. I felt extremely homesick and was stressed out. I gained twenty pounds from eating junk food and sodas because that's all my budget could afford.

Within the first year, I bounced around a lot from job to job. I could not find a decent job because most good jobs needed Canadian work experience to which I did not have. Hence, I was not able to support myself and to fulfill my promise to my friends and family back home in Jamaica. I was so ashamed and embarrassed of myself.

My Introduction to Credit in Canada

In Jamaica, being part of the "have nots," I was not exposed to institutional credit. My mere knowledge of credit was based on bartering or borrowing cash from friends, and the repayment plan was never clear. This was also "the trust" mostly used by our parents, where they would send us kids to the local grocer and take an advance on food items with the promise to pay later – although no clear repayment plan was ever established. So of course, I thought the same applied here in Canada.

To my surprise, I was wrong again. Within my first year in Canada, I received over $20,000.00 in credit even without a good job. I thought, "Wow! I am rich!" By the time I was twenty-one years old, I was in debt for over $100,000. I had to file for bankruptcy with just the shirt on my back and a few more pieces of clothes because most of the credit I had received was used as additional income.

Ironically, I was just starting my career in Finance – working as the Vault Attendant at a financial institution in Toronto.

A quick rundown of my income and expenses for a typical month back then was:

Monthly Income:

    1.Salary: ……………………..………………$736.50 net

Monthly Expenses:

    1. Car Payment: …………………………… $355.00

    2. Rent: …………………………..…….. $350.00

    3. Car Insurance: ……………………… $415.00

    4. Gas for my Car: ……………………. $250.00

5. Food: $450.00

6.

7.

8.

9.

10. Let's stop here and allow you to complete this for yourself.

The Big Turn Around

It all fell apart in the summer of 1989. I was basically using credit cards as an additional paycheck because my current income ran out after about two weeks each month. I could not make ends meet. At the end of the summer that year, broke and desperate, I went back to the only thing I knew: merchandising or hustling. This is what I had learned as a youngster at Bog Walk Secondary School, and what I saw my mom do for years. On Friday, June 30th, 1989, I received my monthly paycheck for $736.00. I took the entire amount to a haberdashery in Kensington Market in Toronto and handed it to the store owner who had wholesale items such as kids' clothing and household items such as towels and bedding. From my cheque, I got back $50.00 and a large hockey bag full of merchandise. That weekend, I went door-to-door, sold my merchandise, and by the end of the weekend, I had cleared $3,500.00 and had about 25% of the stock remaining. On Monday, July 3, 1989, I call my supervisor at the bank and submitted my resignation.

I felt I was in my element, my niche. By the summer of 1991, I had more money than I ever thought possible and earned the nickname "Rich Kid." This pseudo rich kid did not last. By the age of twenty-four, I managed to lose it all. I knew how to make money because I taught myself how to, but I did not learn the art of sustainability. The only thing I ever thought to do with money was to spend it, not realizing that if you are going to spend money every day, then you will need to earn money every day – even when you are sleeping. Hence, I set out on a new journey of how to keep it.

I went back to school to study finance. After my studies, I became a Mortgage Specialist. To support myself while in school, I would wash commercial trucks at night.

I opened a Mortgage office in Toronto in 2004 and I was doing great. I would work in my office during the day and continued to wash trucks at night. My truck washing business, which I had registered a few years back, brought me an opportunity to get in the fuel business which I took and opened a Mobile Fuel Company.

This new company was a hit, and within the first two years, I bought eight new fuel trucks and hired a staff of nine, including five drivers, and had some of Canada's biggest trucking companies as my clients.

By 2007, after operating both the mortgage and the fuel company day and night, it took a toll on me. In the spring of that year, I took a vacation, and while I was gone, my fuel company spilled 8,000 liters of fuel. This single event brought me to my knees.

A few months later, the fuel crises hit the world and the price of fuel went flying high. Then came the recession in 2008, and some of the smaller companies I was servicing went bankrupt with money owned to me – I was done. I closed the mortgage office in Toronto and continued with the fuel company until July 31, 2011, when I closed the doors after being fined hundreds of thousands. I took a four-year sabbatical leave in 2012 and returned to Canada a new man and ready again in 2016. I reopen my mortgage office in May of the same year to help my fellow Canadians with their home financing process. I fully understood the principle of borrowing and lending in Canada.

Once the concept of borrowing, lending, and investing was clear to me in the Canadian financial marketplace, I started to see how truly rich people stay rich wherever they lived. I learned the concept of borrowing money for the right reasons and the role of having good credit plays in the building of wealth. I learned how to maintain good credit and the leverage good credit gives. One primal fact, your credit will always multiply your cash reserve. I was then introduced to the Credit Structure and the 5 C's of Credit that for the most part governs lending in Canada. I have taken the liberty of including them in this Chapter as outlined below.

When it comes to borrowing and your financial health, the key is to understand the 5 C's of Credit and what each one means.

Character

A Lending Institution, such as a bank or a mortgage company, perception of a borrower's personality, credibility, and their general finances. Banks want to lend or do business with people who are responsible and committed to a cause.

Capacity

Banks want to be assured that the borrower can repay the loan or mortgage from their job and income sources.

Capital

Banks want to know that they are not alone in this process on the loan or mortgage journey; that you are willing to risk your own money and not just theirs.

Conditions

This is the current state of the economy and your current situation in life. Is there anything that might affect your ability to repay the loan or mortgage?

Collateral

This is the asset that is used to guarantee or secure the loan or mortgage. Collateral is a backup source if the borrower cannot repay the loan or mortgage.

Today, I am a student of the Mortgage Broker Program and I am in the final phase of studies. Once I had learned the simple system of focusing on my own credit and finance, and the true purpose of credit, the wealth-building process begins.

Brian Henry has been an entrepreneur, for as long as he can remember, in various types of businesses but mainly Fuel, Trucking, and Finance. He also served as Commissioner of Affidavit on behalf of the Mortgage industry from June 2006 to July 2009. Currently, he is a licensed Mortgage Specialist in the Financial industry, servicing the residents of the Greater Toronto Area and the Waterloo Region. Brian is also a non-denominational Pastor for the people of Ontario and is a strong believer in pro-choice. Some of his most fulfilling days are those when he helps his clients with their home financing.

Landing Page: www.kitchenermortgages.ca

www.kwmoneylenders.ca

Instagram: https://www.instagram.com/kitchener_mortgages/

Facebook: https://fb.me/kitchenermortgages

Email: brianhenry2120@gmail.com

Chapter Twelve

Challenge, Heal & Inspire

WRITTEN BY: VIVIAN AMADI

Financial trust can be broken in different ways, but it can also be healed. Even with the promises of healing, it's been so hard for most people to recover from broken trust. The natural effect is to always live their lives full of doubt for anyone they will ever meet. Broken trust forces us, firstly, to acknowledge a painful reality we may not have the choice to ignore; then we have to make some difficult decisions. Now, the trust has broken down. It will take some time to change attitudes, and attitudes are going to be needed to develop trust again. Broken trust is all about the betrayal of trust first given.

After relocating to Canada and trying to put behind me the mistrust and betrayal of the yesteryears, I found out that trust can be shattered in every part of the world and it's not a matter of ethnicity. I am determined to provide my personal experience that will help each of us better understand the world of finance, and take actions that identify betrayal of trust, challenge it, and inspire change – in times of financial crisis and beyond.

I got married in the month of my University graduation in 2000. Together, my husband and I had a good head-start in life. Overall, our level of financial literacy was abysmally low. Nevertheless, we had a target for early retirement, and the key to that dream was financial freedom. After wide consultations, we settled for the Capital Market. The years between 1998 and 2008 were arguably the golden years of the Stock Market business in Nigeria. The country was transiting to a more stable democratic government. Nigeria was a major producer of crude oil and the prices were soaring. An unprecedented volume of Foreign Direct Investment was pouring into the country. Expectedly, the Capital Market blossomed. Other players in the financial sector, like the banks, also flourished.

My husband and I were busy and happy professionals. We were looking for a passive source of additional income without active engagement in terms of time and energy. Furthermore, the return on investment in the Stock Market was considerably high. When the Nigerian economy began to thrive, the Capital Market was the most visible face of that prosperity. For these reasons and more, the Stock Business was an easy choice.

We engaged a popular brokerage firm to handle our investment. We nominated the firm to act as our proxy. By the time we assumed we had attained financial freedom, the first hints of a global economic recession began to filter in. Big companies started to lay off workers in the name of downsizing. Almost all the economic indicators began to fluctuate, and the Stock Market was not left out. In the developed world, mortgage loans were going bad and banks started foreclosing properties. In Nigeria, crude oil prices were dropping at an alarming rate. By the end of April that year, capital flight had begun. Foreign investors were selling off their holdings and repatriating the funds to their home countries. Everything was happening so fast. It was unbelievable! Inevitably, the prices of stocks began to fall. All the indices were looking very bad. We panicked and asked him to sell off our stock investment before it would eventually have a dangerously free fall.

The firm assured us that it was the wrong time to sell. Tragically, we later learned that the firm took margin facilities from the banks to purchase large volumes of shares. The idea was to make a bumper harvest within a very short time frame; liquidate the loans and reap big profits. Expectedly, the banks went after their remaining assets. In other to maintain their solvency status, the firm sold off the stocks in their custody including ours without our knowledge. Yet, the regulatory body suspended their license and they fled the country. We lost everything!

I learned that wealth creation is usually accompanied by a certain appetite for risky investments and adventure no matter how careful you are. Such risk is somehow a factor of trust. However, a prior analysis of the trust you give people in terms of returns compared to the risk versus benefit is required for an informed decision. Typically, you need to trust someone. There is no financial investment that does not require trust. The riskier the investment/trust, the more the benefit you realize, as obtained in every high-risk investment. But once you are hit by broken trust, the effect can be long-lived.

I advised myself to become free from the broken trust and to live today as if yesterday never happened. Understanding that not all people will betray you is key to moving on and recovering from a past betrayal. Just because one person lied to you doesn't mean that all people are liars too. If you fall into a cynical mindset where everyone cannot be trusted, you'll only isolate yourself and breed a toxic mindset that can cause you to feel even more misunderstood and lonely.

The gold jewelry business is a lucrative venture I was inspired to start, by a friend who made a lot of profit from it, when I was in law school. The business exposed me to a lot of acquaintances, and I became friends with other gold jewelry sellers. To reduce expenses on individual business trips, we agreed to contribute money and gave to an individual who would take the flight to Dubai and make the purchases on behalf of others, respecting individual demands. We did that turn-by-turn and we saved a lot of money. We also helped each other to sell. The business relationship was the best I have witnessed. Everything was running smoothly until we contributed money and gave it to a particular lady. Little did any of us know that she was planning a relocation from Nigeria. She took all our money and disappeared into the thin air. The worst is that nobody could tell which part of the world she disappeared to. It was the most devastating event in my whole life!

I realized that there are a lot of green snakes in the green grass. We all have to be very selective about the people we trust. No matter how they present themselves to be nice. Not everyone can be trusted. I picked the pieces of my business together. I got help from family and friends and bounced back to business. I strongly believe that *weeping may endure for a night, but joy [cometh] in the morning* – Psalm 30:5. The nature of my business was to take the jewelry to a prospective buyer's office or home or vice versa. Different customers would call me at will to show them my stock and expectedly, my sales increased remarkably, and even other gold sellers took stock from me to sell for some commission. On a certain day, I took my wares to another city to show a very prominent politician. On my way back, one of the gold sellers who presented an urgent need for jewelry kept calling me. Because she claimed her customer would use it the next day, I didn't want to lose the patronage and was carrying her along with my movement. Immediately when I got into town, I called and notified her of my whereabouts. At the same spot, I was robbed and all my gold jewelry was stolen, including my car. God saved me from being shot.

Luckily, the robbers were caught but the jewelry had been disposed of. Upon investigation, it was discovered that the robbers acted on the instructions of my caller of that day – the gold seller. This was the same lady that came several times to console with me for my loss and was so concerned about the progress we were making in the investigation. Again, trust was broken.

Once trust has been broken by multiple people on multiple occasions, believing in anyone or anything becomes increasingly difficult. Much of the skepticism of our world can be traced back to broken trust.

The provision in Psalm 37:21, *"The wicked borrows and does not repay, but the righteous shows mercy and gives"* has been instructive to my attitude towards family and friends. Continually, people come to borrow from you and continually fail to repay. I do not understand where they have sold their shame to. In the natural observation of the second part of the above provision, we ultimately become addicted to prolonged deceit. After weighing the words in Colossians 2:8, *"See to it that no one takes you captive by philosophy and empty deceit, according to human tradition, according to the elemental spirits of the world…,"* I resisted the ploy. Our native life is that of an extended family system where a fifth-generation cousin can be as close as a sibling. Initially, when family or friends came for a friendly loan, I would give and even without an agreement. Most times, I found myself arguing about figures. Written agreements seem formal and really need not play a part where trust is established. But the constant failure on the part of the borrowers incited me towards leaning on the act. But then, even with written agreements, trust was always breached. I resorted to giving a freewill amount of what I could afford towards the course of the borrower rather than lending the whole amount needed. With that, I prevented a breach of trust in that regard. I know that most people have been in that cycle, but that would be my piece of advice. In other to avoid being hurt severally by broken trust, I treat trust like a vase – its broken pieces can be glued together but it will never be the same.

In Canada, I noticed that financial trust can be broken in the most dishonorable way and yet very official. My first encounter was with a network provider. I was offered a handset and sim card on contract for a certain amount. Lo and behold, during the four months I used the network, my bill was never the same and always increased. I got angry and paid off the balance on the phone. That was an official fraud.

Canadians value the choice and the overall reliability and security of their banking and payment systems. They assume, with good reason, that their transactions will be processed efficiently, accurately, and securely. When bank customers are the victims of payment card fraud, banks stand behind them with their zero liability fraud policies.

However, financial frauds like credit card scams and account hacking are very common in Canada. The only good thing is that insurance has a way of protecting the account holder. But there are situations where the customer simply bears the burden of loss.

There is a particular financial fraud that targets new immigrants to Canada. A case sample: a new migrant made an online application for a job. He was successful and was told that his duties included collecting checks from designated locations and paying them into his account. Next, he was instructed to withdraw 80% of the total and pay a beneficiary in person. The balance of 20% would be his commission. While the checks awaited clearing, this new employee requested a physical meeting with his employers at the stipulated address. His request was declined, and he became suspicious. But it was too late. The checks were returned, and he lost $6000 in indebtedness to his bank. The fraudsters had exploited a banking loophole, which allows the customer to draw on unclear instruments. Trust was broken between the employer and employee on one hand, and between the customer and the bank on the other hand.

In the foregoing, I tried to tell my story of struggles and betrayal. It was not intended to discourage upcoming investors or financial trust. More importantly, I do not advise that people should never be trusted. However, I shall advise the intending investor to explore a study of the *"Cashflow Quadrant."* This concept would give a clear picture of the starting blocks of income earning. An early choice is key to future success or failure, and the prevention of breach of trust in areas your knowledge can control.

The above sad stories illustrate the investment losses that could result from the betrayal of private and public trust, as well as low financial literacy. This chapter is further dedicated to discussions on the basic principles of financial education. Unfortunately, these concepts are not taught as part of a high school curriculum. An early financial education would equip anyone about the best investment routes to take. Admittedly, money commands incredible power. But financial education is more powerful than money. It teaches you how to trap money, engage it to work for you, and ultimately convert to wealth. This state of independence is called Financial Freedom. Financially literate people accumulate assets while avoiding liabilities. In business circles, it is a common saying that the rich acquire assets, the middle-class accumulate liabilities and think they are assets, and the poor have only expenditures.

Secondly, in terms of investment, you may have frequently encountered the saying that "Never put all your eggs in one basket." On the contrary, let me end this chapter with a bite: *"You may safely place all your eggs in one basket, as long as you never take your eyes off that basket."*

Trust is the central pillar supporting any real relationship. Building trust in a relationship takes hard work and commitment. Trust requires that we listen and communicate our wants and needs to our partner. Above anything else, trust requires honesty. Once trust is built, it should be maintained throughout. Once that trust is broken, it is almost impossible to go back to the way things were without the doubt and the fear of trust being broken again. A relationship that thrives on a lack of trust will infuse uncertainties and insecurities in the relationship, either causing both parties to hate one another or the overall relationship to self-destruct. Trusting too much could hurt you, but not trusting enough could torment you through life.

In most cases, healing from broken trust depends on the nature of your relationship, the circumstances of your mistake, and how you act after you've broken the other person's trust. With the right apology, empathy, and healthy communication, you may be able to rebuild a strong relationship. But the question now is: How can financial trust broken be repaired? Mere apology and empathy cannot return the money lost. This is what makes rebuilding trust fail in the aspect of finances. But no matter the situation, we need to forgive for a healthier world.

Healing from broken trust requires a great deal from both parties involved. The offender should admit his wrong-doing and genuinely seek forgiveness. The person who has violated trust in the relationship is to engage in full transparency. This should be something offered up before even asking. If you are the offending party, you should desire to be trusted again. Forgiveness is the first step in healing the relationship on the end of the victim. Holding onto the hate, anger, and negative feelings will only make you feel worse. However, you are doing yourself a favor when you forgive. You are unburdening any feelings of ill will or hurt that has come from that person violating your trust.

Vivian Amadi is a Nigerian lawyer presently being assessed to be called to the Canadian Bar. She is currently a Canadian Immigration Consultant. During her compulsory National Youth Service Corp (NYSC), she served with the defunct Citizens Bank where she gained financial management skills. Vivian worked at the Ministry of Justice, Nigeria until her relocation to Canada in 2018. She is the director of Somanda Investment Ltd. and is married to Dr. Victor Amadi. They are blessed with five children. Vivian has a strong capacity for empathy and takes an optimistic view of human nature. She has the ability to effortlessly function as a team player.

Chapter Thirteen

God is Your Security

WRITTEN BY: SANDRA BOWEN

*F*or a long time, I lived an undisciplined, unstructured, unfulfilled life because I ran after the wrong things in life. I was chasing after wealth instead of God, and I trusted man instead of my Heavenly Father. I had big dreams, but they were ultimately tied to a carnal existence instead of being tied to the will of God. Matthew 6:33 says, **"Seek first the Kingdom of God, and His righteousness (right living), and all things shall be added unto you."** I read this scripture so many times and although I heard it, I did not embrace it. At the time, they were just words on a page; I did not take them to heart.

From a young child, I had dreams of finding my Prince Charming, being a supportive wife working alongside a successful husband, doing my part in helping him fulfill his dreams and desires, and building a healthy, financially sound lifestyle. I did not realize that my dreams would lead me down a winding road riddled with financial woes. Finding Prince Charming was the first issue. Finding a faithful Prince Charming who was committed to working and building a solid foundation was another. From the beginning, I went into relationships with the wrong concept. I reasoned that if I joined forces with the "right" partner and worked hard together, we would accomplish a lot and live a successful, prosperous, debt-free life. My decision was never solely based on God and the things of God. Neither was I concerned about advancing the kingdom of God.

It was about me, my desires, and what my idea of success was.

With that thought in mind, I ventured into the world of relationships looking for my prince. But it was a very unkind world. Instead of a successful, prosperous, debt-free life, I faced times when I was broken, emotionally, and financially, and left in a world of debt, having to rebuild my life. With steadfastness and God, I came to a point in my life when I felt I had started down the right path of putting my life back together again. Although I had to start over in every way possible, I rebounded. Life was excellent and I was settled. I saw the light at the end of the tunnel. Financially, I was finally getting back on my feet. It took a while, but I was beginning to climb out of the pit of debt – one that I had dug for myself because of making the wrong choices. After all the pain and fighting to get back on track, you would have thought I learned my lesson. My immigration firm was flourishing, my children were doing well, and financially I had rebuilt my life. I was alone, but I was content. I was not dating nor in a relationship, and neither did I feel the need to have a partner in my life. Relationships had not worked for me so far. Instead of moving forward, I was left alone, broke, and in a barren place. I vowed to myself that I needed no partner but God in my life.

Unexpectedly, there he was. Without realizing how, when, and what happened, I had thrown my vow and caution to the wind without thinking. Things happened so quickly, I could not fathom what was occurring.

The long and short of the matter is that I placed my entire life into the hands of a man who I thought loved and cared for me. He presented himself very well: intelligent, professional, and established in not one, but two sought-after professions. He made me feel so beautiful and worthwhile – like a queen. He would quickly solve any problems that presented themselves. In short, he became my protector. I was still the provider, but he was the one who determined how, when, and what to spend on. He became the stabilizing force in my life, and irreplaceable to the point where he even replaced God in my life. I trusted him with everything that concerned me as well as my finances. When he said jump, my only question was, "How high should I jump?" I felt that he took away all my worries, and my life would be happy ever after, or so it was supposed to be. I was so happy to have this person in my life. However, after years of entanglement, the harsh truth was revealed that everything I thought I had and knew was a lie from the very beginning.

Misplaced trust is placing your trust in the wrong person. This I have proven to be true. Your misplaced trust will lead you down the wrong path and bring everything wrong into your life. Misplaced trust causes you to lose family, friends, dignity, and yourself. You become so blinded that you cannot see and so deaf that you cannot hear. Your misplaced trust will eventually become broken trust. Several times before my misplaced trust became broken, I would wake up in a panic with the scripture, *"Trust in the Lord with all your heart and lean not on your own understanding; in all your ways submit to him, and he will make your paths straight,"* repeating in my heart. Unfortunately, I was not listening and continued down the bridal path that would lead to my destruction. When the reality of my misplaced trust came to light, I was hit with a tsunami of emotions and realities. They were unbearable. I felt like death was a better answer than to face the financial devastation that I was placed in, along with the emotional trauma that I had to endure. For the first time in my life, I felt truly naked, lost, alone, ashamed, and broken. The shame of not listening to those around me who saw and knew that I was being set up was more than I could stand. The damage was so significant and far-reaching. I would never be able to recover. ***"But God."***

I grew up in the church where I had a close relationship with God. I tried to do the right things as far as my faith in God was concerned, but my faith waned somewhere along the way and I stopped listening to God. My ears became dull, more so, when my spirit started warning me that my relationship is not what it should be. I literally tuned God out and shut down my conscience. I stopped praying and listening. I thought I knew the character of the individual more than God did. If you are a child of God, He will always speak to you. The problem comes when we do not want to listen because what He is saying is not what we want to hear. I exchanged God's faithful guide and counsel for that of a mere man. I thought that my life and financial well-being were well on the way to becoming more than I ever dreamed. I became comfortable in my ignorance. Emotionally, my love tank was full. What more could I ask for? We were committed to marrying each other. Financially the bills were being paid and we were building our business to become a global business. But Psalm 146: 3-4 (NIV) says, *"Do not put your trust in princes, in human beings, who cannot save. When their spirit departs, they return to the ground; on that very day, their plans come to nothing."*

Bitterness, hate, and unforgiveness will contaminate every part of your life if you let them. I was so bitter and filled with hate when I discovered the truth. The more the financial problems were being revealed, the more the bitterness, hate, and unforgiveness grew. I was totally consumed and did not think I would ever be able to overcome it. The truth is, I did not want to. I wanted to keep on hating and I was looking for a way to revenge the evil that was done to me. But God, who is faithful, just, and had begun a good work in me was not about to let me go. He was working in my life even when I did not realize it. Bit by bit, God started chipping away at my heart that had become so hard. He was transforming my heart that had become stony into a heart of flesh. He sent the right people at the right time with the right words of encouragement and financial assistance that I needed. God slowly started to reclaim my heart. *"Fear not, for I am with you; be not dismayed, for I am your God; I will strengthen you, I will help you, I will uphold you with my righteous right hand."* (Isaiah 41:10). Eventually, I realized that by harboring anger, hate, and bitterness, I had poisoned myself. If I did not forgive, I was not hurting the person who hurt me, neither was I hurting God; I was only hurting myself. I had to learn to forgive and let go of the bitterness that had consumed me. Learning to forgive and letting go of hate is painful, especially while working through a financial crisis. However, the more I started to let go and forgive, the more I started seeing the hands of God in my life. The more I started listening, understanding, and trusting God, the more I started to flourish. I had to remind myself daily that I am to love my enemies and do good to those who hate me (not easy). It is hard to harbor bitterness, hate, and unforgiveness against anyone who wants bad things to happen to you and who are mean to you when you pray for them and ask God to bless them.

This time, the way back to financial security was not easy. I had a lot of lessons to learn. It has been the most challenging time of my life. I had to overcome the emotional pain and hurt that was associated with the betrayal that I faced. I also had to learn how to rely on God again because it is He who teaches me and gives me the wisdom to get wealth. I had gotten it all wrong in the beginning. My financial wealth and happiness will never come from man or myself. It will only come from God who directs my path and gives me the wisdom to accomplish what He has set out for me to do. The source of my real wealth and finances is not in myself; it is in God. When I put my trust in God, He directs my path. Instead of becoming intimate with men, I had to learn to become intimate with God. I had to learn to trust the Lord entirely and not rely on my own opinion, but on Him to guide me in the direction to go and lead me in every decision I had to make.

Because of this betrayal, I realized my need to become financially literate. It was an area of weakness that I had to address and overcome – how to manage my finance. Strange as it sounds, I was afraid of handling money, so I desired to have a partner with that skill set who was well-rounded in the area of finance. I would work and he would know how to invest our funds. Most times, we make bad decisions in our lives because we are running away from a truth, or we tell ourselves a lie. The lie I told myself was that I could not handle money and that I needed someone smart who understood money to make my decisions for me. I lied to myself that understanding money is time-consuming and complicated, and I could not do it. To move forward, I had to recognize my weaknesses and deal with them. I realize that it was my responsibility to have checks and balances in place in running my company, and if I did not understand them, I needed to learn. Whether you are married or single, own a company or not, financial literacy is an area that you should know. You do not have to be an expert, but you should take the time to understand the basics so that you become a good steward of the money that God places in my hands. I recognize that I didn't need to be afraid of money; I just had to learn about it so that I can ask the right questions and when I am not sure, get a second opinion. When running a company, having an independent Accountant and Lawyer is critical. Every business and every person needs one. Now my financial decision-making process has changed as I am learning to become financially responsible and accountable.

I have come to realize and believe that your financial stability is dependent on your spiritual stability. When you are spiritually bankrupt, it affects your spirit, soul, and body. Man must be balanced holistically – spirit, soul, body. You cannot be physically balanced when your spirit and soul are unbalanced. We hear of so many financially wealthy people who commit suicide. Why? I believe it is because they are spiritually bankrupt. Physically, they have wealth, but spiritually they are bankrupt, leading them down the wrong path. The question is asked in Matthew 16:26, *"What good will it be for someone to gain the whole world yet lose his soul? Or what can anyone give in exchange for their soul?"* We must be careful about why we are seeking wealth. God does not want us to live a poverty-stricken life; after all, it is He who gives us the ability to create wealth. However, He does not want us to lose our souls in the process. In all you do, check your motives. I realize that I needed to get it right. I had to get back to the source. I needed to be spiritually grounded. My spiritual account needed to be balanced so that my emotions did not outweigh my spirit when it came to making critical financial decisions.

As I am recounting this story, I realize that I am not fully healed. I think it will take some time. What I can say is, "Thank God I am not where I used to be." The pain has dulled, and I am more spiritually, physically, and financially stable than I had been before. I have learned many valuable lessons – the greatest of which is to completely trust the Lord and do not depend on my own knowledge. With every step I take, I think about what God wants and I trust Him to lead me the right way. Joel Olsteen said that *"adversity often pushes us into our divine destiny."*

Today can be a turning point in your life. Wealth is not having lots of money and being sound financially. Wealth is a life that is filled with God. Wealth is great friends and family, a free conscience, a contented spirit, and knowing that God, your heavenly Father, has got your back. God is your security.

Sandra Bowen is the Founder and Senior Immigration Consultant of Bowen Immigration & Services, an immigration firm located in Toronto, Canada. Governed by the Canadian Regulatory Council, I.C.C.R.C., she is bounded by a strict code of ethics in her practice. She holds a B.A. in Human Services from Tyndale University in Toronto and Diplomas in Business Administration, Fashion Design, and Real Estate. Sandra is a Commissioner of Oaths, and the Founder and C.E.O. of Women Helping Women Help Themselves. But her most outstanding achievement is being a mother to her two children, Saidah and Samuel.

Email: info@bowenimmigration.com

Website: www.bowenimmigration.com

Facebook: https://www.facebook.com/bowenimmigrationandservices

LinkedIn: https://www.linkedin.com/company/bowen-immigration-services/

Instagram: https://www.instagram.com/bowenimmigration/

Chapter Fourteen

Daring is a Virtue
Toward Winning

Written By: Moyna David-Ejor

*A*s a person who has been through many challenging times in business relationships, I encourage you to be focused and do not let others influence your vision. If you are a parent of a child or children, especially grown-up children who are trying to find their bearing, encourage and guide them to be independently motivated to their own vision and career. Do not force your dreams on them but rather help them dare to use their abilities to follow their dreams while letting them know that there are outcomes for every choice or action taken. As a parent of three, I have always been cautious not to impose my decisions on the choice of their career but rather advise them to use their strong academic abilities or skills to choose a career discipline, thus creating a passion in their choice of career because harnessing such skills or academic abilities will make it easier.

In an educational consultancy family business I co-owned in Ghana, West Africa, as a registered representative to some universities for admissions/placements, some third parties (family, friends, relatives, and others) that were involved with the consultancy business on a contract basis collected payments from the clients on behalf of the company after obtaining all classified information about the procedures without the knowledge of either myself or my spouse who owned the company. These third parties reaped the benefits of money from the clients. No wonder a popular quote says, *"Trust takes years to build, seconds to break, and forever to repair."* I have now learned my bitter lesson: do not be holistic while disseminating classified business secrets to unsuspecting/unaccustomed third parties and therefore dared to consequently forge ahead in my business life. I now keep a comfortable distance and observe and research contractors who are going to be involved with the company so I can be a better judge of character and avoid the past misfortunes from repeating themselves. Some people lack ingenuity and usually choose to feed off the person with the original vision. The problem is such people usually cannot last long on their own and will look for another idea or vision to feed off.

Magnanimity, although a prominent virtue, can be a problem in running a business. Magnanimity simply means an overgenerous and forgiving nature in a person. This problem is experienced usually with familiar persons. One must particularly ensure to separate general relationship standards from business relationship standards even with familiar persons such as family and friends. The reason for this is when one is not careful with their magnanimous nature in business or life dealings, some people will always take others for granted just because one shows that "overgenerous spirit by being honest or by easily forgiving others and not being persistent ill will at something or someone when wronged." It is really discouraging when people know to the utmost certainty what is right and still behave as if they are ignorant about their behavior when dealing with people. Come to think about it, extreme carefulness should be a watchword as we come in contact with people daily, especially those who have not shown to be truthful to themselves when they are in a relationship. So many times, these people are deceptive, having or hiding under disguise in their dealings. In several times, this situation has repeated itself on different occasions in businesses. Such scenarios have caused a lot of setbacks, leaving one in a shock, and has kept lives stagnant. Because people creep into one's life, feed continuously, and if much care is not taken, by the time there is realization, they deposit all manner of misfortune and then finally leave after sucking all potential, and without investing anything or contributing in the business/relationship. Be advised – always make sure business proposals are spelled out and conditions of operations are put in place before commencing. This should be done to avoid this tragedy, especially in some cases where the cut is so deep to be amended. Stop being carried away by being too forgiving; rather be cautious, reasonable, and realistic so that one does not get hurt all the time as this is not always good when ways are open to evil infiltrators.

Procrastination is the bane of any business relationship, and most importantly affects efficiency. The procrastinator may end up having little or nothing to show at the end of the day.

When we keep carrying over tasks or schedules that should have taken place today to another day, we will be overwhelmed with the additional tasks of that other day. In turn, every penny that comes in hardly counts. This can be seen where such business owners would push the completion of projects to future times, simply because they do not necessarily have the entire funds and would continue to hope and wait for bigger funds. Instead, the wiser option to take is to divide the projects into various parts and focus on completing the most feasible ones; therefore, making the completion of the projects more attainable. As the saying goes, "Make hay while the sun shines" simply implies getting things done on time while the opportunity exists. On the other hand, it is important not to see procrastination as to begin quickly at doing something because some tasks require better timing for optimal results. Always keep in mind that it's not how fast but how far. As a grown-up child, the motherly advice of knowing when, how, and what to do with any resource entrusted into one's hand has affected me. So many times, people tend to look down on you in the business you value and hope it grows one day because of the availability of little funds invested. But people rather would choose to procrastinate on what to do with the seemingly little resources they have at hand and keep blowing it all up with the mindset that the next one will come big. But my spouse would always say to let the little resources handle little projects, while the next big one goes for bigger projects, but don't stop investing since little drops of water form a mighty ocean. More so when there is no indemnity for one to fall back to and life, they say, is very, very short to gamble with.

When one continues in business, it is not strange to perpetually experience so much mistrust and broken relationships in the business because of the type of upbringing meted to us while growing up. Upbringing implies we all have different personalities, characters, and morals. While growing up in Nigeria, West Africa, one is usually taught good virtues and most importantly, to be truthful; unfortunately, not everyone grasps these qualities. Such virtues go a long way in shaping and defining a person and affect their choices and decisions in life. Having realized that business relationships which are often built on "boss and subjects" mindsets that hardly thrive, people need to give their individual best as equal partners. Besides, when one hears people say, "No trust, no relationship" or "You earn your trust," one may trivialize it. As someone who dealt with people on their face value and took them by their words, due to a humble background to be nice to all sundry, so many mistakes were made and lessons learned. For the umpteenth time, experiences have revealed that no matter what, people still have their undisclosed motives and try to take undue advantage, even for businesses they contributed little or no input toward, to the extent of hijacking the proceeds.

Surely the burning light of the Visionaire keeps drawing attention from others, except when one relents or allows the issues of life to interfere with their businesses. Also, most times people expect so much from other people, thinking they have the same level of energy and commitment as the Visionaire. While one gears-up in his or her passionate career daily, all shades of other attractive and futuristic business proposals and promises are made from potential business proxies to spur the Visionaire to accomplish their task. These proxies, when involved with the business, start avoiding or become so difficult to access as soon as their desires are accomplished. As a Visionaire, ensure to assess business proxies before involving them into a business because some business proxies are there to divert attention from clients involved and even go to the extent of exploiting clients with the notion of providing a better package. Sometimes, they go behind your back to even poison the minds of these clients to supplant negative ideas. But the end has always justified the means as such business proxies don't last too long and have always been made to pay dearly for their clandestine acts based on the beliefs that one will not sweat for another one to reap off.

Another set of people are those whose mindsets are that one will never do well or that one will soon meet their end in business and be back to square one. Surprisingly and unfortunately, these are even sometimes family members or so-called friends who are wolves in sheep's clothing that may have written one off based on some primordial yardsticks that may seem okay to them. Like they say, "A prophet is not recognized in his own home," simply meaning that the ones closest are notorious for overlooking potentials and ideas in a person. The cause of this problem is that family and friends who are closest would try to reflect their inabilities on the Visionaire simply because they could not do what is being done by the Visionaire. These categories of people, most times, become the greatest losers as they keep sitting on the fence even when the business is booming due to their negative premonitions. The "pull him down" syndrome is the order of the day. These set go into all manners of schemes to discredit anything associated with the thriving business just to prove their pessimistic point while some later craftily fall in line as they seek to be carried along only to reap where they had earlier jettisoned. Does one blame them? For there is a saying that people perish for lack of knowledge, wisdom, and understanding by remaining in one box and expecting a different result because they are there for one's goods and not for their good. That is why daring is such a vital virtue in winning or being successful.

In all the aforementioned, one just needs to bounce back after every wobble and stumble to wither the storms with a great driving spirit that dwells in a person as doing otherwise and giving up is consequential. Yes, some parents see their children as the highest investment for posterity, but suffice it to say that the orthodox academic education beclouds one's senses to the detriment of total education (that is, an education that entails the physical, spiritual, and intellectual well-being of an individual). Total education can help build up a child completely, who will be ready to go extra miles in business and in life, and be independent in charting a course rather than trying to cut corners. Most so-called "modern" parents now find it fashionable to spend a fortune on their children's schooling, get them cars after school, bankroll their marriages, open businesses, or even secure jobs for them as the case may be. In the case where such parents then withdraw the overbearing support for this monetary show of love, or if the inevitable happens, there is a higher probability of such a child not being able to forge ahead by themselves because of the faulty foundation which may lead to the lack of initiatives or self-confidence in real-life issues. One can now see why some business colleagues prefer shortcuts and some even find it so difficult to fit into the shoes of their renowned parents whose names were written on the tabloids of history. Though arguably, one's child is expected to be greater than the parents so as to say that society has experienced good growth. Thus, any training that is neither holistic nor allows one to experience the circular life should be discouraged.

In conclusion, broken trust is a compilation for a big shake-up and great turnaround as in "never say never" to challenges. Furthermore, in any business transactions, don't be distracted but keep investing and reinvesting. Most importantly, keep daring against all odds until success is achieved. Finally, try to obtain knowledge about your kind of business by going for refresher courses or webinars to update your knowledge. Besides, it is also important to always get in touch with your clients for feedback and their level of satisfaction. By doing so, you can know your clients and be confident to deal with them better. Most times, one should bear in mind that persons can't come glowing if one didn't go through the heat of life. In the heart of the distractors, they believe they'll succeed in their schemes, but unknown to them they're rather refining or helping in the process of preparation. For some persons, this situation could be going through really hard times in life, but instead of dwelling in this dilemma, see this as accomplishing another stage of life. This is always seen as a stage that brings one to achieving the greatest heights with having so many skills to survive the opposition of attaining great success.

Start now by adopting a different role(s) and jettisoning those old attitudes that have failed. It's time to forge ahead. Good success is earned by taking the path of great mentors. So, cruise into a new confidence.

Dedication

My anthology chapter is dedicated to my beloved mother, the late Mrs. Irene Erekosima (nee Amakiri-Tariah), a great matron and a wonderful teacher who was an epitome of Uprightness and Truth.

Moyna David-Ejor is a Nigerian of the Ijaw tribe now living in Canada. She received her education through the YWCA nursery, Township Primary, ACMGS, Elelenwo, all in PH. Moyna pursued a B.Ed. degree in Political Science and Education at the University of Ibadan of the R/S College of Education, and just earned her diploma as an Immigration Consultant. She was featured in the LWL magazine of Co-authors. While growing up with her parents (Michael and Irene Erekosima [nee Amakiri-Tariah]), Moyna acquired business skills in which she rendered educational consultancy services in Nigeria and Ghana. She's happily married with three children.

Facebook: David-Ejor Moyna

Email: moydave@yahoo.co.uk

Instagram: d.moyna

Linkedin: moyna david-Ejor

Chapter Fifteen

Wellness Through Self-Reliance & Motivation 101

WRITTEN BY: KUSH I KROWN

In life, sometimes you don't realize at the moment that you may be going through trials and tribulations. These same trials and tribulations are presented in order to shape you. It's either you get on the road to upliftment or you choose the road to self-destruction. Dive into this chapter with me as I share my story. It will bring you on a rollercoaster ride and will give you hints about what it's like as an African woman to survive in the belly of the beast. But rest assured, it will leave you feeling inspired because you'll see how you can navigate through any obstacle.

"Knock, knock." That was the sound at my door as I walked up to look through the peephole. "Who is it?" I asked. "This is..." and that was the lady's voice. "But wait!" I exclaimed. "I see two."

It all started in 2010: a knock on the door, a brief conversation through the cracked door, and finally the entry that would change my life forever. I thought that it was all a dream but soon had to realize it was my reality.

I had to recover, and honestly, that was the best thing I ever did for myself. My approach was through self-reliance. I would spend most of my time developing myself. I remember writing about four songs in the space of two hours. My first song was entitled *"Live Wise."* It was so therapeutic; the melodies were given to me by the Most High Creator of the universe. The lyrics included *"live in love not hate and think about life's future."* I told myself that I am going to use my music to heal myself. In life, we are constantly healing. We have to heal every day; it's like a flower blooming with new petals.

My lyrics would resonate in my psyche, keeping me calm and militant, and while I've been using my music as a tool in my everyday steps to wellness, my recovery process has been off the scale. With this whole realization of music and healing, my music has been reaching the masses worldwide. The feedback I get is amazing; from Guatemala to Ethiopia, I have realized my calling, and my music is uplifting and inspiring. Call it *"The message in the music."*

KUSH I KROWN: Singer and Songwriter. The name Kush is one of Ethiopia's original names, and Krown came from my childhood "other name." Hence, the name Tiahara was given to me by my parents. My revelation came to me one day sitting down at my computer desk. I realized that no matter where you come from, as long as you are a black man or woman, you are an African. This enlightenment had me knowing myself on a deeper level. I took on to my real self by embracing my natural beauty, and when I say natural beauty, I mean to say "your natural development from the inside," "The real deal," and even better, "just loving and taking care of yourself," keeping in mind that this too is great for wellness on all levels, mentally and emotionally. From this, my songs would continue to uplift and educate. I started writing about the strategies I would use for wellness through being self-reliant, an uplifting situation all around. I can't leave out the fire aspect. The fire approach through music has excellent healing and purging properties, cutting and clearing mechanisms in order to move forward so that I could have maintained a balanced and healthy lifestyle. Sometimes you just have to use word sound and power to get rid of some negative energy.

The reason why I discuss these things with you, the reader, is just so you can get a slight picture of the many ways to wellness through self-reliance as well, and that healing yourself through the arts can also be nourishing for your soul. Our approach to wellness can come in many forms, whether it is offering your care for those in need or ultimately taking care of yourself so that you can pass on the goodness for the reciprocal healing process to begin.

In the year 2011, I also developed my natural skincare line which specializes in Shea butter. The product line name is derived from the names of four of my children who initially inspired me to create. Your wellness on a level like this can be great, it's "Big!" You have now enabled your wellness through being self-reliant to last forever. I have now broadened the horizons of my children, and they too can emulate and choose that road to upliftment. Shea Butter is the fat extracted from the nut of the African Shea tree and consists of vitamins and minerals. The healing properties and benefits from these enriched nutrients is a trip in itself if you ask me! I started to use this amazing nut butter on one of my daughters when she was about three months old. I notice that the raw Shea butter was very hard, brick-formed so to speak, and used it mostly when my children would have rashes, dry skin, and such. While performing our daily routines, I noticed in order to get it to a smooth consistency, I would have to refine it. If anyone knows Shea in its natural state, they would have to literally dig their fingers into the Shea butter, put it in the middle of their hands, and crush it with their palms just to get it smooth. My contributions towards being self-reliant kept me determined; I went on a journey from Flea Markets to events, door-to-door, store-to-store. I had to make sure that I can feel good about myself and not fall into a state where I feel sorry for myself. Yes! There were times when I would get sad and think of all the sad things, but my approach to wellness could not consist of such! This approach to wellness had me very busy with production, inventory, shipping, deliveries, traveling, stage performances, studio sessions, and the like, so there was no time to solely focus on the things that hurt but rather focus on the things that will make others smile as well. It was a balance, and let's just say there is a time and place for everything.

Many of us go through obstacles, but it is how we take on to those obstacles that will determine our outcome, and sometimes it's through your necessities, your struggles, and your will to survive that will have you in that frame of mind.

Take for instance this sudden pandemic that has arisen called COVID-19. Economically, the system has crashed! These are the facts! A lot of businesses have closed and if you watch the news, you can see that a lot of the thriving businesses are the many entrepreneurs worldwide, the people that work for themselves, right? I love this approach to wellness through self-reliance; it builds your character and you learn so much about yourself. Through self-reliance, you can make your own decisions, take control of your life, and honestly when you go through any devastating situation, my suggestion is that you find out what you are good at and find your skills so that you can keep yourself occupied. Develop yourself – it's going to make you feel so good! You will feel uplifted like you're on top of the world because you've now created something that someone else likes and will purchase. With that sale, you're now able to provide for yourself and take it to the next level. I remember one incident during the beginning stages of my cosmetic business. I had a $12.00 profit towards it. At that time, I already had a small customer base, but previous to this enlightenment, I went through a little obstacle, so it left me living off of my products. The $12.00 invested doubled my profit and I was able to make more products. That's just an example of using your skills to survive. Who remembers the term "barter" or "barter system?" In my experience, it still has to be proven if the barter system would work for me. Everyone has a skill and that skill has to be able to earn something in return from someone else that is equivalent to what you can offer them. Apparently, this cashless system worked for many civilians for years. If I had to live off the barter system, these acts of self-sustaining entrepreneurship would force me to keep myself in a positive space. I believe that even if you are facing trials and tribulations, it is important to still remain positive to maintain wellness; and do good because your energy on earth will transcend. All the goodness will follow, just do the good!

I am so happy to share with you my home-based business experience. I encourage you to begin with self-care by being true to yourself; associate only with people who you will encourage you and lift you up. Choose to dedicate your life towards the wellness path, encouraging others to do the same. It definitely broadens your horizons. You may oftentimes have to change your lenses and refresh, meaning you'll have to purposely reconfigure your mindset. It will free yourself from mental slavery. The first signs you'll notice by releasing your self-inhibiting bonds will be that you're not dwelling on something any longer that will hurt you. So, if your experience was negative, you'll be able to find a positive spin on it. You will use the energy from that situation to empower your life, whether it's through entrepreneurship, the arts, or perhaps practicing humanitarianism. Because at the end of the day remember that it's you who needs to feel good. Remember, you have to implement your steps to wellness in order to heal. So, all in all, it's just one BIG healing party that lasts forever. "LAST FOREVER??? Ahhh!" I remember my friend saying this to me one day when she didn't understand my concept. I explained to her that if we realize from the beginning that our expectations should not be in a blind state, meaning there are going to be ups and downs on your journey, yes – healing/rejuvenation lasts forever.

On this path in my journey, I realized that having my life centered around my well-being will continue to help me grow into a better person. As the learning continues, there are going to be more enlightenments which I honestly look forward to. I know that with my skincare line and music, I will be able to continually encourage people. It has also brought me to this place/space within myself where I feel empowered. I know that continuing on this life path will bring about other meaningful interactions on a global level where I can also be the student and learn from others. The connectivity with others on the same life journey will be truly enhancing.

"Emancipate yourself from mental slavery, none but ourselves can free our mind" is a most prestigious and uplifting quote by The Rt. Honorable John Marcus Mosiah Garvey. It is true when you think about it, and when you free yourself, it's like saying "I am going to lift myself out of this situation here that has me "topsy-turvy," for example. You are saying to yourself that you have the power, you have the ability to conquer, and you can do it! When you have that epiphany moment and realize that you get to choose your destiny, you're on to something great and you can be a remarkable person for the good! Imagine if we all had this mindset, this concept of thinking; where we allowed ourselves to heal by acknowledging that we needed to be healed. I believe interactions with other people daily would be a lot easier and global decisions that are made within great governments would be dealt with properly for the betterment of the entire human race.

Now that you have read my depiction of maintaining my well-being, do you see the type of things that are hindering you? What can you do for your well-being? What are the things that you are going to implement in your life so that you can survive and feel balanced? The navigation process is not easy, but at least it will feel like you are in the classroom all over again, so to speak. Isn't that great?

So, during these times of "pandemonium," don't be afraid to step out of your comfort zone, the place you call home. I know it may be hard at times to overcome present economic situations and navigate through the system seeing that a lot of the places have been shut down and are slowly reopening. But believe me, it's worth it to keep your joy and to be fearless, always thinking of the greater things, and allow the solutions in our lives to arrive. Speak your destiny into fruition, declaring that you have already won the battle. You are a conqueror and you're a winner. You're on top of things and you are in control of your well-being. Your positive energy is going to attract you to what you have already meditated within yourself. It is going to be awesome, and as your newfound self-developing methods take place, your path to a brighter and richer lifestyle has manifested its way into your life just like that! Yes, my dear friend, be on that journey, be on that path! You can do it! It's called wellness through self-reliance and motivation 101.

Blessed love.

Kush I Krown resides in Ontario, Canada with her beautiful family. She is a certified Medical Office administrator as well as an international singer and songwriter who is a true woman of Jah. Kush is also the owner and manufacturer of her very own skincare line called *Itaz Care*. She is a co-author in this anthology and is now about to start her own book. Kush recognized that empowering herself is very important and with her gifts, she continues to inspire others to be themselves and have the confidence to overcome any obstacles that may arise as well!

Chapter Sixteen

The Other Side of the Storm

WRITTEN BY: SEYMONDE PETERS CAMPBELL

*H*ave you ever laid down and thought about the things you've been through and how far you've come? One Sunday morning, as I was watching the sunrise from the bay to the peak of the mountain, and then into the valley, I sat there at the roadside on the block, with my mind all over the place wishing for a better life to come. I was tired of living the life that I had: it was hopeless, full of loneliness, and had a lack of love. Something was missing.

I knew that I wanted a fresh start, so I went to my house, sat near the riverside, and started speaking to God. I told Him that if He would only open a door where I could change my life, I will serve Him all my days. Today, I can gladly say that the Lord has answered my prayers and has opened many doors for me. *"Because narrow is the gate and difficult is the way which leads to life, and there are few who find it."* Matthew 7:14 (NKJV)

When we think of open doors, most times we believe the paths to get to those open doors are easy. The reality is that the doors God opens are narrow and few find them. The path to the open doors most times are paved with blood, sweat, and tears, but what I do know is that if you stay the course, you will certainly enjoy the blessings of these open doors. In fact, I am sure I would rather go through the doors that God opens for me. Yes, those doors are hard, but the blessings after coming through the storms will be worth it.

As a teenage mother, I grew up on the small island of Saint Vincent & the Grenadines in a village called Lauders. I am the oldest of six children and due to financial hardships, I had to leave home at a young age. I was mistreated and abused by many and had to live like a prostitute to survive. I can remember having little to eat, nothing but young green bananas with chicken back oil with a tall glass of lime crush for dinner, and pretty plum rose fruit for dessert, which grew in the yard where I lived. I am still awestruck by how far God has taken me. I am no longer a slave to my past mistakes. Thank God for His grace and mercies! I no longer look back on my past with shame; I look on my past as building blocks that God has used to mold me into who I am today.

I had many challenges, but finance was my greatest burden! I knew that I couldn't prosper or be the best I could be if I stayed within my comfort zone, or the village I grew up in. I needed a change of scenery. I was tired of the mundane activities and the feelings of inadequacies. My breakthrough came in 2002 when I got the opportunity to visit Canada. Talk about a breakthrough...or so I thought.

I faced a new set of challenges when I came to Canada. Here I was in a new country, a land of opportunities, but instead of finding peace and prosperity, I found disappointments and broken trust from people who I thought would have my back. My world was in chaos. Despite these setbacks, I knew that Canada would be good to me if I made the most of the opportunities here and worked hard to achieve my end goal – which was to make a better life for myself and help my child back home, as well as my relatives. My mother is an amazing woman. I left my daughter in her care when I came to Canada. I don't know how I would have survived in Canada if I had to worry about the care of my daughter back home. My mother stepping in and filling the gap as a caregiver for my baby girl was such a great blessing.

I remember being thrown out in the heart of winter with nowhere to go. I had no money in my pocket and things started to go from bad to worse. God always has people waiting to assist us when we go through difficult times. I had to call friends to help me by providing shelter. While living with friends, I wasn't comfortable depending on them for my basic needs, so I went in search of a job. My first job in Canada was working as a babysitter. I didn't make a lot of money, but I was grateful that I was able to provide for my basic needs. Now that I was able to work, I was able to pay my rent and send money back home to support my daughter. I finally felt like I was living the dream. It was at this moment that I started to find myself as a woman. I felt a renewed strength like I've never felt before.

This mountaintop experience felt great. I was now on the rise, or so I thought. Fast forward to a few years later when I got into a messy situation with Immigration! I was at the wrong place at the wrong time and now my stay in Canada was in jeopardy. I was given two options: either leave Canada and go back to suffering in my village filled with hopelessness and defeat or apply under an immigration status as a Refugee. I chose the latter because going back to hopelessness and brokenness was not an option for me.

I was referred to several lawyers and each time, they would charge me a hefty fee, but still did not deliver. Denial after denial and mounting debts – at times it seemed like I was fighting a losing battle, but I was determined to come out on the winning side. I believed then and I still believe today that God heard my cries at the riverside in my village many years earlier and even though things were not going how I hoped, I still did not lose heart. I can recall the time I was placed in a holding center and was given a document to sign in order to be deported. I did not fully understand what was on the document, but I heard a voice telling me to look over there. When I followed the voice and made eye contact with another person who was also in the holding center and had been for several years, she mouthed to me that I shouldn't sign off on that paper which was presented to me. I followed what she told me because I saw that as a sign from God. I am so thankful that I followed her instructions because if I didn't, I wouldn't be here today. At that moment, I took that sign as God telling me to hold on a little longer; He was still working things out for me.

While the fight continued, I was given temporary status, so I was able to attend a post-secondary institution. Achieving my Diploma as a Personal Support Worker was incredible. It was at that moment I thought things were finally coming together for me, but disappointments again found themselves right on my doorsteps. After receiving my diploma, my temporary status expired, and I wasn't allowed to work. Imagine this, I fought for my freedom, and in the process, I got my certification as a Personal Support Worker but couldn't put it to use to change my financial situation.

It felt like I was moving backward instead of forging ahead. So, the fight continued. My physical appearance changed, due to all I was going through. It felt like I aged twenty years. I recall not having proper shoes to wear in the winter, and while people noticed and spoke about it, no one stepped in to assist me. Talk about being down and out!

The glimmer of hope came when I met my husband in 2008. Oh, my husband, he was such a good man. He provided for his family the best way he could have. He worked multiple jobs just to ensure we had enough and didn't go without. This continued for years, all the while struggling financially and dealing with the immigration system.

My husband would go the extra mile just to put a smile on my face. He was my sunshine on a stormy day. My second child was born right after I got married, and immediately, I surrendered my life to the Lord and proudly became a follower of Jesus Christ. Again, darkness hovered over my joy because right after this moment, my husband got fired from his job.

God kept us even though we were broken financially, emotionally, and mentally. Our valley experiences seemed to last a very long time, and I wondered (and people even asked me) when we would see the light again. When would our mountaintop experiences come? However, I never lost hope in God. I held on to His words because the same God who provided a way for me to come to Canada will be the same God to keep me in Canada. I was resolute in my faith and trust in God!

I believe that it is in the valley you gain strength and you will know who God really is. There were times I felt like I was going into a depressive state of mind and I would cry out to God and He would deliver me. My husband finally found a new job and things started to look brighter for us. I was working as a cleaner to help out when my husband's salary wasn't able to cover us. We may not have had a lot of money, but what money couldn't buy, we had. We had love, laughter, joy, moments of happiness, and most of all we have our Salvation in the Lord!

In 2015, in the midst of drought, there came a flower blooming in my parched land. I was pregnant with a baby boy. What a pleasant surprise! However, my baby boy didn't see the light of day – he was stillborn at five months. The death of my son was the final straw that broke the camel's back. I went into deep-set depression and couldn't seem to have prayed my way out of this state of mind. I had to seek therapy to help me deal with the loss of my son. This period in my life was a long road to recovery and finding my smile again.

2017 was the year that rocked my whole world. During the Fall, I got devastating news that my husband had an accident at work. It was like time stood still at that moment. I remembered walking into that hospital room and seeing my husband's lifeless body! What else could have gone wrong? I was broken to my core. I went from being a broken teenager to a broken wife. It seemed like I was facing back-to-back pain and depression. When I finally came to terms with the death of my son, I was yet faced with another death. I was so broken in body and spirit – my security was taken from me. Why did this happen to my husband? Was my life meant to be filled with struggles?

After the passing of my husband, things were not the same. There were days I would cry when I thought of him. I barely survived; I wasn't thriving, I was merely existing. But I was a woman of faith, so I knew that the sun would shine again in my life. The burden was so heavy, and life felt unbearable and filled with disappointments, but the Lord has given me hope that never changes and a love that will never fade away.

When I think about the passing of my husband, my heart breaks. My husband was a really good man, one who loved and provided for his family. When I got the devastating call informing me that my husband was killed on his job, my heart shattered.

Some would think that we would have gotten a hefty insurance payout or settlement due to my husband losing his life on the job, but that didn't happen. As I mentioned, we were considered aliens in Canada because we didn't have our proper immigration status. As a result of this, it would seem that my husband's death was in vain.

Talk about brokenness and loss of hope! Despite all these challenges that we faced, my faith in God was still strong because I do believe that He knows what is best. Jeremiah 29:11 (NIV) states, *"For I know the plans I have for you, declares the Lord, plans to prosper you and not to harm you, plans to give you hope and a future,"* therefore even though we were facing tough financial crises, I still believed that God is in control. I thank the Lord for favoring me, and I now know that His grace is sufficient enough to keep me.

The Lord gave me the courage and the resilience to never quit or thrown in the towel, and I encourage you as well – NEVER give up on God no matter how heavy your burdens get or how devastating your life circumstances may seem. Keep your faith anchored in God and trust Him to work things out for your good.

"Weeping may endure for a night, but joy comes in the morning." Psalm 30:5b

By sharing my story with you, I hope that you will also find a glimmer of hope in your personal stories. I do believe that all of the struggles we go through were meant to build character in us. *"Therefore, having been justified by faith, we have peace with God through our Lord Jesus Christ, through whom also we have access by faith into this grace in which we stand, and rejoice in hope of the glory of God. And not only that, but we also glory in tribulations, knowing that tribulation produces perseverance; and perseverance, character; and character, hope. Now hope does not disappoint, because the love of God has been poured out in our hearts by the Holy Spirit who was given to us."* Romans 5: 1-5 (NKJV)

What a great reminder from the Word of God, that hope does not disappoint. So, I am here to remind you that you should keep your hope in God alive because hope does not disappoint!

My joy surely came in the morning, because I am a proud Canadian Permanent Resident. Look what the Lord has done for me. Through all that struggle I had to endure, God delivered me. I came out on the other side of the storm!

Seymonde Campbell is an amazing mother of three who emigrated to Canada from the beautiful island of St. Vincent a number of years ago. She is an entrepreneur, a certified PSW graduate from Maple Leaf College in Ontario, as well a Best-Selling co-author in this anthology. Seymonde is a strong believer in Jesus Christ and has many passions, including spending time with her family and loves to motivate and help others in need. In her spare time, she enjoys going out for walks or doing some writing. Seymonde also enjoys music and traveling.

Email: campbellgail334@gmail.com

Facebook: gaileen peters Campbell

Chapter Seventeen

Purposefully Positioned for Greatness

WRITTEN BY: TENEISHA S. CAMPBELL

"And the vessel that he made of clay was marred in the hand of the potter; so he made it again into another vessel, as it seemed good to the potter to make." Jeremiah 18:4 (NKJV)

Some time ago, the Senior Pastor of the church I am a member in preached a sermon entitled "Marred in the Potter's Hands." For years that was me; that was the state I was in. I felt trapped on the Potter's Wheel. I was marred because of the environment I was raised in, by the people whom my mother entrusted me in their care, by the poor self-image and self-talk. I was a broken person on the inside, but I was resilient and very much tenacious.

I migrated to Canada at the age of thirteen. I left behind my mother, father, and little sister. I came to Canada with my little heart full of dreams and aspirations. I was ready to make a life for myself, get established, and then help my family back home. You see, my mother had instilled in me the importance of education. She would tell me that education was the key to success. Knowledge was my escape from the ghetto or the projects, so I was assiduous when it came to my studies.

Instead of finding the greener pastures in Canada, I found brokenness, hardships, and disappointments. My expectations didn't meet my realities, so

I was marred and felt that my dreams had shattered. I became a single mother at the age of twenty-one, but that didn't stop me. I was more determined than ever before to become a better version of myself, now that I had a little person who depended on me. After the birth of my child, I went back to college part-time while I worked full-time. My days were long, but I had a mission in mind – I was NOT going to be another statistic or stereotype. I was going to be the one to break the generational curses in my lineage, and I was adamant that I was going to live above the status quo. Marred in the Potter's hands, but NOT destroyed. God, the Master Potter, is molding me and making me on the Potter's wheel, removing the broken pieces and failures of my past. He was, and still is, working out the kinks in my life and He will do the same for you as well. Are you willing to get on His wheel?

After years of financial hardships, I was persistent. I was going to purchase my first house and it didn't matter how long it took. In most countries, if you do not own a parcel of land or the title to a house, you are seen as nothing. I refused to let that be my reality, so after years of struggling financially, through lots of trials, errors, and financial blunders, I purchased my first house when I was twenty-eight years old. I used my tax refund and a loan from one of my closest friends. I was ecstatic! Most of the people I told this great news and the turning point in my life to shared in the happiness and my accomplishments, and those who showed themselves to be jealous or envious of the progress I was making, their part in my life's story came to an end. I found that in life, it is okay to let some relationships wither and die.

I came to the conclusion that some people are with you as long as they are above you, meaning they get some kind of excitement when you're at the bottom scraping the barrel. Some people will be your friend as long as you're always crying "Woe is me." Misery loves company, so I gave misery its eviction notice out of my life. At that point, I wanted friends and people around me who were roots – no branches or leaves – roots. Branches break and leaves are eventually carried away when the winds of life blow. Roots stay grounded, roots are deep, they are not easily uprooted. Friends who are roots are not envious of your progression in life.

My first house, which to me represented security, was a sign that generational curses are broken. After a while, it became a nozzle around my neck. Before the laws were changed, people used to come to your door and sell you items you didn't need. If they could have bottled up air and sold it to you, they would have. There I was in my new home, a young single mother who knew nothing about a furnace and how it functioned. In all the places I lived before I bought my house, the HVAC was taken care of. So, the salesmen came and sold me a new HVAC system. This was a lesson I learned the hard way. They were not my friends, they did not have my best interest in mind, and the cost of the equipment was five times higher than if I had walked into a store and purchased them myself. Needless to say, I blundered. My monthly bill became too much to handle, I was behind on my heating bill, and then the inevitable happened – NO HEAT IN MARCH. My child and I were freezing inside of our home. However, being a resourceful Caribbean girl, I improvised. I put to use a portable heater and my child and I slept in the same bed to keep warm. When it was time to take our bath, I would heat water in the kettle as well as a large 24-quart pot full of water on the stove. While I bathed my child, the heater was in the washroom which meant the other parts of the house were freezing. This continued for three weeks until my tax refund was deposited in my bank account. I was able to clear off my arrears and we got our heat back!

I am not ashamed of sharing this personal story in this anthology; this is a part of my journey. That chapter in my life taught me so much. In fact, when I purchased my second home, no one, I mean absolutely no one, could ring my doorbell to sell me anything. The debt I incurred in house one will not be the death of me in house number two.

"Change the way you look at things and the things you look at change." Wayne Dyer

What comes to mind when you think about money? Do the thoughts of money bring you anxiety? Right at this moment, are you having a panic attack just thinking about this question? If you answer "yes" to this question, it means your mindset needs to change.

In being completely transparent, that was me! I used to dread payday! Laughable, isn't it? I was tired of working 40-60 hours per week, got paid, only to see my salary disappear after being deposited in my account. Then it was back to being into overdraft again and again. I was determined to change the cycle of continually being in financial hardships. There are some great tools and resources available online to help you navigate the most common financial blunders that people make. Find them and apply them to your situation.

My perception of money changed when I looked at money for what it is

– a tool. Money is a tool used to conduct business. I shifted my focus from seeing money as my source and put it in the right place; money is only a tool or resource. God is my Source. It is from Him that all blessings flow, so I stopped being anxious about money or the lack thereof.

"Whoever can be trusted with very little can also be trusted with much, and whoever is dishonest with very little will also be dishonest with much." Luke 16:10 (NJKV)

Intriguingly, when I started being grateful for what I had and began to bless others by pouring into their lives in one way or another, my baskets started getting full. I mean, I didn't feel the financial pressures like before. It would seem that the moment I gave God control of my life, including my finances, and began being obedient, I too was being blessed financially.

Things seemed to be looking up. I was progressing in my role as an Accountant, my family was healthy, I was involved in the Church, my child and I had a bond like no other; things were great. Until the end of 2019.

At this point, I was no longer a single mother with one child, I was now a wife and expecting my second child. What should have been my happily ever after fairy tale soon became a bad dream. Needless to say, that relationship ended. A global pandemic has taken center stage and financially, I was back in a rut. Broken relationships can be intensified when you add financial burdens and a pandemic to the equation. However, as I mentioned before, I am a resilient and tenacious person. I do not quit, neither do I throw in the towel. Yes, I cried for months. Mix postpartum depression with financial constraint and you get a mommy who was a mess.

I acknowledge that it is okay to mourn the loss of broken relationships – the what-ifs and the could-have-beens – but what happens next? You must make up your mind to move on from brokenness and broken trust. You can't stay in your graveside clothes for too long; you need to get up and live. You must live because you deserve to.

After that failed relationship, I choose me, I choose my kids, I choose life. Even in a pandemic and broken relationship, God, the Master Potter, has a plan for your life.

I am happy to say that I started a digital business in the midst of a pandemic and a broken relationship. In the middle of my broken relationship, I still encourage those who need a word of encouragement. I speak life into my children, I am progressing in my business and career, but most importantly, I am a Daughter of the Most High God and a mother to my children.

What I failed to mention before was that when my house lacked heat, I was still serving as the co-leader of the Single Mothers Ministry in my local church. While my house lacked heat and was cold, my heart was filled with love, warmth, and encouragement to pour into the lives of other single mothers. I dare you to take your eyes off your brokenness for a while and ask God to use you, I mean, really use you for His glory and see what He does.

Even in your brokenness, you can be a beacon of light for others. I know. I've experienced it for myself.

Therefore, I submit to you that you should take as much time as you need to heal from brokenness, but you cannot stay there too long. Cry your tears, kick yourself about your failures, but get up. Live! You were created for a purpose, and others are waiting for you to find it to speak LIFE into them. LIVE life after brokenness.

Do not renounce your scars; they make you who you are. You've earned these battle scars, so you might as well embrace them. Your scars make you beautifully unique, and they make you who you are. Therefore, love on those scars because they tell your story.

I came to the realization that whatever I am going through, the ups and the downs of life, God has me in the palm of His hands. He has me on the Potter's wheel, and He's molding me and making me into who HE has created me to be – NOT who people think I am. Failures, brokenness, mistrust, disappointments, and the like, they are all a part of His plans for me. That is also His plan for you too; you just have to see the big picture. Marred in the Potter's hands, but He is doing a new work in you and me, and the finished product will be a splendor.

No one knows the pain you're going through or have gone through. They can only empathize with you, but God knows. Maybe you're angry with God for not coming to the rescue when you wanted Him to. In fact, your brokenness could have been caused by someone who says they love God, but they broke you down into microscopic particles. Don't give up on God because He hasn't given up on you.

I've been down that road of questioning and asking Him why He allowed these things to happen to me, but I am always reminded of the scripture which states, *"For I know the thoughts that I think toward you, says the Lord, thoughts of peace and not evil, to give you a future and a hope."* Jeremiah 29:11 NKJV

You are not alone as you go through your periods of brokenness, mistrust, and shattered hopes and dreams. God is using your brokenness as a part of His masterplan. I dare you to have a shift in your mindset. The same way I started being grateful for all I had and blessed others with whatever I had; my cup kept running over. You too can experience the overflow of God's divine design for your life. You were designed with great thoughts in mind. You are purposefully positioned for greatness, even in the midst of your brokenness.

Wherever you find yourself right at this moment, you have a choice to make. You can decide to lay in bed, with the covers over your head with the blinds shut and live in darkness. Or you will get up, dust off the residue of your brokenness, and live. I encourage you to do the latter. I urge you to LIVE. What dreams do you have inside that you've left dormant to collect dust in the attic of your brokenness? Revive those dreams again. Shake off the cobwebs of defeat and move into the direction of light. Let the Son shine on your dreams and give life to them. Step out in faith, and watch God work in your life.

Greatness is inside of you. You were created for so much more. You have the keys to unlock your full potential and to live the life you want to. Repeat after me: I am worthy of more.

Greatness is within you, but you need to access it! You possess the keys to unlock your greatness because you are purposefully positioned for greatness.

Teneisha S. Campbell is a mother of two, an Accountant, an Entrepreneur, as well as a Best-Selling Co-Author of this Anthology. She earned her Diploma in Accounting from Humber College and is working on completing her Bachelor's degree through distance learning from Athabasca University. Teneisha shares her time between studying, running her online business, spending quality time with her children, as well as serving in her local church. She is passionate about encouraging women, especially single mothers, to live above the status quo and be the best they can be. Teneisha is a lover of music, travel, and all things real estate.

Website: https://www.teneishacampbell.com

Email: info@teneishacampbell.com

Facebook: https://www.facebook.com/teneisha.campbell

Instagram: https://www.instagram.com/teneisha_ann

LinkedIn: https://www.linkedin.com/in/teneisha-c-95a42b26

Broken Trust

Chapter Eighteen

Finding Financial Contentment & Happiness in Life

WRITTEN BY: ITOHAN MERCY OSAYI

$\mathscr{L}$ooking back after several years, it became clearer to me that it was not a dream at all. My thinking was more focused, and I could see how the frustrations affected my body surrounding the spirit of lack.

I recall waiting for hours to get a ride, which felt like a decade. No one offers to give a ride to a stranger. Here I was, a total stranger coming into a new area for the first time. The lack of funds and the need to get to my interview was my cry this morning. These questions keep stirring in my mind: How do I get to the venue? Can I walk twenty kilometers? If I lose this job opportunity, will I get another? Should I ask a passerby for some money?

The strength to stand any further decreased as I had not had any breakfast. I woke up at 4 a.m. for this interview with the excitement of wearing one of my new-to-me, used outfits. I took the time to study preview interviews online. The clock kept ticking and my heart beat at the thought of not having a dime on me.

I prayed to break the financial lack in my life that flowed week in and week out. This was a job I knew I could handle, and my resume answered all of the requirements in the job description. I made an effort to look around and it dawned on me that the day had gotten brighter, and more people were filling up the streets.

Many walking by took a good look at my new dress. A dress without a label or brand! I exclaimed to myself. So, they love my look? Hmmm... (I smiled) has become the center of attraction – or so I thought – but God alone knew why everyone was staring at me. As I made an effort to walk faster, a vehicle splashed some water on my shoes. I was happy my well-admired dress wasn't messed up at all. The driver was concerned enough to get out of the car to apologize. In the kind nature of showing how sorry she was, she offered me a ride. I looked around to be sure she was actually speaking to me. With her eyes wide open, she asked again, obviously seeing my surprised face.

I had no words to express my appreciation. I gave a sigh of relief as I realized we were heading in the right direction. "Thank you. I'll be ok at the third intersection," I said. We continued on our way and when she turned into the street, I stared at her and realized God brought me an angel. Tears ran down my cheeks...did I just get help from above? "This miracle must not end here Lord," I prayed silently. My miserable day was beginning to take a new shape. I got my diary to check the address again and behold it was four buildings away. We both got out of the car and laughed. "We work close to each other. You know I can always give you a ride later if you need one," she said smiling at me. "Thank you so much," I replied with tears still flowing down my cheeks.

I ran into the building to join the interview. My name had been called earlier, so the receptionist had concluded I wasn't coming. Everyone turned to stare when the door opened and the team leader asked, "Is she the lady we missed earlier?" I was panting not only from my running but was also anxious about being late and fear that I might be sent back home. I was asked to take a seat, fill out some forms, and join the group. All I could think of was this was my one ticket to provide for my family, something I needed badly. We were all interviewed and given the date and time he/she was to come for the second stage. The lady who gave me a ride earlier had also given me her phone number to call for a ride home.

At the second interview, I was among those who were selected to gain employment. Nothing in the world could top that for me – the joy, the happiness of finally having a job, and a steady income for my family. This was my chance to start a real life. The joy of knowing I had a meaningful and engaging job to empower myself was overwhelming. I needed to read more books on the responsibilities of my new job, know more about working life, insurance, savings, and much more.

I made my financial standard; an order I must not break. This included my tithe (10% of my earnings to God for giving me the opportunity to earn money), my rent (I never want to be reminded by a landlord to pay for the roof over my head), my monthly savings (I believe a little drop every month could become an ocean by the end of the year), family upkeep, and finally finding ways to improve myself on the job.

After a few years, I couldn't remember the location to buy my new-to-me clothes due to some road construction. I only bought new clothes once in a while and sometimes only on special occasions like my birthday or Christmas. I had also moved into my own apartment and purchased a small vehicle to get to work early. The zeal with which I attended the first interview, attended my first training, and took up the job never faded even after a few promotions. I kept praying to never see myself or anyone else in that financial struggle again. The circle has to be broken and self-actualization becomes the key to unlocking the door of our potentials.

In the past, I knew little or nothing about savings and lived paycheque to paycheque. I thought about others around me with no one supporting my business and the debt to educate my children.

Therefore, being an entrepreneur was not reliable. I wouldn't want my goods and services going into the hands of my well-cherished friend whom I have had a great relationship with and at the end of the day becomes enemies. "Why will I make a purchase when I know the payment will not be made in months?" I thought for many and concluded an alternative means was to provide essential services which only the rich and wealthy could pay me.

My thoughts were right, and I began private teaching for families whose parents worked in the banking sector, oil companies, university, and broadcasting elites. It was a worthwhile experience. The ideal process of preparing a well-refined teaching module to instruct the children was successful.

I desired to get back to studying my degree courses. It empowers one to have self-expression and will power. There is certainly no age we can't read or study. Making these facts real was my very first step to freedom which gave me the sweetness of life again. I felt loved and valued. I could work hard to care for my needs and make decisions that had a good foundation. This freedom did not only come by way of money, but also by way of self-acknowledgment: Why am I here? Who am I? Where am I going? And how do I get there? It was clear I could work on a focused five-year plan which included reaching out to the upper class and the lower class. The two classes of mankind: How did the upper class get to where they are? What does the lower class need to change for improvement? In my search, the answer was clear to me: God created both classes, and whatever the status, one should be content at that moment.

This gave me a different life perspective. The knowledge and love for the creator grew without boundaries and I felt the need to know it all. Being rich or poor is a state of mind, but the joy of having all my needs met by the Creator was beyond measure. Waking up from your sleep and being content with your struggle means to be at the top. Put your dreams to reality. Act on your plans and grow with it all. Do not take the failure to be the end. Refresh those written ideas, bring them to the table, and see the long distances become very short.

Your spiritual state is key here as you seek God. Associating with like minds made it easier for me. Never allow your ideas to waste away with time. It came to you as a gift. Such gifts must be used and made a seed to healing brokenness in life. I made a simple budget for home management to save money. This in many ways created a better living. There was a need to cover all household expenses and bills.

Every family purchase was based on a well-detailed budget. This meant getting the needed groceries, clothing, etc. and omitting many unnecessary items. With this, the loans from the bank were reduced for minor projects but strictly channeled to major projects to benefit the entire family. Note, because I once lived a life of lack, I now implement the measures to avoid those experiences once again. Throughout the years, I have taken advantage of acquiring more certificates. By increasing my knowledge, it has enhanced my abundance mindset and provided me with positive opportunities.

Today, I barely remember how tired I was many years ago when I couldn't afford to pay for commuting to my destinations. However, I now tap from the knowledge of patience, education, and life experiences to become who I am today and worthy of my achievements. Indeed, no sacrifices made towards a great future is wasted. I encourage you, wherever you are in your journey, to look at the abundant resources in 2020 and make decisions that will last a lifetime. Embrace the steps to see tomorrow in a brighter light. Stand tall to declare your victory over lack and poverty in your life.

If you are struggling with financial issues, I suggest you adapt the following points. I suggest sincere answers be rendered to these questions. Say it raw to yourself. I did many years ago and realized it was indeed a personal decision to overcome financial lack.

1) Tell yourself what you really want or desire. I never realized my focus until I decided what I wanted.

2) Give yourself a timeline. What's the goal you are planning? What does your schedule look like? Don't see yourself as wasting time or a season.

3) Find a solution. For example, each season for me came with a different job, with the long holidays came a sales job alongside the home tutorials. Sales were from my clients purchasing my study guides needed for their further studies. I sold them to the families because busy parents needed books and I solved their need and the time it took to browse the shops.

4) Apply your action plan: Find a good mentor. Who has the experience you need and how can you follow in their footsteps? What training would lead to the next step?

5) Be simple: Be yourself. Remember, your answer must be genuinely and uniquely yours.

6) Be ready, always: Never wait for anyone to awaken your dream. Great entrepreneurs of our time are always on the move.

7) Build your shock-absorbers: This is a full topic in my life. Be ready for various disappointments, praises, well wishes, awards, and

disapprovals. Through it all, brace yourself and follow your dreams to break out of lack and poverty.

8) Business funds: No matter how little the investment, let your business take off with that little step and strategize. Do you want to involve family and friends? Would it be wise to take a loan?

9) Link-Up: Ensure you are not left on an island. Attend workshops in line with your plans. Go online to search for recent solutions and ideas. See how your ideas work in other places. Be a part of a related social platform with positive support. This gives you clearer competitive knowledge to work with.

10) Times and Seasons: Never be stagnant with your ideas. Every season in life has its purpose. Create wealth at every changing factor. I got into a new society and saw the need to brand events, I did research and noted its size of need. It was a positive breakthrough and the demand was higher than I had expected. Different opportunities will provide multiple streams of financial resources. The e-commerce market is ideal, and many products are in demand and stand out. I am keyed in and each day I am content with my results.

11) Invest and save: When the profit comes in little drops, don't neglect savings and investing. Many new "financial step-ups" eat up their profits and want to celebrate when they should be laying stronger financial blocks. Make sure all your business profit is not lost on elaborate spending. This is when a great financial budget must be applied.

You can be successful and step out of poverty, or living paycheque to paycheque today, by being a master of finding great hidden opportunities around you. I know it sounds simpler now, but many years back when the internet was hardly available and social media was not within reach for everyone, we walked the "manual" approach and the results were still great. However, better results in financial stability and well-being always work in my experience for disciplined households. I pray for my readers never to get to a point of giving up, but that everyone will find the financial breakthrough and healing they are looking for.

Wealth is a state of mind that requires the foundation of faith and peace. There is no competition with others, but only the desire to be greater than you were yesterday.

Finding contentment in life is the greatest gain, so I encourage you to seek a simple lifestyle of satisfaction with a sound budget and invest in your future for total financial freedom and happiness in your life today.

Osayi Itohan Mercy is a mother and career personality with a passion for developing women and building stronger personalities. She has a wide received her diploma in Mass Communication at the Auchi Polytechnic; her Bachelor's at the Delta State University, and her Masters from the University of Lagos. Osayi's work experience includes a Public Relations experience at The Quadrant Public Relations as a trainee Executive, customer protection, and Counselling. She previously worked at LAPO Microfinance Bank as Client Protection and Support Manager, and currently works with Culture Link community services in Toronto, Canada-volunteer. Osayi also holds a Canadian Retail and Customer Service certification.

Facebook: Mee Deedey

Website: https://mercyosayi.canada.juiceplus.com

Whatsapp: +1-438-873-4088

Chapter Nineteen

The Pursuit to Happiness

WRITTEN BY: KIMBERLY TRÉA MANNING

$\mathcal{A}$t the age of sixteen, I was kidnapped for ransom, orchestrated by a friend in whom I'd trusted. Later in life, I decided to put up walls to prevent myself from being hurt. I would closely analyze everyone with whom I came into association. Being separated from my family for what had turned into months, I felt very alone and abandoned. I know it was the best option in keeping me safe, however, this caused me to develop a very strong feeling of detachment from my former friends, family, and everyone in my acquaintance. Yet still a child who was distressed, depressed, and confused, my life took a permanent turn; one that would determine where and who I would be as a by-product of my strength or weakness in a new land. Canada had been known as a place that provides safety, security, diversity, opportunities, and growth. The place now became a place for me to grow.

In my loneliness, I vowed to set aside my academic aspirations for a time in order to procreate. In the striking foolishness of how this sounds, I wanted a son – yes, a "man-child" whom I would nurture, love, and grow into the best person this world would have. I wanted someone that would never leave. I would never be alone again, and I would love and cherish him till the day I died.

My parents had sold most of their assets and were here now. One day, my father had inquired about me furthering my education and asked me to choose whichever university I wanted to apply. He would pay for it, but little did he know that I was about to give him his most disappointing news – I wanted to have a baby. While this sounded immensely insane, I had my reasons – my deeply rooted reasons.

My parents had never understood what my kidnapping had done to me. They thought that I was somehow responsible for what happened, and they were right; to some degree, I was irresponsible for trusting a stranger who had just entered my life. He was able to convince me into leaving the comfort of my home, venturing off to a place unknown to me. My parents' absence at that time had made it somewhat easier for me to give in to teenage curiosities. They were away on business.

Something my parents never understood was that my experience was very real – so real that it had changed me. The details of my kidnapping were never discussed, but I did seek help. I'm happy to say that I am very blessed because the help which I had was very effective.

I spoke to a very trusting and amazing psychologist in the city where we lived. Her work with me was very effective because not only was she well experienced, she was good at her work because she loved what she did. I was healing and was smoothly brought to understand things about myself which I had never understood. She was able to elaborate on my cognitive state as to why I felt and wanted the things I did at that time. Soon after, I was ready and prepared to start all over again.

In life, people will judge you for what they see; their systemic conceptions implemented by the social construct in which they live would have them feel even justified in doing so. I had to make a really tough decision, one that was based wholly upon my pursuit to happiness. In turn, I would come to raise a very happy and special little child.

I remember going to church and being showered with so much love but pity, positive words but scorn, encouragement but decrement, and at the very same time, perceived as a very little girl who had made a very big mistake. I was viewed as a child who had sexually explored myself at too young an age. I was not the "ideal" model of a friend that any parent would have wanted their children associated with, but for some reason, I was not bothered. My goal was to have this child so that I will never feel alone again. They did not know about my kidnapping, and my parents didn't know that I was also almost raped. No one cared and I needed not to explain myself. No one asked.

During the time of my pregnancy, I was so afraid to lose this precious soul that I went up and down the staircase using arms, legs, and butt. My mother thought it was funny but admired how dedicated I was to protect my unborn. She said I "worship" my belly, and she was right. I modeled before my pregnancy and here I was modeling my pregnancy with my younger sister as my personal photographer. I prayed every night while looking at a very bright star. That star brought comfort and somehow a promise to me – that God was with me all the way, even to the end of what would be, a very painful pregnancy.

My child was born and upon holding him for the first time, tears came to my eyes. I had never seen anything so perfect and beautiful in my entire life. He was healthy and so was I, so healthy in fact that I was able to walk us home, carrying him in a handheld car seat.

I had my beautiful baby boy and we lived with my parents who had bought a gorgeous home in a quiet town called Orangeville. I was the happiest young girl and was now ready to begin raising who is now, today, the most intelligent and amazing young man and person I have ever met! I made many sacrifices to give this beautiful angel everything I had and more.

My parents enjoyed feeding him and putting him to bed. My older brother would take him to the garage to hang out with him and his friends. One of his friends took my son on walks in his stroller to get him to sleep. He was loved and a village was raising him already. One day I decided to get out for some fresh air and came across the guy who took my baby for his daily walks. He looked at me and quietly asked my brother who was I. My brother responded that I was the mother of the baby he was so taken by. We got married about four months later when my baby was eleven months old and raised an amazing child together for many, many years. My son's first word was "VICTORY!" For his first birthday, he was already taking steps. He was reading at three years old and learned to ride his first bike without training wheels in just under two hours. For his first time on ice, he just began skating, never fell, and was already doing spins. He began walking on his hands when he was six and could do backflips at eight, hands-free. A born acrobatic and a good swimmer, he was never taught. He has traveled a lot and is currently an "A" student. He scored the winning goal for his football team, loves God, and loves to help people.

As I have grown older, and hopefully wiser, I've come to understand life on a much different platform. As human beings, we are educated by many things. Consider the mere fact that our children spend more time away from us when they begin attending institutions such as daycare centers, kindergarten, and other places of supervision so that most of us can get back into the workforce to better provide for our children. Our children aren't really raised by "us." We are a product of education systems, Netflix, news channels, social media networks, commercials, TV shows, political systems, the music we listen to, and I can go on. The people within your association – friends, families, co-workers, church members – have been programmed in the very same way, different country. Maybe, but the same model.

The question for you is: do you think they have something new to offer? It's like living in a house with many rooms – east wing, west wing; it's a really big house. The thing is, within this house, there is a special ventilation system providing you with the quality of air perfect to sustain your human survival. If any of you were to go outside, you'll die! Nobody has been outside. You want to know what life is like out there, so you begin asking questions. You've heard so many different stories, but you still ask questions. All versions told are so amazing. The guys in the kitchen, the folks in the basement, the family in the attic, people in the east and west wing, they all have amazing versions, but of the same story. They are so satisfying to your curiosities, but have they offered something new? None have ever been outside. All they have to offer are different versions of what they've heard, what they think they know.

Moral of the story: No one has anything new or truly satisfying to offer you but yourself. If you want to experience something new and beautiful, you have to experience it yourself. The best part of that story is, upon going outside through those sealed doors, the air is not toxic, and no one has to spend the rest of their lives in that house anymore. They are safer out there than being in the house. They have fresh air and discover ways of growing their food without the use of a greenhouse or other devices.

Lessons are best learned when we experience them. It's polite to listen and learn from other people's experiences and it's wise to use the knowledge for the better, but you have to know what's best for you and only you would know that.

I had taken it upon myself to break social conformities. I did something that was viewed by the majority as a violation of my self-respect that would bring great limitations to my life. I wasn't "cool" anymore by my peers, but that's okay because what I had done, despite my disposition, was to create something to inspire me, encourage others, motivated myself, and made me want more out of life. Something that always gave me the strength to never give up, even to this day. I'd bought my first property at the age of twenty-three. I had the down payment but not the credit, so I received the help which I was so grateful for. Things didn't turn out the way I wanted and I've come to the understanding that it may not have been a wise decision to have someone put their name entirely on what was supposed to be my house. My little boy and I ended up in an even worse situation than before. The house was sold without my consent and I was never shown the documents upon the sale agreement. What that did was help me thrive to buy another house in my own name, and so I did. We have to understand that everything will not always go as planned. We may be robbed of six years of our entire lives, but we don't give up. It's never too late, or too early, to start over again. We take the good and leave the bad behind, but we move forward.

On my child's 15th birthday, we stayed up from 3:00 a.m. to 6:30 a.m., laughing and chatting. Our talk ended with him telling me that I was the only person he could talk to like this; and like I always say, if I had to do it one million times over, I would choose to have him every time because, in everything we do in life, the end game for every single one of us is to find happiness, something he taught me last week.

Our social systems were designed to orderly arrange our individuality, social groups, and our institutions. They do this for us to live our lives in compliance with their standards, rules, and laws. This is supposed to support a blueprint that ultimately keeps us "safe." These systems do provide a degree of stability and order, but they also frame our minds to do things in a certain way, for example. Your husband takes advantage of you while you are sleeping, and you can charge him with rape, but really?! Do you really love him then? Another example, if your husband or wife cheats on you once, everyone will tell you to leave them, take the kids, and take them to court. Right! It's the right thing to do! Oh, come on...WRONG! The right thing to do is what's in the best interest of everyone, kids incorporated as well. Now, do you want to get an STD? No, but you also don't want to raise your kids alone, have an entire family court experience where ultimately the kids would spend a lot less time with their dad. What I would do is have a conversation – everyone deserves a second chance. We must always put ourselves in the other person's shoes and ask ourselves how we would feel if the tables were turned. We should not allow these things to steer us into forgetting our natural-born instinct in our "pursuit to happiness." Everyone deserves a chance at happiness.

Abraham Maslow developed a hierarchy of human needs. My son and I had discovered that individual needs on every level could all be derived from one universal need: "HAPPINESS." In a nutshell, we wouldn't be happy without air, water, food, sleep, sex, clothing, safety, money, good health, intimacy/relationships, freedom, and we strive to find purpose in life because that also is another contribution to our "happiness."

I've gained knowledge, strength, resilience, inspiration, and most of all, "HAPPINESS!!" I've been ashamed, misconceived, exploited, misjudged, neglected, underappreciated, and depreciated by total strangers and my very own family; but by knowing that these experiences which I've faced would leave me with the building blocks for a foundation to succeed, I did.

I am not what had happened to me, I am what I choose to become. Life is filled with many lessons that must be experienced to truly understand. There will always be hurt and happiness through relationships in this life – that is living – but we can take these experiences to help us aim for success. Something I always say when someone tries to put me down or tries to hurt me is, "That's fuel to my fire! Add it!" And that's what it should be. We can prove people wrong by just being a good person. Strive to always become better, pray even if you don't believe, and you will attract the right people and things into your lives that will in turn bring you HAPPINESS.

166

Kimberly Tréa Manning is the founder and co-owner of Trey and Manning Company, studied Social Sciences, and has also fulfilled studies as a medical assistant. She began writing at an early age of sixteen; however, this is her first published material, and is a very passionate writer. Mrs. Manning is currently in the process of writing her very own book as she has many more empowering experiences to share. Her academic aspiration in life is to acquire a Law Degree as she aspires to help people with a much more direct approach.

Snapchat: kimberlytrey1

Facebook: Trey & Manning Company

Facebook: Kimberly Manning

Email: treymanningcompany@gmail.com

Web page: www.treymanning.company

Broken Trust

Chapter Twenty

Powering Through Adversity

WRITTEN BY: SHERRY RICHTER

Brokenness happened to me due to a trail of unfortunate circumstances that led me to become a teen mom at the tender age of fourteen.

Terrified of the things to come and wondering what I would do with a baby, how would I cope, what would my friends think, plus marry a man when I was barely fifteen years old? Crazy! And I had many thoughts running through my mind, wishing I could go back in time and pretend this was all a dream...but it's wasn't. More than anything, it seemed like a nightmare. He was the best guy. There was something so different about him, but how would I even know that since I was so young. Somehow, I knew and felt he was the man of my dreams.

Feeling ashamed and alone, my friends were all heading back to class in the fall of 1976 and here I was planning a wedding. There was a special teacher who tried to convince me not to drop out, but to come back to school. He told me that we would make this work, but I was just too ashamed. I tried to do the homework my younger sibling would bring from the school on the bus for me. He went to the same school and the teachers would package up the homework and tell him to give it to me. Wow! Imagine, bringing homework home to a pregnant sister. So weird.

This all played a role on my mental health. The brokenness had challenged me and I felt that letting my parents down was the biggest disappointment of all.

How could I possibly look after a child when I was still a child myself; and not an underage woman? There were so many scary moments from that time until the wedding in December.

I had no money, none…what would I do? Not even a bank account. My husband-to-be was a bit older and had a job as well as a profession, so that would have to do. A young couple starting out with a baby – I had no money and he had some. Likely isn't the best way to start out a new life, right? And I had no idea what to do even if I did have support.

When you are that young, no matter how much family you have, you are alone with your thoughts at night. You feel this baby moving and you think, "What have I done and how will I fix this? How did I get myself into this mess? Why did I let this happen?" When you're a teen mom, you blame yourself. You don't blame anyone but yourself. I was devastated that I allowed this to happen to me.

I did the homework for a while and then I just couldn't do it any longer. It was so hard – in many different ways – not just the academic part. I felt like shutting myself off from the world. Who wants to be part of this and how did this all happen? I had such poor self-esteem and no confidence. So many judgments from others and the shame were almost suffocating. Her mom was so supportive and even though they didn't talk about a lot of things, she knew her mom was always there for her. Here I was going to be a mom, and I didn't even understand what that meant. Truly, I was fourteen years old, pregnant, and didn't have the best opinion of myself.

Well, back to the pregnancy. Fix it, but how will I fix it? Someone mentioned terminating the pregnancy which I would not allow, no matter how young I was. A life is a life, and they are precious.

There is no fixing anything. It happened and now we had to deal with it. Being pregnant at my age was traumatic…and positive at the same time. I needed to get away from someone and maybe this is how it would happen.

It was exciting to have a new baby arrive, and for some in his family, the first grandchild. I'm certain it wasn't the way they had planned or dreamed of it happening, at all. The first time I felt that baby flutter was truly amazing. My doctor said it would feel like a butterfly flutter and that is exactly how it felt.

Meeting the family was nerve-wracking, to say the least. I had been invited to a family wedding with my soon-to-be husband and was scared to death.

The emotions running through my mind were crazy but I was determined to make this work. His family was so kind, so much fun, and loving. They greeted me with open arms, although I'm certain they wondered where this young girl came from out of the blue! And likely thought, this is crazy too. My soon-to-be husband was so amazing and I honestly loved him, so going through this experience with him was wonderful.

I enjoyed planning a wedding although being so young, how would I know what I wanted? Was this all a fairy tale? I had no idea what to think, what reality was, or what would be. Because I was so young, I had seen older people do things and thought that would be it. I watched movies and TV shows and thought that's how to live and do things. However, those things weren't reality. They were all fairy tales, not real life but that's what I had. As time went on, plans came together and many things were made for me: dresses by someone close, invitations ordered, and fruit cake made with love. Things were coming together for my wedding, but I was still so young. By now, I was fifteen years old. Who in their right mind thought they'd be married at that age. Not me, that's for sure. I still didn't know if this was the right thing to be done. At my age, it's considered statutory rape. I had to get the appropriate permission which is obviously what happened. I still thought this was crazy. Was it really happening or was this all a bizarre, mixed-up dream?

I hid out. I didn't go anywhere because I felt so worthless and ashamed. But I had someone who loved me and I felt so incredibly grateful for that. He was amazing, he truly was. Small towns have their own dynamics. If you have ever lived in a small town, you will know. Your business is everyone's business and they all think they know the real story.

People talked, people made assumptions, and some of those assumptions were derogatory. Although my perseverance was strong, I also came from a good family who was well-liked, respected, and very giving. I think my parents were proud of me for doing what I did through all the hard times (perhaps not the getting pregnant part), but following through with all this stuff. How would you feel if your daughter was fourteen years old, pregnant, and then got married just a few months after her fifteenth birthday? Nuts. You'd think it's ridiculous and who in their right mind would let this happen. I was blessed, truly blessed. But there was something else at work here. I didn't know that at the time, however, as time went on, I would soon realize it to be true.

Some girls that got pregnant very young were sent away to the city to go to school and live there until they had their baby. Ashamed wasn't even the word. They were rejected from society which is so wrong! They went to a school in a nearby city where the windows in the basement were blacked out so you couldn't see in because all these teenagers were pregnant. Shame on that system!! We were all members of a contributing society, we all had something to give, and this just made me feel sick. Lucky, or blessed, or something else, but I had a loving, caring family and I went down a different path.

When graduation came along for Grade 12, I truly felt disconnected from the rest of the class. I knew everyone but didn't feel like part of the class that I had gone to school with. It wasn't their fault, at all. They were graduating, and I had three kids by that time. Seeing them graduate was so nice. They were my friends and I had known them for a long time. They would be starting their lives and moving forward, which was awesome, however, I was in such a different place in my life and had already accomplished a lot. Completely different circumstances, that's for sure!

Is this the life I wanted to lead? Yes, it was, as it played out…I loved farm life, my hubby, and my kids. I was proud of the family I had. I persevered and had gotten through some of the most difficult times of my life. There were many struggles, many financial restraints, and so much to overcome, but I felt like I could do anything I set my mind to and I was here for a purpose.

I got a job, a real job which I never really had before. Because I was so young when I got pregnant and married, I never had a chance to work or even drive for that matter! So I was very limited to what I could do. I was terrified and knew I'd overcome the fear sooner or later. I was just so grateful to have a job. Money was very tight and I needed it to help support my family. I started working at the local hospital in the kitchen when my youngest wasn't even two years old. Farming is a great way to raise a family, but raising three kids is also tough too. I worked a lot and it really helped out to put food on the table and pay bills, so I was proud of that as well.

I loved doing things with my family. I knew how to cook and clean, and I loved gardening. Seeing things grow is the best thing ever! And you can save a lot of money doing that too, so I canned and froze vegetables from the garden. Having the job at the hospital kept me busy as I worked quite a bit, but it helped us out on the farm too. Providing for your family is important and I was grateful for the opportunity I had to make a difference.

I became more interested in therapeutic diets as I worked in the hospital kitchen. It was part of something I had dreamed of doing. I wanted to help people become healthier and heal. Life has a funny way of paving the road to where you're meant to be.

As years went on and I became more educated, I completed my GED and started taking other classes. I did not see myself as being smart, though. I always thought I was dumb, but as I started to learn more about nutrition and the healthcare industry, I realized I was actually quite smart and had a lot to contribute!

Most of the courses I took were in a nearby town through distance education and online. Dial-up internet took forever but where there's a will, there's a way! I completed my classes and I was so proud of my accomplishments! I even took two university classes because I wanted to prove I could do it.

So here we are. I didn't finish high school but I did take my GED, received my Grade 12 designation, and then took Biology 100 and English 100. I bombed them both but didn't care! I had tried and that is what's most important. Don't ever give up; your dream is right there around the corner.

If you think you're not worthwhile, you're wrong. You are put on this Earth for a reason. God has a plan for you even though you may have no idea what it is. You are the only you there is. You're amazing and are going to change lives. God puts us all on this earth for the greater good. Now maybe you don't believe in Him, but you must believe in something. Believe in yourself…if nothing else. You are truly amazing! Look in the mirror and tell yourself every day, "I can do anything I set my mind to," and you will. Look for those who light up your life and believe in you if you can't believe in yourself. We all have a purpose and it's our job to figure that out. Listen to that little voice in your head and if you have someone you trust, ask them for help.

If I can get married when I was fifteen years old, have three kids before I was twenty, and raise my family plus build a career – you can too. Don't listen to any negativity or why you cannot succeed. Success is possible. It really is. I am here to tell you that if you have a strong enough conviction, you too can do anything at all! I'm not saying it will be easy, but life often isn't easy. However, it is totally worth it to give it your all. Keep a positive mind and have a good heart always. See the good in people as much as possible because that will bring out even more of the good from you!

We all have so much to give. I never thought I'd be where I am today, however, I was determined to succeed. I was determined to not be part of some statistic that someone has decided to keep track of. Now, go out and change the world! We all have dreams and hopes. Get out of your own way. I know you have it in you.

This year I've had to adapt to so many things with COVID-19 coming into the world and all the uncertainty that goes with it. I was part of the front line due to working in healthcare at the time. Such a scary time for so many with so much uncertainty, but we're getting through it. I've endured many hardships: being pregnant at a young age, getting married, taking classes, and getting an education. Now we're fighting a worldwide pandemic, so distance education has become very important again. Social distancing is our new normal.

This is just part of my story. I survived and persevered, and through adversity, you can too. Believe in yourself and hold your head high. I did.

Sherry Richter spent many years in Food and Nutrition management. She is also a former member of the Canadian Society of Nutrition Management, as well as the Saskatchewan Society of Nutrition Management. Sherry held a position on both of the CSNM and SSNM Board of Directors. She has deeply enjoyed being on many community boards over the years and volunteering her time, especially with a teen mom program. Sherry has since retired; however, she continues to be that amazing entrepreneur as always. She is a co-author in this anthology and is presently living in Regina, Saskatchewan.

Twitter: @RU11Bon

LinkedIn: Linkedin.com/in/sherry-richter-58a3aa60

Email: sharaleerichter@gmail.com

Facebook: https://facebook.com/sherry.richter2

Section Three

WELLNESS

Be authentic and trust the process of your growth.

Rose Marie Young

Birthing New Wings From
A Place of Healing

Written By: Rose Marie Young

I believe that our main goal in life is to have and live a happy, healthy, and well-balanced abundant lifestyle. Although we were created naturally to feel fully-well in our bodies, our minds, and in our spirit, unfortunately, sometimes certain things happen to us that can directly affect and cause us to feel otherwise. Such things can and may be influenced by our body's internal environments as well as external environmental factors. However, it's all about the degree of our pain, our beliefs, how we understand each situation, as well as how we view ourselves. The question is who and what caused us to be unwell and broken? And can we become unbroken?

For me, I was extremely broken in all areas of my life. My brokenness was caused by not one, but two major life-shifting car accidents. I can still remember the pain I felt after that first devastating accident that has now become my testimony. Back then, I felt the anger as it boiled up inside. I felt all the frustration and the fear of an unknown future and great uncertainty. My entire life was completely altered the day it happened – April 4, 2008.

It was unbelievable and totally shocking to find myself again a few years later in another four-vehicle accident where all the cars were completely unfixable. As before, my life was uprooted, and I did not understand what the universe was trying to say to me. All I knew then was that my life would forever be transformed, and nothing would ever be the same. It was as if I was traveling through a very dark tunnel while trying to find my way to where there was some glimmer of light. I was in a very dark and lonely place where I struggled to find myself. There were moments that the pain was unbearable; I could hardly breathe. Yes, I felt pain before, and yes, I have been through some ups and downs, but this experience that I am speaking of was far more intense than anything I have ever felt. It was crippling to my well-being as well as my health. As my future and my health were slowing diminishing, I also became depressed and a stranger to my children and myself. My emotions were all over the place. Suffering from PTSD and severe pain, I was unable to mentally and physically function for six full years. At times, I wondered if the pain was ever going to end as various aspects of brokenness engulfed my life.

Certainly, the road that I have traveled was not an easy one, but through it all, I kept pushing forward. Even though the days were long, and the nights were even longer, I was committed to getting better. I knew if I did not, I would become lost in the dept of my anxiety and despair. I was fearful of being lost in a place of no return. My only way of becoming well was to focus entirely on healing. I realized that I was not going to get any results lying or sitting around in my dark room feeling sorry for myself. My healing and breakthrough began the minute I started to shift my mindset. I also began to witness a feeling of healing the minute I stopped trusting all the negativity that had been sent out to the universe about my health and my well-being. Be aware of the words that are being sent out into the world and the universe about you. Words can be used as very powerful weapons against us. However, they can also be used as great tools for our success.

It was a difficult journey, but somehow, I made it through the tough times. I told myself I would...and so I did. I accomplished what most people, as well as medical experts, had told me was not possible: I *thought* myself better. After both car accidents, I was told that I would not recover and be rid of the pain without back surgery. Yet, I refused to believe that was my only option and the sole solution. The thought of it was rather very stressful. I definitely could not. Truly, it was by God's good grace why I am here. He was with me every step of the way. It was Him who blessed me with some amazing good doctors, like my chiropractors, who helped me to regain my courage and the strength to overcome. I am still seeing one of them even now.

With each passing day, I made my future my road map. I developed new mottos to follow. Some of my favorites are "Think from the end," "Think of yourself as being well and being victorious," "Think of having a pain-free life," and "Think of a life where you can trust others who are honest, ones who show you kindness, respect, and are empathic to your feelings." As for now, be very thankful for all the good and positive things about your life right where you are in this present moment. The world is yours to discover as you work towards growing and discovering yourself. As you begin to live a life with an attitude of gratefulness, the universe will eventually give you more things to be grateful for. And without even realizing when, you'll have found that you've birthed new wings from a place of healing.

Life can be very twisted, and at times it shows you something different than what your naked human eyes are seeing but give yourself a moment to take another look. Behold the bigger picture and think outside the box. It took me a while to understand this because it was far beyond my human comprehension to view the beauty that was buried underneath my pain and anxiety. It took me a while to see the reason and the purpose that God has for my life. I had almost given up but almost doesn't count. What matters is I didn't. And you shouldn't either. I became driven by my ambition and my will to survive. I had no choice but to make peace with my past and work hard to manage the pain each day. I prayed, I exercised, and I diligently kept all my doctors' appointments. Most importantly, I began to love myself again.

Always love yourself and do good unto yourself as you do unto others. Never be unapologetic for loving yourself and who you were created to be. I also encourage you to pray with the right attitude of hope, trust, and believe that all will be well. You don't always have to be strong. Start with just believing that you can be...and you will be. Believe that you are stronger than all your insecurities. You may not think that you are perfect, and others may look and see all your imperfections, but always remember that God created you perfectly and He has a perfect plan for you and each of us.

Although it may not be our intention, sometimes we are left with no choice than to transform with the changing of the circumstances. For example, during this period of Covid-19 where so many millions of people have been affected in one way or the other, adaptation is necessary. Accepting and adjusting to so many changes is not only good for an individual, but it's imperative to all life existence of the entire universe. Changes help us to become aware, and it enables us to evolve in our humanness, and although there is so much brokenness in our lives and the lives of others around us, it's important to have faith and practice self-care. Do your part to maintain a healthy lifestyle for all. To be well is to stay well and feel well not only in your body but also in your mind. The stressors of life can be very overwhelming. So, stay focused and be very mindful of what happening in and around you. In every situation, be sure that all your physiological needs are met as well as all your other basic human needs. It is very important to maintain your physical health and strength. Always remember that your body is a masterpiece created by God himself to be appreciated and loved.

Be mindful and know what's important and relevant in your life. Pain sometimes helps us to grow, and at times, even helps us to find our divine purpose. Be positive and try to accept new realities. Create in your mind a future of unbroken health. By doing so, you can make a great difference not just for you, but in the lives of others. Do not let the negativity of the world change nor break you. Instead, adjust your perception of how you view the world. Change the way other people in the world are viewing you and be transformed by the renewing of your mind. Stay optimistic – you will be well by navigating all your thoughts and feelings to positively strengthening your mind. Let the pain that you feel give you the ability to become empowered. Take time to enjoy your life. Love yourself and love your life. It is the most important priority.

"I can do all things through him who strengthens me"
Philippians 4:13 ESV

Chapter Twenty-One

The Purple Warrior:
A Battle of Epilepsy

WRITTEN BY: AMANDA ROBAR

*Y*ou never know what life is going to throw your way until you get hit. The question is, are you strong enough to take the punch?

Some of us don't get a choice – I sure didn't. I have been fighting epilepsy since the day I was born. I have several different types of seizures. Some of these include simple partial, complex partial, myoclonic jerks, and growing up I had my fair share of tonic-clonic seizures.

As a child, I did what almost every kid does. I took swimming lessons, gymnastics, karate, and trampoline lessons. I also participated in musical theatre as a youth and as an adult.

You see, I am a very determined person. I was a strong-willed kid and epilepsy wasn't going to stop me from living my life.

I won't lie, my condition can be exhausting at times. Sometimes my smaller seizures, where I go temporarily blind, can knock me out for a good two hours. I really have to listen to my body. If it says I should rest, then I should rest. If I overexert myself, I am just asking for seizures. Everyone has a threshold and it's important to know when to stop for your own health.

There are many things that can cause me to go into a seizure. Some of these triggers include heat, reflection from a water's surface, and pixelation from screens such as televisions, tablets, and cell phones. Other triggers are lack of sleep, too much caffeine, or constantly being on the go with little rest.

I have been through a lot. I've tried seventeen different medications over the past thirty-five years. Some treatments made me aggressive, some extremely depressed, while others caused me to be incredibly dopey or drunk-like. I even suffered double vision on some medications when the dose was too high.

As a kid, I was told on several occasions that I could outgrow the seizures. Childhood epilepsy they called it. I was twelve years old when I told my pediatric neurologist not to lie to me. I knew this wasn't going to be the case, at least not for me. It was an empty promise and false hope.

Growing up and into adulthood, I hit many brick walls where there were no new medications available. This was beyond frustrating for me. As a kid, I was lucky if a medication helped control my seizures for six months to a year.

When I was first given stress balls, I thought they were stupid. Little did I know how handy they would become in my life. They helped in relieving some of my anger and frustration. Some I would squeeze until flat while others I would chuck against the wall with a hard thud! I would then crawl under my covers, crying tears of helplessness, and fall asleep.

Before I left a well-known children's hospital in Toronto, I was told I was a candidate for brain surgery. It was a decision not to be taken lightly, but at that point in my life, I was out of all other options. I said yes and they began running all the pre-surgical testing.

At the age of eighteen, I had resection surgery done to try and stop the seizures. The surgery did not go as planned as there were severe complications. My brain swelled up, my eyes were swollen shut, and I couldn't talk, walk, or move at all. I could hear though. I heard my brother crying and felt him holding my hand. The only things I wanted to do were to squeeze his hand back, tell him that everything was going to be okay, and not to cry. I couldn't though and that killed me inside!

As I lay bedridden, I continued to listen. Some of the things I heard made me angry and this just made me even more determined. How dare the doctors tell my family what I would or wouldn't be able to do in the future!

I worked very hard relearning everything from walking and talking to reading and writing. I progressed from using a wheelchair to a walker. I worked the stairs with someone either in front of me or behind me. I spent countless months doing rehabilitation both as an inpatient and an outpatient. I worked with physiotherapists, occupational therapists, speech therapists, and recreational therapists to help me regain my skills.

In the long run, the surgery was worth all the painful struggles. It helped remove almost all of the tonic-clonic seizures, something I never thought would happen in my lifetime.

As part of my post-surgical brain therapy care, I was connected with a community support organization. At this point, I was still having daily seizures. The people from the organization suggested that I look into a seizure response dog for my safety. Since I required the dog to do multiple tasks, it took a while to find a company willing to take me on.

I was finally paired with Kramer, a 4-year-old golden retriever. Kramer became my lifeline and best friend. He prevented me from walking out into traffic, assisted with my vision loss, and responded to my seizures ensuring I was safe. He saved my life no less than twelve times.

A decade passed as I went through several new and experimental medications with little success controlling my seizures. I became incredibly frustrated with the visits to my neurologist. He had no new treatments to offer and anything I brought forward either wouldn't work for my type of seizures or wasn't available in Canada. I was drowning and any form of hope faded away.

On November 24, 2013, Kramer passed away from an unexpected heart attack. I was beyond heartbroken. Kramer and I had been a team for four years. We had taken care of each other and together we had educated the community about service dogs.

After his loss, my life began to spiral downhill. It got to a point where I couldn't even fake a smile.

On March 16, 2015, I hit rock bottom. My meds weren't working, one of them was making my depression even worse, and I was grieving Kramer's loss. My heart and soul were shattered and I felt so lost and alone. I just wanted to die and be with my friends who had passed away from SUDEP (Sudden Unexplained Death in Epilepsy Patients).

After a very long, painful day with my family trying their best to offer me support, I admitted myself to the Mental Health Ward at the hospital in Newmarket.

The first three days were the worst. No one was supposed to have any electronics. Music was the only thing that helped calm me down and now it had been taken away. I probably would have passed out from hyperventilation if the staff hadn't returned my music player to me. It definitely helped get me through my two-week stay.

When I left the inpatient ward, I was far from ready to be at home. I signed up for the outpatient day program. It was very supportive and and every lunch hour, our group would watch the same game show on the television.

The program was six weeks long. During this time, we were introduced to a national mental health association, programs available through a regional women's center, government support programs, and if we wanted, information on getting back into work.

As the program came to an end, I began to bond with my new service dog, Kira. This was a huge step for me. I never thought I would bond with or love another dog the way I had with Kramer.

I was progressing slowly but knew I still needed more help. I signed up to take the four-part program at the women's center. The program was amazing. I learned so much, but more importantly, I grew as a person and built up my self-esteem.

It took me two and a half years before I felt worthy and hopeful again.

After graduating from the program at the women's center, I could feel myself becoming flat. I needed something to stimulate my brain, so I put together a fundraiser event for the cancer society. This gave me a purpose until the event was over.

Knowing I needed to keep myself busy, I decided to join a network marketing business promoting wickless candles. I watched training calls, bought business books, and attended the local and international conference. I now have friends from all around the globe.

If there is one thing in life I love, it is traveling. Thanks to my service dogs, I have the confidence to travel by myself.

My first solo trip was with Kramer. We flew down to Cancun, Mexico. What an amazing feeling it was to have this kind of independence! When I returned home, I felt like a whole new person. If I could do this, I could do anything!

As for Kira, she and I have an annual trip to Anaheim, California every November. We represent a community-based epilepsy agency at the Epilepsy Awareness Day & Expo in Anaheim at a world-renowned resort. Representing my epilepsy agency internationally to over 2,500 people is a tremendous responsibility and an honor.

It is also an honor to meet with specialists who take time out of their busy lives to speak to us about new treatments for epilepsy in the works.

The Expo is held over a two-day period and the entry fee is free. Everyone deserves more education about epilepsy. The Expo has over 100 booths to visit, and between manning our booth and listening to educational speakers, I am lucky to get the chance to visit them all.

On the third day, everyone puts on their purple t-shirts in support of epilepsy awareness. We then head outside where we have a giant group picture taken. Seeing this sea of purple gives you hope and lets you know that you are not alone!

I am quite a strong advocate when it comes to epilepsy awareness. I am part of an epilepsy support group on Facebook. If I see the same questions or concerns pop up over and over again, I will go live and talk to everyone. I have done presentations in schools and for seniors about how a seizure response dog helps someone who suffers from epilepsy in their everyday life. For example, if I go into a seizure, I will call Kira. Her job is to lick my hand as this helps bring me out of the seizure faster. Kira keeps me away from the roads and if we are out and about and I have several seizures, she will guide me back home. Kira is also trained to hit an emergency button if I go into a big seizure. Thankfully, she has never needed to push it.

Kira also reduces my anxiety and stress; two other things that bring on my seizures. For me, it could be as simple as meeting a new person, heading to the city, or going through security at the airport. Having Kira beside me helps me breathe easier and the motion of stroking her helps a lot.

I believe that having updated data is very important, especially when it comes to your brain. I asked my neurologist if he would set up a time for me to go into the epilepsy monitoring unit. The data collected indicated that electrical activity was coming from all areas of my brain. I wasn't too surprised; it was more confirmation that things were changing and not for the better.

Knowing what my brain was doing gave me the chance to explore and research alternative therapies, one of which was the Vagus Nerve Stimulator. I had seen it down in California at the epilepsy expo and the following year in Toronto.

After speaking with representatives from one particular company three times, doing in-depth research, and much thought I pushed my neurologist to consider me a candidate for the VNS. It took a while, but on March 21, 2019, I had VNS implanted.

It took a bit to get used to the feeling of the electrical pulse and my voice cutting out, but I knew I had made the right choice. The first thing I noticed was a positive change in my mood. I wasn't as depressed as I had been before, and I was able to lower my anti-depressants a little bit.

When I reached the nine-month mark of having the VNS, I noticed that it caught a bigger seizure. I also know it is catching seizures while I sleep as I am more clear-headed in the mornings. Every month, the VNS gets a little bit better as it learns my body and brain activity. I have been told that the battery life is five to seven years. After that, I will get an upgrade to a newer updated model.

Throughout my battle with epilepsy, I have discovered how strong a person I truly am. I have learned how important it is to advocate for yourself, why you need a good support system, and the importance of surrounding yourself with positive people.

Living on your own is possible for most of us. All you need is an emergency system in place in case something happens. It could be as simple as having a call button, or medical alert bracelet.

Find your passion and go for it! Don't let people tell you that you can't do something.

Last year I started a podcast. It covers a variety of subjects such as what epilepsy is, possible triggers, preparing your child's teachers in advance, requesting an IEP, SUDEP, and how people with epilepsy are just like everyone else.

As you can tell, I am very passionate about assisting other people with epilepsy. I try to help them understand their disability and help their families appreciate what their loved one is going through.

I came to realize that this is one of the reasons why I am still here. I am meant to continue spreading awareness and letting others with epilepsy know that they are not alone.

Don't be afraid to go out and live your life! Some days I go out to lunch or catch a movie on my own. I also love going to see live musical theatre.

I know how hard it can be at times but living in fear and depression is far worse. After falling into the darkness and rising back into the light, I know that the only things I want in my life are to be happy and surrounded by positive people.

There is so much joy to be found in life. Open your heart up to new adventures and enjoy every minute of it.

Amanda Robar is an entrepreneur who lives in Newmarket Ontario. She is a graduate of George Brown Community College in Toronto, Ontario, enjoys writing as well as other activities and was featured in the very first issue of the LWL Lifestyle magazine. Amanda has many passions which include her family time, animals,and educating others about epilepsy. She started a popcast in the hopes of reaching and helping those who are feeling lost and alone in the world of epilepsy.

Facebook: https://www.facebook.com/amanda.robar.5

Twitter: www.twitter.com/@AmandaCScentsy

Instagram: www.instagram.com/amanda.amanda.robar

Chapter Twenty-Two

Upside Down and Inside Out

Written By: KAYLA BARAN

I have come to believe you should live upside down and inside out. Imagine an arrow pointing vertically down; now imagine the same sized arrow directly in the center pointing from one side to the other. This symbol represents living upside down and inside out.

Upside down represents living from your spirit into your mind and from your mind into your physical body. You are a spiritual being, you have a mind, and you live in a physical body. From a scientific point of view, all we are is matter, and all matter is simply energy. You are not your thoughts but are an observer of your thoughts; therefore, you cannot be your thoughts. You are not your body, but you live in your body. You do not say, "I am a hand," or, "I am a foot." No! You have a hand, and you have a foot.

As spiritual beings, we always want to grow, learn, and get better at what we are doing. Having a mind that we can use to create our thoughts and feelings makes it so that we can shift our actions, which changes our external world. In my opinion, we are the only creature on the planet with an intellect. Our minds have mental faculties such as imagination, will, memory, reason, perspective, and intuition. We have been given these faculties to use to create pictures of how we want to live. Everything is first created in the mind and then in the physical. The body is an instrument of the mind. The body does exactly what the mind tells it to do.

I believe the phrase "inside out" represents living from the greatness inside us, out into the world. The opposite is letting our external environment and outside circumstances influence how we feel about ourselves, our abilities, or what we can achieve in this lifetime. If someone else tells us, we cannot accomplish something because we are too young, too old, undereducated, or anything else, we should never let this external condition stop us from what we truly desire. Instead, we should focus on the internal reasons why we desire our wants.

As a physiotherapist, this understanding has turned my practice into a holistic-focused care model. When I treat my clients, I view them as a mind, body, and spirit. When I was solely focused on the physical components of an individual's health, I addressed the symptoms and never really got to the root cause of the problem. When treating this way, it is only a matter of time before the same person returns with another issue.

I tore my anterior cruciate ligament (ACL) when I was twenty-one years old, at a trampoline park. At that time, I was a long-distance runner, and running was the love of my life. I ran to clear my mind, ran to think, ran to feel, and ran to show love to myself. This whole experience dramatically shifted my life. I remembered feeling the jump, the pivot, and twisting mid-air on the trampoline. I heard and felt a pop come from deep in my right knee. At that moment, I knew that I had torn my ACL. It felt the same way as described in the textbook. I fell to the ground, holding my knee close to myself.

I did not want anyone to see that I was hurt. I stood up and tried to walk a little, my knee collapsed inward, and I knew in my heart what had happened. I started to become very fearful about what was going to happen. I was unable to bear weight on my right leg after the injury and was using crutches to move for a couple of weeks. I needed help to get up the stairs and into the bathtub, which was embarrassing for me. I had been completely independent before and never experienced this much pain. Therefore, I was having a hard time keeping a positive attitude. I was mostly grumpy, upset, or sad. I spent a lot of time complaining, expressing worry, doubt, and fear. I was angry at myself for what happened and tended to lash out at those around me.

After three months of physiotherapy rehabilitation, I found that I was walking well again, however, I still felt a significant weakness and instability around my knee. I was then referred to a surgeon who looked at my knee, wiggled it around, and said, "Yes, it is an ACL. I will fix it for you." Perfect, I thought, it could be repaired, and everything would be back to normal. I had trust and faith in the doctor and my upcoming procedure.

Through this experience, I realized a large part of my life and identity was changed after the injury. For instance, I missed moving freely, feeling good, being independent, and running every day as I had done before. I often got angry with myself when our family walked on the beach while camping. I hated not leading at the front and I kept repeating to myself, "You are so slow," in my mind, then mentally beat myself up. My knee was in constant pain and it was a continual reminder that caused me to get extremely upset with myself and others. I think this was because I believed I couldn't help myself, and no one else could make me better. I continued with my appointments and physical training until my surgery. This was extremely frustrating as I frequently had to stop during my runs due to ongoing pain. For some reason, I was under the impression that after surgery, the road would be smooth sailing.

After the operation, I found myself in unbelievable pain, limited mobility, and a range of prescribed drugs. I wish I had never got the surgery as things became much worse than before. During this stage, it felt like it was slowly healing. I attended physiotherapy for the entire post-surgery period with a kind and positive woman. It was then I decided that I would become an understanding, compassionate, and positive physiotherapist. I decided that I would be the best I could be in supporting others through their healing.

One year after my injury, I was accepted to the School of Physical Therapy at the University of Saskatchewan. I was still unable to return to long-distance running due to muscle weakness and knee pain. I was told by the surgeon that this was as good as it would get and that I should find a different sport and should not consider becoming a Physiotherapist if I could not handle the physical pain. I remember feeling so disappointed that I was not physically where I was before the injury. I was very upset that the doctor had not acknowledged my concerns about my physical limitations or treated me with respect I felt that I deserved as his patient. I only believed in what the doctor suggested so mindlessly. I let his opinion about my knee impact me emotionally, which led me to believe that I would never be a runner again. I focused on the pain, limitations, and lack of running in my life. I left running behind for four years. During this time, I enjoyed spin classes, yoga, strength training, biking, and rowing.

I often share my story and use it to guide my clients through their exercise therapy and healing. This helped to increase their faith in their body's ability to heal.

I began coaching clients on the importance of positive self-talk, visualization, and holistic care during my time as a new graduate. I received many comments from my clients about how mental and emotional acknowledgment and encouragement were just as beneficial as their physical therapy treatments. I supported my clients to have faith and patience to know that they can heal through their pain or injury. I even remember showing some clients my scar and telling them my story to support them in understanding their body's ability to heal.

One day at work, we had a presentation on ACL construction rehab. I remember listening to the speaker and all the stats and facts that were repeated. At the end of the presentation, my knee was throbbing with discomfort. At this point, I hadn't experienced knee issues for at least a year. I began to analyze my thoughts over the past hour, and how the thoughts of my past injury and pain created those same issues at that moment. I started to play with the new ideas that I wanted to fill my mind with. I put an image of running with ease on the sand in my mind while smiling. I tuned into how I was coaching clients to reach goals and how our thoughts can affect our health. After hours of deep thought, study and reflection, I heard the voice of one of my mentors say, "Your biggest limitation is the use of your imagination." At that moment, I decided I would run a marathon.

After many years without long-distance running, I opened up my mind and started to visualize myself running with ease. I wrote affirmations out and got emotionally involved with the idea that I could run again. I started training and didn't let my body convince me of any limitations. I decided to place the image of what I wanted in my mind and held it there until I believed it could be true. I started to act as if it could happen. My beliefs around my body started to change, and I began to run longer distances. I achieved my marathon of 42.2 kilometers in the summer of 2020. That was the longest I had run since my record of 21 kilometers in the summer of 2014. I was very proud of this moment. After achieving this, I became aware that my mind was in control of my body and that my body was an instrument of the mind. I reconnected with an activity that fed my soul, connected me to nature, and gave me deep satisfaction and happiness after years of believing it was impossible to return to my previous level, let alone far past it.

When I reflect on why I let my favorite activity go, I realized it was because I let what was going on in my physical body get me emotionally involved in the discomfort, lack, and limitations. I was looking at my physical results, getting emotionally involved with the ideas, and then believing that my current reality would always be my future. I was giving energy and momentum to all the reasons why it was hard, it hurt, or why I could not run. This was the moment when I realized that I changed my way of thinking. I started focusing on how my restoration helped me express more empathy, understanding, and healing for others. I stopped making excuses for all the outside circumstances that were in my way and started to express my desires and intentional beliefs out into the world. My personality changed significantly, and therefore my reality changed. I instantly started to study this, do research on the mind-body connection, and how I could integrate it into my practice.

I had come across research that taught me our beliefs and emotions can enhance or regress healing. It has been proven in science now that our thoughts can make us sick, which inversely suggests our thoughts can help us heal. This is now a passion of mine, and I love to teach clients and athletes the power of visualization.

We now know in medical science that your thoughts can cause physiological stress in the body. Stress is the cause of the majority of diseases in our world today. Worry and overthinking can cause physical illness in the body. Our stress arises through the habitual repetition of our negative memories, thoughts, feelings, and actions. Most of what we worry about is out of our control or little importance. Only 8% of what we worry about actually has the potential of happening. This causes me to believe that choosing faith over fear will always lead you to better thoughts and feelings.

You do not have to let your current physical situation influence what you believe you can do. Think from the upside of what you want down into your body (upside down). You also want to live by expressing your desires and greatness from within you out into the world (inside out), rather than letting the world tell you what you can and cannot accomplish. It takes training, practice, and self-control but is a skill that can be mastered just like any other. The more you put into it, the more you will get out.

To make massive growth in your life, you need to know where you are and where you are going. You have to define in your life the way you want to live it. If you are like a sailboat in the ocean and you do not decide on the direction you want to take your life, the wind will push you around and you won't know where you will end up. But if you carefully point in the direction that you wish to go and progress towards your goal with faith and persistence that you will reach it, you will meet with success.

I realized that I had been unconsciously and unintentionally living from the downside up for years. I committed myself to focus every day on becoming better at living from my goals and dreams into my reality while expressing the greatness within me. When I was living from the downside up, I was letting my current reality control the way I was thinking about my current state and focusing my thoughts on where I was. When I was living this way, I had a constant flow of mental mind chatter. Over time, I learned to slow this chatter down and start to consciously choose the thoughts I wanted to become emotionally involved with. From my personal experience, I now believe that our thoughts can help us to heal.

In summary, living from upside down is flowing with your creative potential. We all can tap into our spirit or energy and come for our highest want. We can easily hold that image on the screen of our minds by using our will. Eventually, we will get emotionally involved with ideas in our intellect, and it will be expressed with and through the body. We must define how we want to live our lives. Then ask for the resources we will need. We do not need to know how it will occur. Once we believe with faith that it will come, we will receive all that we need.

I encourage you to be brave enough to explore the depths of who you are. When your inside world changes, everything outside begins to follow.

Kayla Baran is a Physiotherapist and business owner from Regina, Saskatchewan. She graduated with distinction in 2015 for her Bachelor's degree in Kinesiology, majoring in Adapted Movement Science and Human Kinetics. She completed her Masters in Physical Therapy at the University of Saskatchewan in 2017. Kayla believes it's essential to have a holistic approach to health and uses acupuncture, myofascial release, and education as part of her treatments. Her areas of special interest include educating on visualization, goal setting, and the hypersensitive nervous system. Kayla promotes love, gratitude, and forgiveness, and enjoys studying personal development, physical fitness, camping, fishing, canoeing and traveling with her love, Nick.

Website: http://kaylabaranphysio.ca

Website: http://infusedgemstones.ca

Broken Trust

Chapter Twenty-Three

When Everything Falls into Place

WRITTEN BY: TAMMY CHINN

Sometimes you have to sit alone in the dark with yourself in order to find your light.

On February 14, 2016, my lights went out. What began as a fun evening out with my husband and friends to celebrate Valentine's Day, ended with a heavy hit to the floor; one that would leave me with no recollection (to this day) and a visit to the hospital. I was forced to retell an embarrassing story that I only remembered partly – whether it was the alcohol, the hit to the floor, or a combination of both, my husband had to fill in the missing pieces for the doctor. Needless to say, I had suffered a serious concussion and was ordered to do nothing for the next few days and follow up with my family doctor in one week. No work, no phone, no computer, no television, no reading, absolutely no brain stimulation – it was literally all lights out for me.

Over the next few days, I just laid on the couch, alternating between pain medication and ice to ease the hammer that was pounding in my head. I was completely alone with my thoughts that were racing through what still felt like the worst hangover ever. Despite the pain, confusion, and fear, I hadn't felt this much at peace in a long time. You see, the days, weeks, and months leading up to this were filled with anxiety and a feeling of emptiness, like something was missing from my life. Always the outgoing, talkative, seemingly confident, party-loving gal, I felt like my flame was burning out. I was seeking meaning and had recently made a birthday wish that resembled more of a desperate plea to the universe to show me my purpose. I knew there was more to this life than the robotic routine of my days. Although I had a family who loved me, a brand new grandson who brought so much joy to my world, good health, supportive friends, and co-workers, every morning was a struggle to feel motivated and muster up the strength to just smile and wave my way through each day. No one understood my pain. I don't think I even understood what was happening inside of me. I was tired of being strong and putting on fake smiles for everyone when all I wanted to do was hide from the world. I felt disconnected from my true essence, my soul, as though I was drowning in this deep abyss while the world continued to spin out of control around me – until now. Everything stopped.

Days turned into weeks. With every doctor's visit, there was some improvement but not enough to send me back to work. Bright lights, crowds, and socializing left me with headaches, confusion, and irritability. I was also still struggling with memory loss and insomnia. Although physically, I looked and sounded like me on the outside, my inner self was struggling and begging to be healed. Aside from these lingering symptoms which warranted an MRI confirming no apparent lasting damage to my brain, I felt completely alone as no one could understand what I was feeling. Almost two months had passed, and I was still far from fine.

Music and podcasts became my daily dose of therapy and encouragement. I listened to everything from self-empowerment, building a successful business in one week, to manifesting your life's dreams, but nothing resonated until, during one of these inspiring talks, a citrine crystal was mentioned for attracting abundance. For some reason, I decided to write this down.

Just days later, my doctor felt that it was time for me to return to work. I was devastated! I thought the universe had given me this opportunity to figure out my soul purpose. That night as I sat up wondering what the point of these past two months was, I remembered those words I had written down a few days prior...*Citrine Crystal*. I googled them. I can't describe the feeling I had when I began reading about this crystal, its healing properties, how it helped the solar plexus, and what was a chakra system anyways? I had always loved gemstone jewelry and the little meanings attached to them, but something happened to me on Monday, April 11, 2016. I read for over three hours that night (without a headache), and after four hours of sleep, woke up never feeling so alive and charged up about anything in my life up until that moment. I had a sudden overnight "obsession" with this alternative healing modality. Something had clicked for me and resonated deep within my soul.

I found myself wandering into my first new age store the next day. I was overwhelmed with everything! I had no idea what I wanted, what to do, or how to start. I was guided to a bin of crystals and told to trust what I was drawn to. Without even realizing it, I was being given my first lesson in following my intuition. I picked up a few to which the owner showed me their names and meanings. He then handed me a book to investigate further. I was shocked to learn that every crystal I had chosen contained healing properties that I was needing at this time in my life. I had made a connection with their energy! I bought the book and the handful of chosen gems, one of them a beautiful citrine, and back home I went to sit with their energy and learn.

Over the next couple of weeks, I worked with each crystal. I slept with Amethyst under my pillow to bring peace, ease the headaches, and insomnia. I wore Garnet inside my clothes to fuel my new passion and Rhodonite to find the courage to discover my potential. I carried Black Tourmaline in my pocket to ground and protect my energy and Smokey Quartz to absorb all of this negative energy that had been consuming me, while I attempted to meditate with my magical rainbow-filled Citrine to raise my vibration (another new term) with an abundance of happiness and hope. I could not focus on much more than these crystals. It was as if they were calling out to me and demanding my attention. I was listening.

A few magical events took place over the next two weeks. It was decided that my risk of re-injury and recovery setbacks were not worth my returning to work until September. The lingering symptoms from my concussion not only seemed to lessen and almost disappear, but my overall sense of peace, health, and well-being had improved. I was excited to wake up each morning for the first time in a very long while. I just felt this connection within myself that I had never experienced. It was a union of mind, body, and soul, all working together. I felt whole but did not fully grasp how my energy had shifted in just two short weeks. I had to learn more. On May 1st, I opened an exciting new door when I signed myself up with a private instructor.

What began with the intention to learn about crystal energy, actually became the start of my healing and transformation. Every week, I drove to my lesson with more excitement and enthusiasm than I had ever experienced throughout all of my past education. My drive home was always one of awe and gratitude for what had transpired that day. I was receiving so much more than what I had signed up for. I was learning to trust my intuition and experience the effects of energy as it connects us together. Layer by layer, I was shedding my old skin to reveal this version of me that had been hiding beneath. Somehow my broken pieces seemed to fall back into place, but with a better fit. Although this was all new to me, I felt connected so deeply as though I had dug up some ancient knowledge that was buried within me. Before I knew it, I was certified as a crystal healer and was now ready to practice on willing family and friends.

Over the summer months, I learned to make bracelets and wire wrap pendants to design my own line of crystal healing jewelry. I always had a passion for bling, so why not create jewelry with a purpose? Ideas were flowing through me continuously. Journaling became part of my daily routine, something I hadn't done since I was a child and would highly recommend to everyone reading this. Our days become so filled with duties and obligations that we rarely take the time to acknowledge our thoughts and just how powerful they are. Just five minutes a day spent journaling and meditating will do wonders for your health and help you to connect with your inner guidance.

As expected, I had mixed reactions to my newfound passion from some family and friends. I was told that I was crazy, this was just a fad, and I should go back to work...but I didn't care. I knew beyond a doubt that this was something I had to do for myself and without the approval of anyone. This was HUGE for me. As a lifelong people-pleaser, I had never made a decision without asking others for their advice. I was finally trusting my own guidance. When you just know something is meant to be, there is no turning back, despite how off the beaten path it seems. I didn't know how, but I knew why I had to begin this journey. Friends and family noticed the positive changes in me. I was happier, more patient, and wanted to help everyone feel the way I felt about life now. I wanted to inspire and share with others how my life had transformed in such a short time.

Something incredible and magical happens when you trust in your heart and no longer allow fear to hold you in that comfort zone. The energies of the universe come together to assist you. People and opportunities just seem to appear out of nowhere to guide and encourage your path to freedom – freedom from the outer noise, the doubt, the fear, and the lack of courage within yourself. Life begins to flow as you are brought into alignment with your true soul path. There is a fire that burns passionately from within, igniting your light to shine.

I had this vision that led me step-by-step to design and launch my heart and soul-based business that I continue to run out of my home today. I will never forget the courage and the glass of wine it took before I launched my brand-new Facebook business page on Friday, August 26, 2016. I closed my eyes and just couldn't believe I had done it. I had officially come out of the crystal closet for the social media world to see! It was both terrifying and empowering at the same time.

I had built my own little niche. I had no idea what I planned to do with this platform, other than to share whatever little tidbits of crystal wisdom or inspirational words that resonated with me and to connect with others who were seeking a holistic approach to healing and spiritual guidance. This step led me to so many beautiful friendships, soul connections, and opportunities, including sharing my story in this inspirational and empowering anthology. I am still pinching myself! This was once a dream.

As I sit and write this, I think back to four years ago and how differently I now see the world and myself. I have realized that our purpose is not something to be revealed all at once. It's about following those little nudges, whispers, intuitive guidance, your soul, source, whatever resonates for you. Trust in your path, taking each step one day at a time and basking in every moment as you learn and journey towards your true authentic you. Embrace the darkness and the days you feel broken. Be vulnerable. Be grateful and forgive. Forgiveness of ourselves and others is key to healing and inner peace. It is when we acknowledge our shadows and weaknesses that we crack open our ego to allow the light to shine out through our soul. If I could describe the journey that I have been on, it would be just that – breaking through each layer of ego and armor that kept me safe from failure, rejection, judgment, and hurt, to open my heart to live, trust, and love with intention – fearlessly! Healing is an endless journey of self-awareness, spiritual growth, and discovery. It is being mindful of how and where we spend our energy and thoughts. We may not be responsible for our traumas, but the healing is completely up to us. We have the power to transform our lives at any moment. Happiness, wellness, and peace is a conscious choice and must always come from within first. In order to love and be loved, we must first love and accept who we are. Setting boundaries and acknowledging that we can't possibly help anyone without helping ourselves first has been a hard lesson to learn for me. Self-love is not weakness or selfish. How we treat ourselves determines how others treat us.

So, as for my purpose. Is that really the point? I believe that I found purpose in every moment of each day. It is not one thing but instead how we choose to live our lives. We can allow the pain, hardships, and suffering to break us down or we can see them as gifts to help us to learn and grow into who we are really meant to be. My intention every day is to empower others to believe in their strengths, gifts, and dreams. When you start believing in yourself, others will too. Our reality is a perception based on our mindset and intentions. Taking a few moments each morning before my feet hit the floor to state an intention of gratitude sets the tone for my day. Although I am still human and experience stress, anxiety, sadness, and all of the other emotions and battles we face daily, I have learned to allow myself the grace to be in the moment and embrace it for what it is. The job that I once dreaded has meaning now. The challenges and obstacles I am confronted with have meaning. Life has become meaningful. I am grateful for all of it. The good, the bad, and everything in between. Working with crystal energy woke me up to connect my pieces (mind, body, soul) back together to bring me into alignment with who I am and why I am here. Life is all about the journey and it begins with that first step out of your comfort zone and into the unknown. Are you ready?

Tammy Chinn is an education assistant and an entrepreneur who is currently living with her family in Bowmanville, Ontario, Canada. She is a Certified Crystal Healer and guide. Tammy combines her practical university background in Sociology with her alternative/holistic methods of health and wellness to create a powerful union that helps others find their inner strengths and alleviate pain, suffering, and addictions. She offers a natural remedy and spiritual approach to health and healing all through her deep connection to crystal energy. You can connect with Tammy through the following social media platforms:

Facebook: @ Crystal Groupie Designs and Therapy

Instagram: @ crystal_groupie

Broken Trust

Chapter Twenty-Four

My Journey from Anxiety to Serenity

WRITTEN BY: NICK LARSEN

*M*y intention for the following story is to inspire and motivate others across time and space so it may be used as a guide, a bright light, and a system through which you may navigate your own experience of life. You may connect with the experiences I have gone through, or you may not. Still, throughout these pages, you will discover and unlock some fundamental truths of life and our universe that will resonate with any situation that you may be experiencing in this present moment. It's been said that when you hear the truth, you know it because it resonates with the essence of you. As you continue to read, keep your mind open and in a receptive state so you may accept these truths and begin to integrate them into your behavior and, therefore, your results. I encourage you to read over these pages multiple times in search of these hidden truths. It is in the repetition of the ideas of growth and transformation that I am about to share with you that you will experience the change and improvement you seek.

What You Are Seeking Is Also Seeking You – Rumi

Let me start by stating very clearly the most fundamental truth of all: *We Become What We Think About*. Before you pass this off, I encourage you to keep that marvelous mind of yours wide open and begin to *Think*.

Thinking is the highest function that we are capable of, and it's how we use this function that determines the direction and outcome of our lives. We are all seeking something more, and that want for more comes from the essence of who you are; this is the spiritual side of you. Now, every thought holds with it the seed of its physical equivalent, and by its very nature must be drawn, like a magnet, straight to you. The process I am about to describe through my story is in no way the only answer, and I do not pretend to know it all but only to share my truth and understanding. I have become a daily student of life – the study of me as I call it. What I have found is that the more I understood myself, the more I was able to understand others and help them overcome their challenges.

The Other Me

Understand this, you and only you are in control of your reality and when you learn to harness the infinite power that lies within, you too will begin to separate from your current perceived self and transform right before your very eyes into the ideal version of who you want to be. There is absolute perfection in the center of your consciousness.

I was five years old the first time I passed out. I was lying on the floor dressed as a vampire for Halloween. My mom had put fake blood on my lips while I looked in the mirror, and a few seconds later, I felt myself becoming conscious again on the bathroom floor. Little did I know that this would become a regular occurrence. "The kid who passes out," "The shy one," "Nice but quiet," were a few labels that were used to describe who I was from elementary school to university. Over those years, I found myself slowly spiraling down into a reality of chronic anxiety and almost weekly passing out due to the anxiety. I hated it! I hated that it's what I was known for, and I detested that I felt as though I had no control over it. Was this how the rest of my life was going to be? After years of Councilors, Psychologists, Testing, Medication, Hypnotherapy, Meditation, alternative medicine, and so many more, I had concluded that I would be an anxious person for the rest of my life. I had lost trust in myself and in those who said they could help me. I felt like I would never find a sense of peace, confidence, and happiness.

Now, what happened next was my rock bottom and an emotional impact so significant that it jerked me out of my habitual way of thinking. While finishing up my final year of education, my dad suddenly passed away.

It seemed as though the carpet was pulled out from underneath my feet, I had lost my foundation and found myself hitting rock bottom. I was very close to failing my internship, overwhelmed with anxiety, and grieving over my dad's passing. The waves of emotion came full force and on a quite regular basis, but as time passed, those waves came less frequently and with less intensity. After a while, I began to notice that my thinking had started to change. I began to think more "big picture" and beyond my singular struggle. I realized that if I continued with the same thoughts I did yesterday, last week, and the month before, then nothing in my outside environment would change. You see, everything you are experiencing right now is a direct reflection of the past thoughts and images that you have held in your mind.

Here's how it goes…you choose your thoughts – your thoughts cause your feelings – your feelings produce your behavior – and your behavior produces your results.

The combination of anxiety, overwhelm, and my dad passing away was a huge wake-up call. Something started to change in me. I thought to myself, "Is this all there is to life?" "Am I living my life the way I want to?" "There's got to be more for me than this." Clearly understand that nothing is good or bad in life, but rather, it's our thinking that makes it so. Now, when I first heard that I thought, you've got to be kidding me! This is bad. But what I didn't know at the time was that these experiences and events would serve me in such a way that I would be able to help a lot of people navigate through similar difficult times. There is a natural law in our universe that states everything has its opposite, which means that if something is really bad, then the opposite side of it must be really good. Wherever you are in your journey, know that there is always something good, even if you can't see it. Out of the difficult times in your life will blossom a beautiful experience and awareness that will bring you joy and confidence.

My Starting Point

Lying in bed one morning a while after my dad passed away, I went into a full-blown anxiety attack. But this time, something different went through my mind. I said to myself, "Never again! I will never be here again!" This was my starting point and the beginning of my journey to discovering who and what I am.

I know without a shadow of a doubt that if I can do it, so can you! Make a decision right now that this is going to be your starting point, that no matter where you are at or what you are experiencing, you are, in this very moment, capable of creating a life that you genuinely love and enjoy…in a relatively short period too. There is absolutely no such thing as coincidences – everything in this universe operates in an orderly way and by law. You may connect with my story and think, "What a coincidence that I would read a book that included a story so similar to my own." The truth is that it was no coincidence at all. You see, what you are seeking is also seeking you. You are in harmony with this book, this story, and therefore attracted it into your life in some way or another. There are always signs being presented to you, intuitive feelings, that nudge you in new directions or to take action…trust them, act on them. They will never fail you.

The Process

What I am about to share with you may strike you as far-fetched, silly, or way too simple to be true, but I assure you that it works and will create some profound changes in your life with immediate impact. Before I go any further, I want to clarify that the process I am going to describe is a never-ending process. Yes! That's right, the process of self-development never ends. Think about it. You are a being of infinite potential; there is no end to the good you can experience in your life. Steve Bow said, *"God's gift to you is more talent and ability than you will ever use in one lifetime. Your gift to God is to develop and utilize as much of that talent and ability as you can in this lifetime."*

Awareness was the key that unlocked my potential and continues to do so every day. To get from where you are to where you want to be, you must begin to gain awareness. The only reason I was experiencing anxiety was that I was unaware of how to create confidence. This led to the first step in my process: to gain awareness about how to build confidence. At this time, you must abandon the old thoughts of anxiety and focus your mind and attention on confidence. Have you ever noticed that when you have your sights on a new vehicle, you seem to see it everywhere you go? It's in your awareness. Well, you must set your sights on confidence, and you will begin to attract that experience into your awareness. Before too long, you will notice that your inner world is more saturated with thoughts of confidence. Because the external is a reflection of the internal, you notice that you are surrounded by confident individuals who encourage and support you to feel more confident. One of these individuals for me was in the form of a mentor. A mentor sees potential within you that you don't see in yourself and then encourages you to express it. I would not be where I am today without that mentor, which is why I have decided to dedicate my life to mentoring others through their personal development and awareness journey.

When expanding my awareness, there were two areas that I focused my attention on. First, my awareness of what confidence was and what that meant for me. Everyone is confident in something, so I had to gain an understanding of what I wanted to feel confident about. Second, and most importantly, I gained an awareness of who I was, my potential, and how the natural laws of this universe governed my being and results. Through this understanding, I gained the most confidence, and because I had this new awareness, I started to act upon the new ideas that were resident in my mind.

Now, the start of any process is the most difficult. When you want to improve in any area of your life, you must step outside of your comfort zone and begin doing something completely different from what you have been doing in the past. Doing this will cause you to feel uncomfortable because it is going against your current way of thinking, but clearly understand that it is only temporary. When I was lying in my bed having an anxiety attack, it took everything I had to stand up and take conscious control over my thinking. No matter who you are or what you are experiencing, if you wish to improve yourself, you must begin to take conscious control over your thinking process. Chances are you have been thinking those same thoughts about yourself or your life for years. These become so deeply ingrained in us that we begin running on autopilot.

As you continue to read these pages, I want you to start your process by making the most critical decision you will ever make; this decision will determine what happens next. I want you to make a committed decision that you are going to make a change, that today is the last day you are going to live your life this way. You may even say something similar to what I said at my starting point, "I don't know how it's going to happen, but something incredible will come out of this. I am going to become a new and improved version of me." Remember, your thoughts and words are the most powerful things you have. With them you can be, do, or have anything you seriously desire.

Next, you must get crystal clear on what it is that you want. Do you want better health? Improvement in relationships? Increased abundance? And what exactly does it look like for you to have this in your life? Be detailed, be specific, and build a clear picture in your mind. It's the clarity of the image you hold in your mind that determines the clarity in the universal mind. It's this infinite intelligence that will then clearly manifest this in your results with and through you.

It took me a while to get the picture of what I wanted for myself clear and then to transfer that image into words. I sat down with a pen and a piece of paper and began writing a description of the person I wanted to become and the life I wanted to live. Since that day, I've had to rewrite my story multiple times because I had become that person and achieved that life. Once I got there, I realized that I had to move on to a further expansion of who I was meant to become. I went from an extremely anxious individual who was sometimes incapable of leaving the house and passing out regularly to leaving a job that I didn't enjoy, putting myself out there, sharing my story, running a small business as a healer, purchasing our first home, and marrying the love of my life. Now to learning from my mentor and becoming a consultant with him to help change the lives of individuals all over the world. I love what I do and the impact it has had on my life and the lives of those around me.

If I had to sum up my journey and transformation in a few words, I would say that you must begin to think, feel, and, most importantly, ACT like the person and life you wish to manifest into your present reality. Do this, and you will notice very quickly how your inner and outer world begins to transform right before your eyes. You are in control, you are in the driver's seat, you are the designer of your life experience, and it can be incredible. Step out there and become the person you always felt you were. The universe and world are waiting for you to become who you were meant to become. Set yourself a goal that is so worthy of you as an infinite being that you are propelled forward in the attainment of your true desire.

Nick Larsen, CPGC, C.R.M.T., B.Ed, is a Proctor Gallagher Consultant, Energy Healer, and Educator. He began his journey as a substitute teacher in Regina, Saskatchewan. During his time teaching, Nick was very involved in studying and researching human potential, the power of the mind, and healing modalities. This led to a passion for helping others heal as well as learn to harness the power of their minds in the creation of the life they want to live. Nick now spends his days working with individuals to remove blockages, create a clear picture of what they want, and tapping into their infinite human potential.

Website: www.nicklarsen.ca

Broken Trust

Chapter Twenty-Five

What About the Child?

Written By: Pearl Sinclair

You would think that after a divorce, two remarriages, and decades gone by, I would get over this, but I'm still not convinced this is something you ever really get over. This was by far the hardest thing I have ever had to go through. I know this was a union between two people in a marriage, and there are complexities I could not comprehend at the time, but no matter what anyone told me, the issue *was me*. It never ceases to amaze me how I can remember specific details of random, insignificant events, but the most devastating day of my life is mostly a blur. I cannot tell you what year, month, or day of the week it was. I don't recall how old I was (although I am told I was ten), what I was wearing, or what I ate that day if I ate at all. Yet, the way I felt is as potent today as it was then. Forsaken, lost, but above all else, unworthy. It was the first time I felt the rug being pulled from underneath me. I was devastated. Life as I knew it no longer existed. With all the missing pieces of this day, I can still hear the echo of her cries. In my short time on earth, I had never heard this pitch leave her body. It was piercing, it was loud, and it was the soundtrack to the end of an era.

I sat with pen in hand for days hesitating on the words that would flow through; I realize this isn't just my story, but the story of my biggest heroes. This isn't an indictment on them in any way. It was simply, life. I write this story as a way to release the little girl who felt, and in many ways, still feels abandoned.

Healing isn't a final destination, but a road that gets easier to travel, if you allow it. My observation has been that no matter how old we get, one of the most painful things for us to do is relive the darkest secrets buried in our youth. The key to our healing is tucked neatly in the crevices we often never visit. It is my hope that in my journey of discovering freedom, you too can release the child that is waiting to be redeemed. This chapter is dedicated to the children still living inside us all, whose trust was immeasurably broken.

Trust, Broken

My hero was a man with impeccable style who was larger than life to me. He had this uncanny ability to always do everything to perfection. Oh, how he could do no wrong. He and I were inseparable and I adored him with every fiber of my being. He was all the things my soul needed: present and so very loving. This love made me feel full and validated my existence in this world. I was the apple of his eye and he could do no wrong in mine. In his protection, I was fearless, confident, and absolutely nothing seemed impossible or out of my reach.

It started on what felt like a Sunday, and by all accounts, it was a good day, like most. We had dinner and after spending some time talking and laughing, I retreated upstairs to my Toy Room as he made his way to the Family Room. I must have gotten bored with my toys at some point and decided to call my friend. I made my way to my parent's bedroom and picked up the receiver of the house phone. I could hear his voice on the other end but didn't recognize the man who was uttering the words. I held the phone to my ear and immediately knew something was wrong, inappropriate even. The tone in his voice and the words that came out of his mouth were a betrayal to us, but I just couldn't seem to put the phone down. What I heard next plays in my head like a broken record. "She doesn't know about you," I heard him say to the woman he was talking to. He called this strange lady by her name and I heard her unfamiliar voice. As I felt a lump growing in my throat, I gently put the phone back down. I could not move. I was in shock by the complete shift in my atmosphere. The man who was so perfect to me was betraying the trust of his family. The admiration I had instantly became disgust.

Later on that evening, I heard him call me from downstairs. He and I would often go bike riding in the evening; however, this evening I wasn't the least bit interested in spending time with him. I replied to him in a sharp, stern, "NO!" when he asked if I wanted to go outside. I could see the shock and confusion on his face; I had never spoken to him like that before. He looked at me, paused, but all he could muster was a hesitant, "Ok." I don't remember another exchange between him and me during that week. I have no recollection of how I processed what I had heard. All I remember was the intense need for it to be a nightmare. I don't know how many mornings passed after that day. For all I know, it could have been weeks before the dreadful morning I was awakened by the sound of her unfamiliar cries. I lay paralyzed, knowing what I always knew in my spirit – it wasn't a nightmare. My family would never be the same again.

As I developed into a young lady, the brokenness I felt grew into anger; I'd even call it rage. By all appearances, I was confident, smart, happy, and secure, but inside I was withdrawn and kept people at arm's length. I was cold and often distant. The betrayal I fell victim to claimed dominion over me. I did a great job at burying the pain, though. I mastered that class like a pro although I lacked faith in humanity and knew eventually people would show their real side, no matter how much you loved and adored them. I slowly developed a compulsive obsession with everything around me appearing picture-perfect, all in an attempt to mask what I felt, inherently flawed. I developed an insanely competitive nature. I joined the debate team, all the sports teams, band, student council, won speech competitions to show myself approved, but the more I achieved, the less fulfillment I felt. The void increased over time no matter how colorful I tried to paint the picture, for perfection is only an illusion. Nothing could blanket the day that I froze and the things I subsequently told myself as to why my family was torn apart. I realize I have always been overcompensating for feeling inadequate. I now look back at the friendships and relationships I entered and wonder if I subconsciously tried to recreate that day in an attempt to convince him I was enough for him to stay. Perhaps it was me that needed convincing.

Healing - Find Your Outlet

What can you do for hours but feels like minutes? What gives you joy? Don't let go of those things that make you who you are. I reminded myself of all the things that brought out my raw excitement. I remembered what was true to who I am and what made me like no other human on this planet. Having something you can focus on can be such a great and rewarding part of your healing. I channeled my energy into the things that brought me serenity. For me, using my hands to create is what did it for me.

Writing this story has definitely been one of the hardest yet rewarding things I've done. The challenge of putting your heartbreak in print is daunting. This was a vulnerable time for me and it made me reflect in ways I didn't think I'd ever have to. How ironic – during the process of writing how I got to the place of healing, the process healed me. As I said earlier, it's a journey, not a final destination. Being this open released another layer and I'm eternally grateful to have been blessed with this opportunity.

Picture Michael Jackson's music playing in the background, a glass of Merlot on the left, and a paintbrush in my right hand. This is where all my energy goes when I'm in a creative vibe. Time seems to stand still and every idea comes to life with each brushstroke. The paint lines smooth the canvas to the rhythmic pulse of the music. For me, peace lives in this moment. My emotions are released and then redesigned into a tangible piece. It is truly art in every sense of the word. I started painting any and everything I could get my hands on. I allowed my creative juices to flow through. I got energized about trying new techniques and colors. There was an excitement about creating something out of nothing that was a thrill. I can get caught up for hours perfecting techniques and trying new colors. Painting brought me back to a time I was free to create my heart's desire.

Sisterhood

As far back as I can remember, I've witnessed a bond between women, a sisterhood that grew so effortlessly before my eyes. The first time I remember seeing the power of Sisterhood was sitting in the hair salon at the tender age of five. I adored those days watching women walk in the salon to get beautified. These stunning women would pamper themselves to makeovers fit for an Ebony magazine. I witnessed how to be vulnerable from these women as they would share their innermost fears, dreams, hurts, and triumphs. I learned that we share more similarities than differences. I understood that life can get hard, but the character that is built while gracefully moving forward is unmatched. Not only did they look amazing on the outside, but they were equally as amazing on the inside, bravely sharing their unique stories of broken trust. It was through this experience of being in this space and having women from all walks of life come together in Sisterhood that I understood true therapy is in the details.

True sisters may not come across your way often but when they do, they are to be cherished. There is a familiarity when you're in the presence of women that even in complete silence, the communication never ends. There are stories that need no explanation when it comes to them. It is so important that the women you have in your corner, walk a life of purpose and intentional living. Trust in your intuition to be able to identify what your soul needs from a strong sisterhood; a woman of virtue who leads by example each day. Without even knowing it, this has been my therapy many times. I leaned on the women in my life that I respected and felt safe with. My Sisterhood circle is a powerful part of how I've been able to relieve myself of feelings of doubt that seep in at times. My sisters are there to remind me of my greatness on the days I may forget, while allowing me to express myself with honesty, staying true to my authentic self. These are the women who can bring me to tears with their loving correction. They are there to ensure I remember that there isn't anything I cannot do and unapologetically command I knock down the door of every obstacle. They are there through the ups and downs providing a shoulder to lean on if the weight of the world gets too heavy. My sisters are not afraid to tell me when I'm wrong and celebrate my every win, no matter how small.

Solitude

It was through the COVID-19 pandemic of 2020 where true healing began for me. Everyone was socially and physically distancing themselves from one another, by choice and by force. For the first time in my adult life, I was still. The sounds of the birds chirping replaced cars honking. The hours spent in rush-hour traffic were now spent gardening. Journal writing substituted email responses. I started to spend more time with myself and ultimately foster the relationship I had with God. I spent time in prayer, and in silence. It was through this silence I involuntarily re-encountered the pain I was carrying around with me like a Scarlet Letter. All the distractions had vanished and I could hear myself, and the girl who was trapped inside. I allowed myself to drown in every feeling, the good, the bad, and the very ugly. It never occurred to me until then that I never mourned the family I once had or the loss of my innocence. I had never shed a tear for that girl who was stuck frozen in time. Some days were unbearable as I shifted through each emotion, but I am thankful for the silence. I am thankful for the space that was given to heal, to recognize, to face the demons of yesteryears, and the ghost of the past waiting to transition.

Being still is now an essential part of my daily routine and I encourage you to find time in your day where you are alone with self. Healing doesn't always come in the form of a therapist listening to you regurgitate your life's heartbreak. Sometimes healing comes from solitude. Sometimes healing comes from being in, and one with nature. For others, writing is the right amount of exhale needed to exonerate the parts inside that have been bruised and forgotten. I cannot tell you what the future holds or that people will not break your trust more times than you deserve, but I can tell you that you are worthy of everything that is good. We often define ourselves by the scars that have been left behind, but you will never be free until you begin to define yourself, despite how anyone else sees or treats you. All that you need is right inside of you. You are worthy.

I want to express my sincerest and heartfelt condolences to all the people across the globe who have lost a loved one to this contagion. To everyone who is a survivor, I am happy you are alive to share your testimony. Thank you to all the frontline and essential workers who risked their health daily to provide the rest of us with the necessities and oftentimes, the luxuries of life. I have no doubt this experience has taught us all something about how precious our time here is. Let's make it a healthy one, physically and mentally.

"I've learned that people will forget what you said, people will forget what you did, but people will never forget how you made them feel." – Dr. Maya Angelou

Pearl Sinclair is a Jamaican-Canadian international Best-Selling published author and entrepreneur who grew up in Southern Ontario. Pearl studied Political Science at York University, and Arts & Science and Paralegal Education at Humber College. In 2015, she became Miss Caribbean Canada's 1st Runner-Up where she advocated for Sickle Cell awareness. Pearl went on to pursue a career in law, specializing in accident benefits and small claims, and currently works for the public sector. She proudly manages and facilitates a support group and social media platform, SIS – Strength In Sisterhood, a space created to empower Black women.

YouTube: Niquey Clair

Instagram: Niquey Clair Official

Facebook: Niquey Clair

Twitter: NIQUEYC

LinkedIn: Niquey Clair

Broken Trust

Chapter Twenty-Six

Faith & Hope Over Anxiety

WRITTEN BY: SHONTELLE WEST

*I*f someone told me six months ago that I would lose my teaching position and go through a season of depression and anxiety, I would've told them they were crazy for thinking such a far-fetched story. To be utterly honest, I didn't even believe anxiety was a real thing. I thought it was all in people's heads and if they simply made the choice, they could just get over it. Through the past couple of months, I've come to the harsh realization that is indeed not the case.

Truth be told, my story did end up in a dark season of my weary soul. However, it did not start that way.

I was a thriving business owner and a mother to a beautiful daughter. We had a great life, lots of friends, great family support, and a peaceful farm home with plenty of furry creatures to keep us company. My daughter had her own horse which she raised from birth. This experience gave us both a strong work ethic and to fight for what we wanted – to live in the country and live wild and free. Needless to say, we were very blessed. God had surrounded us with so much. My life was on track. I only dreamt that we would arrive in this life and here we were, living it. I could never have imagined it could get to such a dark place filled with so much trepidation and uneasiness.

Before I was plagued with this crippling mental health issue, I had decided to close down my salon and go back to university to get my teaching degree. I left my daughter behind and headed to the big city for school. Looking back, it really all started there. The pressure of keeping up with my studies, while also supporting my daughter from a distance, began to weigh heavily on my mind. One morning, all of the stress hit me, and I was paralyzed with Vertigo. It felt like I was seasick on a boat destined for doom with no hope in sight, like my eyes were spinning and wanted to jump right out of their sockets. To be brutally honest, it felt like I was dying. By the grace of God, I was able to somehow get my parents on the phone and they drove three hours to pick me up and bring me home. After many days of distress, the dizziness, nausea, headache, sweating, and ear-ringing subsided and it was like nothing had ever happened.

Without a second thought or an attempt to discover the root of the problem, I continued with schooling and landed my dream retirement job. At almost forty years of age, my life had come full circle. I thought I had finally made it; a secure job, a pension plan, summers off, and no more worry. I thought to myself, "Praise God, I made it. He made me a promise and it has finally come into fruition."

Little did I know that this job was just a stepping stone and not the rest of my life. I loved my job and even more, my students. They are what drove me to be a better teacher; to be who they thought I was and looked up to. My job became my mission field. The kids would come to my classroom to talk, some would come for help, and some simply for comfort. I had made it my life's mission to help all my students that needed help, whether it be prayer or just a friend to listen. My co-workers often poked fun of me for "always being held up in my room," but little did they know that I was in there feeding someone lunch or sharing a cry with someone who just lost the "love of their lives." They were teenagers – for them, that boyfriend/girlfriend was their everything. I loved being able to be my students' advocate and someone they could trust. I thanked God every day for my job and the life I had at this school. I was so busy with life, my students, and preparing for the departure of my daughter to university that I didn't have time to even think about taking a break or resting.

Then COVID-19 hit and everything came crashing down. My principal came into my classroom one morning with the news that I wouldn't have a job in the fall because they were shutting down my program. It was like all of my hard work and dedication was for nothing. I was completely devastated and didn't understand how they could just do this to me. I was supposed to sign my permanent contract that week but instead, I lost the one thing I put all of my efforts into. Even though I was let go, I was still expected to be there for the rest of the year until summer break. It was like opening a wound every day I walked back into my empty classroom and seeing pieces of my heart put into my room in an effort to make it a safe and comfortable space for my students, knowing that I would never get to see them again. One morning in my classroom, I was plagued with the ugly presence of anxiety. This would last for the next five months. I thought God was calling me home or that I was doing something terribly wrong and was being punished. The racing thoughts, the sleepless nights, and straight terror and fear…it was enough to make someone think they were going crazy. But in all seriousness, I was not going crazy, I had simply hit a wall and crashed hard. But, like most things in my life, I suppressed it and tried to move on.

Finally, after all of my turmoil, I thought there was a light at the end of the tunnel. I had met this wonderful man who at first, I thought might be the one. Deep down I think I knew he wasn't exactly what God wanted for me but after eighteen years of being single and the quickly approaching day of my daughter moving out, I just wanted to have my person. I compromised my morals which inevitably led to an open door to the attacks of the enemy. I stayed in this relationship out of fear of being alone when all along, God was bringing me through all of this to draw me closer to him. In our darkest times or moments, it's what brings us closer to one's faith and my being in God, I needed Him like I needed water.

One night I heard Him say that He wanted me to rest in Him and that He would show me great things. He said to my spirit that I would never have been quiet enough to hear Him tell me anything.

His message to me was so profound I knew I had to do something. I ended my relationship and focused on myself and my relationship with God. I had to learn how to trust and depend on Him instead of on my own strength or any man in that season of life. He healed me and taught me how to deal with my feelings. It wasn't in an instant – it's a work in progress. Every day you have to wake up and make the conscious choice to tell yourself that you can get through it and that God is right beside you walking through it with you. Even when you only see one set of footprints, it's because he was carrying you all along.

In one of the darkest nights during this fight with anxiety, I heard God tell me that He wanted me to go to bible school, then write a book to help empower His children to get through anxiety and dark the seasons when all hope seems lost. I thought, "Wow. What an honor to be trusted doing this huge responsibility. Now all I can do is get better so I can go out into this world and help the hurt and suffering."

In my teaching position, I was convinced that was "it" for me; those were the only students who got to hear my wisdom from God. It was easy and I thought that if it was easy, then it had to be from God. But truthfully, some of the best things are just behind a hard season. Oftentimes, there are enemies and/or giants next to a promised land. That "Goliath" is often a sign that you are in the right land. Abraham and his descendants were called to Canaan, the "Promised Land," but where the promised land was, Goliath, the giant, was. The Israelites could've said, "This giant is too big. We could never defeat him." But instead, they remembered that nothing is bigger than God. They defeated their giant and fulfilled God's purpose for their lives.

After everything I've gone through, I know that no giant is too big for our God; with Him and through Him, I can accomplish anything.

> *"For I know the plans I have for you," declares the Lord, "plans to prosper you and not to harm you, plans to give you hope and a future."* Jeremiah 29:11 (NIV)

However, the giant I faced at the beginning of this journey was all too frightening to defeat just on my own. Let me share some insight and tactics I learned to win this battle.

When the ugly giant of anxiety was full-blown, I tried to breathe it away. I tried to go for walks and run away from it, but as soon I came home, it was right there like a huge wall hitting me in the face. You see, what I learned on my journey is that you cannot run away from anxiety; you must stand up face to face and fight for your life back.

I learned that you need to face your thoughts head on and tell them they do not control you; YOU control them. This had become a very helpful strategy in my tool belt moving forward in my fight. I also wrestled with the fact of whether to medicate or not medicate. I'm not saying medication is bad, it just wasn't what I needed during that time.

You see, I'm an advocate for natural living and natural foods. I also love using my essential oils to aid in pain. So, let me tell you that I used every essential oil I had to fight this anxiety. I used it while I prayed, while I sat quietly doing my breathing exercise, while I cleaned dishes. Leaving the house was a huge thing for me, and of course, I used oils. You see, everyone needs something they can lean on when going through this, whether it be a person, medication, prayers, or oils. Whatever it is, every little thing helps. Although it won't fully do the job, it just is that extra thing to help you get through the bad days. It never fully helped until I realized I needed to actually deal with those toxic thoughts when they came rushing in like a flood instead of just putting on a "band-aid." Of course, all of the little things help but for them to have their full effect, we need to get to the root of the problem first.

It wasn't until I was out for my daughter's eighteenth birthday for a spa day when it dawned on me: I needed more help than I could give myself. If you are reading my chapter and have been fighting this alone and not getting relief, get help. Talk to your doctor because there is no shame in taking medicine for our brains. If it's ok to take insulin for diabetes or antibiotics for a sickness, then it should be ok to take medicine for your brain while we learn to deal with all the underlying reasons we are suffering.

It won't be forever; maybe it will only be for a short season while you change, grow, and learn how to deal with the stress of grief, loss, or trauma from past experiences. After years of brushing all of these feelings and experiences under the rug, things can pop up in the most unexpected time. And mine, unfortunately, was right in the thick of huge life changes.

I am learning that we don't always have to be strong on our own; we can trust in the medical field, in God, and in yourself because you are strong. Trust that feeling deep within because you know what is best for you. Just remember that it is ok to reach out to those who walk with us through this hard journey while we also grow in self-strength and independence. I have gained new friends and unexpected friends through this experience and each one has helped me get one step closer to a new and improved me. The way it works is, you talk it out, hear different advice, learn more about yourself, learn how to take the advice with a grain of salt, and use what you know is right for you.

The hardest part of this battle was being so vulnerable after years of holding in my thoughts and emotions. I had to open up to people in a way I never had before. I had to ask people to be my friends and help me walk through it. For a forty-year-old, strong, independent woman, this was the hardest thing I ever had to do; reach out and ask for help. When I did, God did a thing and opened up new doors with new people who came alongside me to help me heal.

I have learned these few things: strength comes from within when you least expect it, don't ever give in to that manic thought that you are losing it or crazy cause you are not, and human suffering is always for a reason, season, or a time.

Remember that if people cannot be there for you in the way you need them to be, don't be too harsh with them because they cannot fully understand what you are going through. But appreciate the little ways they help.

I am a proud daughter of two of the best parents a daughter could ask for. Mind you, I did have to go to them a few times to sit them down and tell them I needed them to be there for me and just be my friend. This was also hard to do; however, I am so blessed beyond measure by my loving parents. Without them, I could do nothing.

God knows what we need. Just ask and have faith while you wait and fight your Goliath. Remember to take those thoughts captive; don't let them win. You are in charge of what you let in and what you release. You can win this fight. Be Strong!

Shontelle West, originally from Cold Lake, Alberta, resides in Bonnyville, Alberta with her beautiful daughter Isabella, who will be starting university in the fall. Shontelle has been a veteran hairstylist for the past fifteen years. In those wonderful years as a stylist and business owner, she discovered her passion for teaching. She later took her next step and became a Secondary School Teacher. Shontelle would like to dedicate her chapter to her best friend and biggest supporter, her daughter, Isabella. Thank you for being you. Where I lead, you will follow.

Facebook: Shontelle West

Instagram: lady_bellas_salon

Email: shontell@ualberta.ca

Chapter Twenty-Seven

Forgiving Myself

WRITTEN BY: CHERYL FINK

*I*t was a calm and fresh summer morning and I was sitting all alone on the deck at a farm where I used to live. As I was taking in the beauty and the peacefulness of the countryside, I found myself beginning to tear up, and a wave of sadness fill me up. It was hard to understand what I was experiencing. How could I be experiencing feelings so tranquil and at the same time feelings of deep sadness?

I then realized the feelings were coming from memories pushing up from deep inside that I had buried for many years. It was from a time where there was discontentment, hurt, selfishness, guilt, and insecurities when I was in a relationship that was breaking down around me.

As I sat there, I began thinking of how different things might have been had I known then what I know now. I thought to myself what if I had I been more compassionate, more self-aware; things could have been so different. Instead, I missed all the beauty and the opportunities to live a wonderful life.

I took so many things for granted and was not grateful for what was in front of me. I was in a place trying to prove myself to the people in my world. I missed seeing what was right in front of me. I neglected opportunities to show my love, to be supportive, to encourage and nurture the relationship I was in. I just was not emotionally mature enough; I was ignorant of what it took to build a relationship. I believe that we could have experienced a life abundant in love, joy, happiness, purpose, and lived a fulfilled life had we both been able to understand ourselves, our reasons for thinking the way we did, and better able to communicate our wants, needs, and desires. Even though there was love, we were both so insecure in who we were that it kept us stuck. I was not alone on this misguided journey. There were many things about each of us that impacted the breakdown of our relationship and our inability to save it.

Like most failed relationships, there was blame on both sides because we did not know how to process the untrue feelings of being inadequate and not enough for each other. Nor did I think that I should be wanting to figure out, in my mind, there was nothing to figure out. I was now taking responsibility for my part of our relationship not lasting a lifetime. The power struggles, the need for recognition, the constant competing instead of being creative, and fighting for our relationship.

I can say that now, but at the time I lacked the understanding of what it really took to make a relationship work. At the age of seventeen, being a young mom and a new wife, I was just trying to figure out who I was expected to be.

How was I supposed to fill my new roles and be what everybody assumed I would be? As the years went by, I felt that I was losing myself and was feeling very small in my world. I was never being recognized for who I was, or a least that's how it felt to me. Funny thing is, I kept telling myself I did not want to lose myself, but I didn't even understand who I was or what was I trying to hold on to. I did not recognize where all this was coming from.

Why was I doing the things I was doing? Why was I seeking validation? Why was I always insecure? Why was I oblivious to the fact that I was behaving that way? I had no clue that I lacked self-awareness, self-confidence, and harbored some misguided beliefs and behaviors. Hence, my need for self-preservation was born and my fear of losing myself became more and more real with every rejection, every conviction of guilt, and every broken relationship.

I was extremely clueless even though I believed I had it all together. I knew I was a very hard worker who did what it took to get a job done; someone who worked tirelessly to help support her family, was frugal, and never wasted money. So, if I was all that, why did I feel like I was never enough? What more could someone want in a partner?

Lack of communication played a huge role in the breakdown of our relationship. We never talked about what we wanted for our lives as individuals much less what we wanted to work towards together. We never told each other we appreciated one another or talked about our relationship at all. This meant we were left to figure each other out, which left a lot to the imagination and much to be assumed. What I came up with was that I was inadequate and not enough to make him happy. Heck, I couldn't even make myself happy and I suspect it was the same for him. I choose to believe now that in our own way, we both admired one another. However, I know that I was ignorant about how to show it; ignorant that I just didn't know how.

I somehow managed to justify it all because I told myself that I was doing great. I was getting the things done that I needed to do to, and always doing more than my share. It was more than what anyone could reasonably ask, and I believed that wholeheartedly.

After I began to peel back the layers of my fake self, I realized that I had no idea what I was doing to myself since I had no belief or faith in myself. How much I was holding myself back from experiencing life? I know now that it was all there – all I was seeking was right in front of me, but I just couldn't see it. I was too insecure to believe that I was enough and worthy of all the good there is in the world. Over time, my poor self-image and all this angst inside deepened as I continued looking for approval in all the wrong places.

It wasn't until I was in my 50s when I began my journey of self-discovery or should I say self-recovery. Discovering who I truly was on the inside was no easy task and I learn new things about myself all the time, and I suspect I always will. I'll continue having new experiences in my life that will bring more of me to the surface now that I understand how to allow that to happen.

After two failed relationships, and my third one on some uneasy ground,

I knew that if I wanted to stop sabotaging my relationships, I needed to figure out who I was, what I genuinely wanted, and to honestly believe that I was enough. I finally decided to take a good hard look inside myself. I needed to ask some tough questions and be honest about my answers. What did I actually want? What was I truly looking for? Why were my relationships not lasting? What did I want in a relationship and why was I not getting it? Also, what would I be willing I give to that relationship that I had not given in the past?

Let me tell you, this "looking inside stuff" required me to get honest and vulnerable with myself. I needed to peel back the layers of my false self and to recognize my true self. I had to expose my codes of emotional survival layers of protection. I would have no choice but to go through this if I wanted to forgive myself about what I had lost due to my misguided behavior. I wanted to fully understand why I did the things I did, acted the way I acted, why I hid what I hid, and why I was attaining the results I was getting. This took some serious reflection and courage. It's what I needed, regardless of how painful, embarrassing, humbling, or how many tears I've cried. I had to go there.

And so, my journey of self-discovery began at the age of fifty and now, at sixty, continues with every passing day. This was all a very humbling experience. The self-reflection and the effort that I put forward to understanding *ME* was so worthwhile and is still a work in progress. This effort is making my life more meaningful, more joyful, more expansive, and is unfolding in ways that I never thought possible.

I began to understand what my belief system had in its arsenal and it told me the story about who I had become. My results were defined in my beliefs. If I was going to change the results, I would have to first figure out what was causing them.

On my journey to enlightenment, I discovered many things. The first thing I had to admit was that I was a people pleaser – looking for approval and praise from others. I came to realize that no matter how much outside approval I got, I was still looking for more. Weird thing is that deep down, I did not believe any of that outside approval anyway, therefore, I was not able to change those feelings of being unworthy, not enough, less than, and on and on it went.

Unable to get past all these false beliefs that I was in denial about, my first relationship ended, and nothing changed in my life. I moved on to another relationship with all the same issues and even more baggage to work through. My patterns of people-pleasing and seeking outside approval continued. I kept on with my same old behaviors, thinking that at some point I would experience the approval I was so desperately seeking. Well, that did not happen. There were so many moments of self-destruction, blame, guilt, and never being enough to keep my relationship together.

So here I am in my third long-term relationship, and all is well during the honeymoon stage as per usual. I have not really changed at all – no behavioral changes, no better self-image to speak of. However, what's different is that the person in my life now is much more self-aware than I, much better at communication, and I know that I truly want to be in this relationship, even after the honeymoon stage is over.

Oh, believe me, this journey has come with its own set of ups and down, games of tug-of-war, and we have to remind ourselves every day that we must work together, respect one another, support and love one another, even on the days when we don't like each other very much.

We look at ourselves as a work in progress and we get better and better every day. I feel that he understands me better than I understand myself. He opened my mind to begin thinking about myself in a new light, I had many things to be proud of, and that I needed to be satisfied with myself. Not because he was proud of me, but because I believed I was worthy, and I was enough. He talked at length about the man he strives to be every day and I admire him for that. He has inspired me to truly be the person I want to be – a person who believes in herself. It may seem like that goes without saying, however, when you think you are already giving yourself fully, and that you do believe in yourself, having to come to terms with the fact that you are not, isn't easy to accept.

You see, for many years I thought I was giving so much of myself to my partners, and in some ways I was. However, I was holding on to an unhealthy self-image which I could not get past. Until I did the work to improve my self-image, begin seeing myself with all the gifts I had and gave myself the approval I was looking for, nothing would change on the outside. My results would continue to repeat themselves.

When I started to seriously look for answers from inside of me, the flood gates opened, and that needed to happen because I needed to make sense of what had happened. I needed to see the mistakes and shed the guilt I was carrying from those mistakes.

Before I could do that, I needed to accept that what I referred to as "mistakes" were just part of my journey, a part of growing into who I am now which, I believe, is part of our purpose here in this life. To grow and expand in awareness is to live a fuller life and along with that comes opportunities to learn. To me, that is what our "mistakes" are – opportunities. I did not always think this way, but it has become what I now believe, as have so many other defining moments and I am aware I will never be that person again.

The growth I have experienced is something that I will cherish forever, and I am continually grateful for what I learn each day about me. I did the work, the reflection, the tearing down, and building back up of who I was, who I want to be, and continue to do so. It is much easier now because I understand the process and the importance of this growth in self-awareness.

Today, I fully understand that we cannot outperform our self-image and that we can not expect others to believe and have faith in us if we do not have it in ourselves. I have grown so much in self-awareness and my self-image as improved immensely.

Through my journey of self-discovery and healing, I have been able to forgive myself for what I did not know, for my role in hurting two people that I loved, and who were a huge part of my journey. I understand they were also on their own journey and that our time together was an opportunity to grow and to learn from each other. I miss them both and have asked for their forgiveness which I truly feel has been granted.

With all the growth I have experienced on my journey, I have matured so much in self- awareness and development of a healthier self-image. I have increased in confidence, believe in my potential to be, and can do anything I choose to. I am able to do these things now without seeking the approval of others. I am now able to accept me for me. My self-validation is all that is required for me to live a fuller, more purposeful life.

I can give my whole self freely to my partner and together we are creating a life that is loving, nurturing, and supportive.

Cheryl Fink was born and raised in Saskatchewan where she still lives with her partner of twenty years. She has two grown children and is a Gramma of two amazing granddaughters. Cheryl was employed with Social Services for almost thirty years before retiring in January 2017. Since then, Cheryl has immersed herself in personal development and has a greater understanding of who she really is and why she operates the way she does. While on her self-development journey, along with her experiences while employed with Social Services, Cheryl created her own personal growth program which she hopes to have implemented in the very near future.

Facebook: Cheryl Fink

Email: Cherylfink60@gmail.com

Broken Trust

234

Chapter Twenty-Eight

Double Blessings

WRITTEN BY: LOU MACAULAY

𝒲ho am I? I'm exhausted but I keep pushing. No breakthroughs as of yet. What is wrong with me? I'm failing...in more ways than one. I'm not a friend. I can't be a mom. Who am I? I dunno...I'm hard to love.

I'm not okay that they told me, no babies for me. How dare they! I can't be a mom?! It's not that I don't want to be, I just can't be. But I want to be a mom. I have to be a mom. If not, then what's my life purpose?

The hurt in my heart was pounding so heavily I can still feel the throbbing in my chest all these years later. I remember not being able to focus on anything else for so long. I was told that due to medical complications, I would not be able to conceive. I was shocked, devastated, and I felt sick, thinking this must be a horrible nightmare. Wait, I'm waking up. It's not a nightmare. This is my reality. I am not ever going to be a mommy.

Could I recover from this? I was experiencing brokenness and all I felt was bitterness and hate inside of me. I hated myself for not being able to do this one thing – to become a mom. No matter what people told me or what they said, I was broken and felt no self-worth.

I had so many dreams as a young child growing up. I played house and pretended to be a mom. I had imaginary children – two children, in fact

– a boy and a girl. How perfect! I even had a name for my boy, "Dylan." I didn't have a name for the girl, or not that I can recall. I spent many hours setting up my porcelain tea set having tea parties with my kids. We went to school together as well. I was their teacher – poor kids, or maybe they were lucky. I recall practicing printing in my printing journal. We would work on crafts, and of course, I also drove the school bus, singing the song *Wheels on The Bus* all the way to school, laughing, and having good times. I don't recall having arguments, defiant children, or crying children. We were always laughing! Laughing out loud!

My childhood home was full of laugher, love, and a lot of company. How fortunate I was to have a family that offered me so much. I was always supported growing up. I was so lucky to have such an amazing upbringing. I can never thank my parents enough for raising me and showing me what family truly meant: work ethics, honesty, loyalty, respect for others, just to name a few. Most importantly was to have faith in our Creator, something I will cherish the rest of my life!

I'm sure you have heard that time heals all wounds. This, my friends, is a crock of bull crap – not in the reality I was living in at that time. I couldn't see it clearly at all, but maybe another day. I was blessed with friends who shared their children with me. It was always difficult and as the years passed, I was able to overcome my envious jealousy, unhappiness, devastation, and self-worth. It wasn't easy but truth be told, time could heal wounds. This was my year. I've decided that I am healing, overcoming my emotions, and moving forward. I could see a clearer vision now and I believe the pain can still go away.

I recall that it was a beautiful fall day and I was traveling to work, but something was not right. I wasn't feeling good. I know that I wasn't myself and felt nauseated. I loved orange juice, but I could hardly get it down. Did I have a rare sickness? This is it, this is why, my answer, why I am not able to have children? I have an illness. Instantly, I can't see. The water has filled my eyes with tears, and I pull over on the side of the road, wiping away my tears. The ride to work was harsh and the ten-minute commute felt like an hour. I barely got the car parked, opened the car door, and ran inside directly to the washroom, vomiting. My head was pounding. "I will beat this" was playing in my head. I told myself that it was a mind-over-matter situation and that sickness would not get me. I took a few deep breaths and started to feel like myself. The day was long and finally, it was quitting time, home time! Yes, rest time!

The next morning, I found myself not feeling like myself again. "Dang it. This is real." The same symptoms as yesterday were starting to strike force at me again. "Dear Lord, what is happening to me?" My ten-minute work commute seemed like an hour again today and I needed to get to the shop quickly before I started puking again.

After work, I agreed to stop at the drugstore, not sure what I was looking for. I walked through the cold and flu aisle. "What do I need?" I came around the corner and a home pregnancy test was the first thing I saw. "Wait, that's it! I'm pregnant!" "Stop it, stupid," my mind tells me. "I can't get pregnant, remember? Why even consider pregnancy?" So, I grabbed a home pregnancy test and headed home.

I can't forget how on the way home my mind was playing all kinds of tricks on me. "What if I am pregnant?" My mind responded, "You're not pregnant, not possible!" I arrived home, quickly read the instructions, and complied with everything I was instructed to do. I took a deep breath, closed my eyes, and when I opened my eyes, I looked down and saw that the test was...POSITIVE! What?! Positive?! I grabbed the instructions again to make sure I read them properly. My heart was racing at this point and I was crying. I just knew to trust my self-worth and trust in my gut. I just proved to the world that I beat the odds of not conceiving. "Holy moly, I'm having a baby!"

I loved, believed, hoped, and trusted myself. I never gave up on myself or the Lord. My faith and prayers were answered! Trust in God for He is good! Fright, excitement, and tears of joy filled my eyes. I was so darn excited, I kept telling myself, "I'm going to be a Mommy!" I was laughing and crying all in the same emotion. All I could think of was, "This explains my sickness."

I made a doctor's appointment to confirm the home pregnancy test, but I was so nervous. The soonest I could get scheduled was a week later and it couldn't come soon enough. The rest of my week was a replay of the first couple days: sick about an hour in the mornings, with an added feature that I couldn't even get my toothbrush close to my mouth. As soon as I brought it to my mouth, I started to dry heave because of my morning sickness. "I'm not sick," was my new normal and I had no complaints!

As I approached the doors of the clinic, I got this knot in my stomach. The thoughts playing in my head were questioning me, "What if I'm not pregnant?" I then felt myself starting to sweat; my mind was playing games on me. Soon, I would have a confirmed answer. I started doing some deep breathing to calm my mind. The test confirmed did the due date.

I looked at the doctor and told him boldly, "I'm having twins." He looked me in the eyes, started laughing, and said, "Really, that's interesting." I then told him about my dream I had a few weeks prior where I was walking in the forest holding hands with my two children. They were very small, I didn't get to see their faces, nor did I know their sex, but we were running, skipping, and laughing! It was the best dream ever; truly breathtaking. Besides, at this point, I was showing a lot already. How could there possibly be only one baby in me? Twins also ran in our family. The doctor then sent me for an ultrasound appointment.

I can still remember how many times I would go to bed praying for a baby; asking God to answer my prayers. I often cried myself to sleep, quietly, too embarrassed to share how this impacted my life. I had many self-talks with myself over the years. I believed in myself and our Creator. I asked forgiveness for my behaviors and actions. I had to love and accept myself for who I was, which was the hardest part. Perhaps I overreacted. Thank you, God. Thank you for listening.

On the ultrasound day, I prepared for the examination. But I was disappointed because I thought I would be able to see more on the monitor. The x-ray technician told me that she was finished and pointed at the screen saying, "This here is baby A," and drew a circle around baby A with her finger. "Here is baby B," and drew a circle around baby B. I was stunned and asked again for her confirmation. She calmly said, "This is baby A, and this here is baby B." My dream was becoming my reality. "God has blessed me with twins," I thought as I wiped the tears from my cheeks.

It was super fun sharing the news with family members and friends. Most were in disbelief; watching the reactions of others was fun.

For the next appointment at the doctor's office, I found out about my delivery date and burst out crying as it was on my deceased father's birthday. What a beautiful gift! Dad is my angel. He helped send these babies to me; I just knew it. My faith and beliefs are so strong, stronger than ever now, and God is amazing as I trust in Him.

My morning sickness was starting to get better but there were still those awkward mornings where the smell of coffee was a trigger, and brushing teeth was far too difficult without gagging...or worse.

After another ultrasound in December, I received a dreaded call from my doctor requesting that I come into the office as soon as possible. Something was wrong. My appointment did not go well, apparently, and I had been diagnosed with placenta previa complete. This can cause serious bleeding during pregnancy and during the labor, which could put the babies, and me, in danger. My babies were now at high risk of prematurity, which included breathing difficulties, cerebral palsy, and hypoxic-ischemic encephalopathy. I could lose one of my babies and my life was at increased risk as well. I was so worried, scared, and in lack of understanding everything at that moment. My doctor placed me on strict bed rest until the babies were born.

I was so grateful to have someone come live with us to look after me with bathroom privileges and strict bed rest. I spent the majority of my days crying with worry and anxiousness. What if I lost a baby? What if I died? God must be tired of me, asking Him for so much, just for me.

I also remember going for blood work, which was something to look forward to as on appointment days I could get out of bed and out of the house. My blood tests indicated I was also a gestational diabetic. Great! Something else to add to my growing list of worries.

On the evening of April 3rd, I started experiencing some weird belly cramps, but I didn't think too much about it. I tossed and turned all night and told myself it was just the normal pregnancy symptoms. The next morning when I woke up, I discovered that I was hemorrhaging in my sleep and had to get to the emergency department right away. I was told I was having false labor because it was too soon for the babies to be delivered and the nurses put a catheter in me because I was being transported to a larger medical center that was better equipped to deal with my urgent pregnancy situation.

A few hours later when I arrived at the Edmonton hospital, the medical team addressed my ongoing hemorrhaging immediately. The Gynecologist was determined to keep these babies inside me until week 36. I was given steroid injections to help the lung development of the babies. There was so much going on at the hospital: heartbeat monitors and machines around me constantly beeping and making a lot of noise. I recall that the days were long, but I was so grateful to have people around to take my mind away from all the stress and fear. I missed my immediate family dearly as they were back home which was approximately 2 ½ hours away.

Since my admittance, I hemorrhaged three times and the medication was not helping me anymore. This was it, I was told. That night, on April 12th, the babies would have to be taken out of me. It's getting too risky and it was a life or death matter for all three of us. My family all waited anxiously to hear the ongoing reports. I was wheeled down to the surgery room as it had now become the only way for the babies to come into this world – through emergency cesarean.

The surgery room had a medical team for each baby and me. I recall being scared to death, but I trusted that God would still take care of us all. I kept on praying and praying.

"Mrs. Macaulay," I heard a nurse say, "I'm just here to take your vital signs." I felt lucid like it was late at night and was confused. So, I asked the attending nurse where were my babies were, and were they healthy? The nurse confirmed that they were born and that we now had a champagne family – two healthy babies. One boy and one girl.

In the morning, I visited the NICU. They were both so perfect and tiny. My daughter was born first, weighing 5 pounds 3 ounces. My son was second and he was 4 pounds 11 ounces. The babies were very big and healthy for 33 weeks. I didn't have the babies on Dad's birthday, but I felt his presence with me during all the excitement and times of chaos. My dad is my angel; he is always with us.

Today my twins are eighteen years old – my double blessings. I am forever thankful that I never gave up on my self-worth. I constantly encouraged myself to keep trying, and the reward was remarkable.

I hope I have inspired you through your broken trust. Know that God is here, and He only gives us what we can handle. Believe in your hope and faith! The world awaits you. Live your dreams. Thank you for many blessings, Lord.

Double blessings to all of you!

Lolita Macaulay, aka Lou Malo, is a graduate of St. Albert Catholic High School. She is an entrepreneur who is currently living with her beautiful family in Bonneville, Alberta, Canada. Lou enjoys writing and is a co-author in this Best-Selling anthology. She is also spotlighted in an upcoming edition of LWL Lifestyle magazine. Lou has an amazing personality, as well as a genuine and sincere love for all.

Broken Trust

Chapter Twenty-Nine

A Journey Within

WRITTEN BY: KESHA CHRISTIE

Life is a tricky production and this live-action drama has no rehearsal. For me, it meant mixed up scenes, forgotten lines, and missed intermissions. I would have liked a commercial break or two to catch a breath or even edit a scene, but it is LIVE and it's life.

One of the advantages of life is that no matter what you are going through, there are always lessons in all of it. There is one lesson that I wish I had taken seriously as a young woman – the notion that everything begins with a decision. Whether it be good, bad, or indifferent, we always have a choice and it's important to remember that doing nothing is also a choice.

I am not a person who loves looking in the rear-view mirror of this journey, but there are times when it is necessary to glance back at where you have been to see how far you have come. Confession time: I have come a long way. To see me today, you could not imagine the baggage I carried and most of it was self-inflicted.

I was lost and disoriented on my path with no sense of direction! The chaos in my head showed up in my life in so many ways that I denied both myself and everyone around me. I resented the woman in the mirror because every time I saw her, I looked less and less like the woman I wanted to be. And facing her meant I had to admit that I was avoiding being honest with myself about my confidence, my size, and my feelings. I felt abandoned. The shame of it caused me to internalize guilt, anger, and loneliness. I spent too much of my time searching for approval outside of myself and it often resulted in disappointment or upset for swallowing my voice and not speaking up. I lived life on autopilot and completed tasks like a do-to list, but never enjoyed the life I had been given. Instead, I stayed guarded and held myself hostage by my "past." At the time, it made me reluctant to explore what the future held for me. I simply existed. Deep down, I knew that existing was not enough, but it was all that I permitted myself to have. My professional world had its own challenges, but I could go with the flow. As for my personal life, my best option was to feel nothing. Loneliness was crippling and my feelings of unworthiness clouded my judgment. Emotions were so confusing, partly due to my many unresolved issues and the need for love and acceptance. I was an overthinker. My family would say that I would stress myself out. I had all symptoms of anxiety but in the 1990s, that was not a word used in my culture. Food became my comfort because it never rejected me and tasted so good. I remember a time when my younger sister's father, who had been MIA most of her life, mentioned in casual conversation that I always had an issue with weight. I thought to myself, "You don't know me like that." Yet, again I said nothing, and it haunted me for a long time. One more thing I had to think about that added to my insecurity.

I believed certain truths about myself, like my body shape, commanded attention from the neck down. My skin tone made me a different kind of beautiful, yet I was so intelligent that I could pen poetry like no one else. But I kept my voice strictly to paper. I believed that no one would listen to a hypocrite who had great ideas but was too afraid to act on them. That was why apart from my many notebooks, I keep my views to myself. I was awkward in my own skin. During this season, the people I was the most vulnerable with tended to drift away. Maybe I was not enough or perhaps too much of something. I wanted love and security badly, but it eluded me amidst all my efforts. Somehow, I always ended up alone or betrayed. The labels I wore read "Easy," "Naïve," and "Co-dependent." Instead of creating my own self-image, I relied on others and believed their options of me, completely. I became an expert at swallowing my emotions and giving the "right" answers. I spent more and more time in my head imagining scenarios where one would think that everything should be sunshine and roses. In my mind's eye, people were out to get me for one reason or another and I had to be on guard. I was a victim of circumstance and excelled at pushing people away; at least creating enough distance that they would lose interest in my friendship. There is a quote that says, "Those who think they can and those who think they can't are both right." I made sure I was always right, which would have been amazing if I were portraying my best self. Instead, I made myself miserable. I built a wall of protection, but it did little good when the enemy was within.

At this point, not all my adult decisions were winners: I moved too fast, left home too early, and created self-isolation instead of emancipation. I rushed out into the world on my own to find brokenness and heartache. I could not understand why my reality looked nothing like the images I saw on TV or the scenarios I read about. Barely an adult going to school, work, boyfriend, and no family to share it with. I craved connection – anything to make me feel alive. I clung tightly to people who needed their own space. I didn't notice until they pulled away. Life was tough but livable if only I could see things differently. I thought about suicide, but it would have been too much work for me and those I left behind. I figured my life was enough of a burden.

During those college years, I disrupted my stability and moved so frequently that I stopped unpacking. My phone number changed so many times that friends and family stopped writing it down. I couldn't pay my bills on time, much less rent. I needed a lifeline to ground me and bring back to some of the stability that I had at home.

When my first child was born, I prayed that the madness would cease and allow me to provide a stable home for her. My mindset changed from being all about me and what I needed to make sure this little girl had everything she needed either by finance or by hand. I remember being so broke that I could not buy a scarf for my daughter. This was long before the popular dollar stores existed. The daycare politely informed me that without a scarf, my child would not be admitted. After I shook off the embarrassment, I made that sucker by hand and she was admitted that next day. This is the first time I saw the grit that would get me through the upcoming trials ahead. Until this point, I saw glimpses of my future self but nothing that I could hold on to. When my daughter was born, I realized my determination to succeed and I refused to fail. I had no way of knowing that this random skill would change my life.

Before this epiphany, I would hit a few speed bumps and experienced some evasive maneuvers that I needed to overcome: walking away from a long-term relationship, discovering childhood traumas and all the brokenness that followed, and embracing a new relationship that felt more like trial by fire. I would do almost anything for love but learned quickly that love did not love me. Truthfully, I did not love myself so how could I expect that from a partner. I learned how diamonds are made through firsthand experience. I withstood the pressure and found myself in the process. Amidst the arguing, put-downs, emotional and physical stress, I faced the woman in the mirror and told her off. I no longer wanted to be her. I decided deserved better.

One of my favorite quotes is from T. D. Jakes. He says there is nothing more powerful than a changed mind. I am living proof of this! We all reach a point in our lives when we decide that today is the day for change, and act on it. I no longer wanted to feel sorry for myself. I chose to move. No more self-doubt, no more hiding. I will open my mouth and share my voice. I decided to show up for myself every day.

Cold truth is, I did not wake up the next day as the woman I wanted to be. I knew who I did not want to be and had to recommit becoming the best version of self, daily. Much like my transformational weight loss journey, I made little changes regularly until they became a lifestyle. I did not allow the options of others to distract me. Knowing that others cannot see your dreams and goals the way you do, so there is no way you can expect them to understand your journey until the results are in. The more I showed up for myself, the more it reflected on my relationship.

There were a few bridges that I needed to cross. I realized quickly that to make a permanent change, I needed to get to the root of some things, and I could not do that on my own. I sought out counseling and had some real conversations about past hurts showing up in my current situation. I learned a lot about myself; most importantly I learned about forgiveness. A funny thing about forgiveness is it has nothing to do with the other person and everything to do with you, especially when you are learning to forgive yourself. Through forgiveness, I was able to repair relationships with family and friends. It also gave me the courage to leave and let be those relationships that did not serve me. I realized there was no need to be angry at myself or the other person. They acted simply based on what they knew at the time: their hurts, their experiences, and yes, even their joy. I know now that I am vibrating on a much higher frequency and decided that there was no need to revisit – my closure is in the lesson I gained from the experience.

Healing in a process and it has many steps. Counseling was the first step and continues today in various forms. I am not a finished product, nor will I ever be. With growth comes change. Sometimes we all need a little help processing all of it. The next phase of my healing was to regain the things that I had deprived myself of. That meant increasing my confidence and unleashing my voice. To do that, I had to get out of my own way and burst through my comfort zone. A television celebrity wrote a book that I read, loved it, and decided to try it.

I started volunteering, joining groups, and began meeting some amazing women who are elite in their fields. I listened to their stories and shared in their triumphs. These women revealed their vulnerability and proof to be stronger than their circumstances. They were socially conscious and started businesses to help others and fill a need. I saw my generous nature rise-up and pay attention. I started to see the small degrees of connection that I shared with women I did not think I knew personally. I felt inspired and connected to these women who knew family and friends who are dear to me. This experience made sliding into my new sense of self much easier than I expected. Standing in the middle of all this positive energy, I had a moment where I felt like an imposter in this circle. I had no business of my own; I was new to women's empowerment and lifting each other up instead of standing on the sidelines. "What if someone figures out that I do not belong here?" I finally found a group of women who were just as authentic as I aspired to be. I could be as honest as I desired without judgment. I made the decision to belong! The love I was seeking outside of myself – I turned inward. Filling my head with motivation speeches, quotes, and allowing myself to dream were big starters. I realized that it is okay for me to find my own way in my own time, God's time. Somewhere in the mix, my youngest daughter was born, and I promised to be the woman she could be proud of.

To do that, I needed to know myself. It became the most important journey I could take – exploring the multiple layers that make up who you are is a class in mastery. Journaling is an amazing way to listen to your heart and trust your intuition again. It gives you the capacity to grow on a level you may not have expected and the ability to see how far you have come. When I started journaling, I did not have much to write about. Then I started to write about the things I was grateful for. Soon, my journal held answers to questions I would ask a partner, quotes, along with my goals and dreams. I used my journal to get into my head, in a good way. I used the power of journaling to trust myself again. As the African proverb says, "If there is no enemy within, the enemy outside can do no harm." Journaling helped me to quiet the enemy.

Vision boarding had a huge impact on my year of "Yes." I am a visual person and vision boarding helped me to see my dreams both consciously and unconsciously. I completed my first vision board on New Years' Eve about four years ago using four magazines. I mostly wrote words, quotes, along with some pictures, and focused my energy on how I would feel when I accomplished my goals. Looking back at that board and all the subsequent vision boards, I see all that I have accomplished and am destined to achieve. I could never have imagined life this way.

The woman I see in the mirror now is no longer hiding behind her weight or crippled with self-doubt. She is confident with a clear purpose. She is a warrior for women and desires to add value to her community. This woman has done great things, like becoming the president of a Toastmasters Club, starting my business from the ground up, becoming a cultural curator, organizing community event(s), performing on stage in front of hundreds of people, teaching youth leadership, and becoming a podcaster. She is a writer and author, and every time I see this fearless woman in the mirror, I ask her, "What's next? What's next for you?" Don't remain broken but be that fearless leader.

Kesha Christie is an animated Afro-Caribbean storyteller and Motivational Speaker. She volunteers for several community-based organizations, campaigning as a warrior for women in the areas of mental and physical health. As a cultural curator and storyteller, Kesha is the founder of Talkin' Tales, a platform that promotes oral traditions and preserving culture through various performances and vendor marketplace. The event is called *Talkin' Tales: A Celebration of Afro-Caribbean Heritage*. Kesha has recently added podcaster to her accomplishments and can be found on Spotify, Google Podcast, and other platforms. Kesha also inspires youth, ages 14 – 17, through the Toastmasters Youth Leadership Program.

Instagram: speaklife2inspire

Facebook: Kesha Christie

Twitter: km_christie

Website: http://www.talkintales.ca

Broken Trust

Chapter Thirty

The Girl Who Found Peace

WRITTEN BY: IDIAKHOSA ONAIWU-OSAYI

I lay still in my bed with my mind wavering to the ticking of my night clock and I faded. I sat on top of a mountain and waddled my feet in the clouds. The Lord sat beside me and said, "You can tell me, child." "I am scared, Father," I replied as the tears I had held in for so long spilled down my cheeks. "What are you scared of?" "I don't know, of failing? Of falling?"

"Hmmm, when you fell as a child and had no one to lend you a hand, what did you do?" "Well, I...I placed my hand on the ground and pushed myself up. Why?"

"Failure is the level ground that helps you push yourself on the path of success," the Lord said while ruffling my hair and patting my back. I realized that I stopped climbing my mountain for fear that I would fall, and I stopped trying to succeed for fear that I would fail. "Thank you!" I screamed, expecting an echo in return but instead, I heard a resounding chuckle that felt so far yet, so close that it wrapped me up in its warmth.

With a smile on my face, I awoke. The feeling of happiness was charging my body, and I decided today was my day. I was going to feel everything. Every single emotion belonged to me, so I didn't have to be scared of them. Today I was going to begin my wellness routine which would then become a habit.

I started my day with a little yoga to give my mind the freedom it needed. Stretching the body early in the morning prepared my mind for the day ahead and also gave balance to my body and mind. And for a power boost, nothing beat a great shower after a morning of exhilarating yoga. I waltzed out of the bathroom freshly showered and sang a song as off-key as I possibly could because there was nothing better than singing a song and not knowing the lyrics while feeling like you're the queen of the world. My bathroom robe swept around my feet while I danced to the kitchen to have a light breakfast and if there's anything about this girl (namely me), her definition of a light breakfast is a bowl of cereal in one hand, a spoon in the other, legs crossed above the countertop (which I must say is not at all hygienic), and listening to the radio playing the latest ranking songs.

I wanted to look good for the day. I mean, it was autumn and a girl has always got to be prepared for the chilly autumn breeze with...the right coat, of course. Autumn might mean a pop of color in the fashion world, but that was a little too bold for me. Denim overalls, a brown tee, heels? No, a black converse and camel-colored coat were just right. I arranged the fly of my coat while I stared into the mirror and said to myself, "Today I will actively pursue my wellness. I will experience happiness and open my eyes to see the beauty in the world." It is my choice to enjoy each passing moment. Today was in my hands and it was left to me to decide how it played out. But then, there was a subconscious part of my brain that had constantly stopped me from doing this earlier, saying, "What if you find out you do not have a choice to make? What if you don't get to achieve this peace of mind that you are yearning for?" This inner voice taunted me, mocked me, laughed at me, and spat in my face, daring me to begin anew and realize how much of a failure I would be. The fear I had faced since I embarked on this journey of wanting to find who I was resurfaced, ridiculing me to pieces by questioning, "What if you fail? What will you do then?" But I replied, saying, "Oh, you have forgotten the most important question of all. What if I do succeed? What will YOU do then?" How happy it made me silence the part of myself that had made me stop trying to make myself happy in hopes that I would not achieve happiness. What I wanted was to get away from all the hustling and bustling, all the hurrying. I just wanted the noise to stop. Lately, that is all I could think of. The world was just too loud for my soul to handle. "What does it have to take for my world to quiet down? Moving to the countryside or living on a farm? No, none of these will do," I said as I stared into the mirror again. "I can find peace and quiet in my current life by changing my perspective on my day-to-day activities. "My well-being is in my hands," I reminded myself while I belted my coat.

I stepped onto my balcony and stared at the used bicycle I had bought on impulse when I had first thought of doing this wellness thing. We all know some plans fall through, but this time I would seize the day – not just this day, but every other day going forward. I checked to see if the bicycle was still functioning and praise be to God, it still worked. I never really got to take a ride on it after buying it. It had been laying on my balcony looking like something out of a vintage story, abandoned by the one person who thought they could treasure it. With this notion in mind, I felt sorry for the bicycle and mad at myself for never taking the time out of my busy days to actually ride on something so beautiful. I also felt sorry for the beautiful bike for being bought by someone who couldn't enjoy the simple luxury of riding a bicycle and feeling the freedom that came with it. There was a little something on the handle and as I pressed, it made that tingly bell sound that comes from children's bicycles when I pass by the park. "Oh my," I laughed heartily while I continuously pressed the bell to my heart's content. It was so much fun that it made me feel childlike again. You know, those little things that remind one of what it feels like to see the world through the lens of a child. That's the best way to appreciate the world – with the heart of a child and the mind of an adult. I took the bicycle outside, sat atop it, and started riding. It felt so good to do this again after so many years had passed. I smiled merrily knowing this was what it felt like to be free with the wind in your hair and the smell of spices in the air.

The smell of spices only reminded me that I was very close to the café. I parked my bicycle and was already preparing in my head what I wanted to have. "Oh, this was going to be good." I stepped into the restaurant and the jingle announced my presence. "Hi there." I greeted the lady at the counter with a wave. I'm a regular customer because this is my weekly stop on my way to and from the publishing house. I made my order for a large cup of iced coffee and some Scottish shortbread cookies. If this wasn't the perfect combo, I don't know what is. You might be asking, why iced coffee this season? It's simple. I am not a seasonal girl, so I am not into all those pumpkin spice and peppermint things, but a cup of iced coffee on this day seemed so perfect. And if there are no shortbread cookies on the side, the question isn't, "Why should there be?" It's, "Why shouldn't there be?" I completed the articles that needed my urgent attention and munched at the same time. Eating stimulates my brain and food just makes me happy – I don't know why. I crossed out article completion and editing off my to-do list. Next on my list was crochet.

Crochet is the one hobby I have (aside from anything that has to do with food) that gives me so much joy and confidence. I picked up my crochet hook, brought out my printed crochet pattern, and started working on the piece. This reminds me that I need to stock up on cotton and velvet yarn. They are my favorites at the moment – not together, just separately. The thing with crochet is that you may not realize but the day goes by very fast while the action continues. I looked at the piece in my hand and it reminded me so much of how life was woven and connected and resulted in something so beautiful just like the piece I held in my hands. I am a fine print of woven experiences and that is what life really is. "Um, we are about to close, Pearl," the waitress reminded me. "It's 7 p.m. already? My God, how time flies. The coffee and cookies were good as always. I don't know how you do it," I said and of course she laughed because this was the first time I had complimented her homemade cookies and topnotch barrister skills. It felt like it was time to go home, but it wasn't because the day hadn't come to an end for me yet. Last stop was the old bookstore a few blocks away.

The bookstore was in the basement of a building that looked like it fell out of the Victorian era pages. The top was used as a Papeterie, or stationery store, and they were both run by a husband and wife who I had come to know through my search for new stationaries. The bookstore was more of a bonus to visiting the Papeterie. Stepping into the bookstore felt otherworldly. I hadn't been there in a long while and I sure missed it. There's something about the smell of old and new books in one place that calls to a reader's soul and a writer's heart. I didn't know which to pick: old books that looked raggedy and told the tales of the hands that had touched it through the times, or new books waiting to be explored by an adventurer and delved into by the wanderer in me. I picked both; by both, I mean old and new books which amounted to, let's say, sixteen books altogether. The fact that I had unread books at home didn't change my mind about buying them. I bought them all!

It was a tough decision to make – whether to sit in the rocking chair in the bookstore (it is placed there for those who would love to read while being surrounded by books) or go to the park across and read under the night lit stars. I remember that rocking chair had been with me on many of my worst days, rocking me back and forth and reminding me of the comfort found only in the pages of a book. The days I had no idea on what to write in my articles, or the days when writer's block visited me often, and even when I almost lost my job, I always came to this bookstore, bought a book, and dove into it immediately with a cup of tea in my hand which the owner always gave to me. That woman had enough tea to serve the whole country and she keeps stocking up on more. I tell her that she's a tea collector, but she doesn't believe me.

I chose the latter as I had never been to the park in the evening and curiosity ate its way up to heart like it always did and I sure gave in, as always.

I walked over to the park after paying for the books and once again, forgot to collect the receipt. I still don't know why I do that, but I never collect the receipts for what I buy. It's become a habit and I don't know if it's something that needs to be broken or not. On my way out of the bookstore, I saw the other owner closing up the Papeterie and it didn't take him long to recognize me, though he keeps reminding me of how he is; an old man who doesn't see clearly these days. I said hello and we talked briefly even though we had a lot to talk about. If I stayed too long, we might end up standing in the chilly breeze with all of his travel stories. He never gets tired of telling them to me. Even though some of the stories are repeated, I do not have the heart to tell him I've already heard those stories. And as always, he asked how I am and if everything's okay as he hasn't seen me in the past three months. I could tell he was concerned about me by the look in his eyes. He knew I visited the bookstore too often to be absent for three months, but it just wasn't the right time to tell him I had been on a personal journey trying to figure it all out. Even though I had a lot to say, I kept quiet and he understood. It always surprised me how he could always understand what I wanted to say even when I was silent. And I was more surprised by how someone who wasn't in any way related to me could care so much about me.

The stars looked so beautiful. I had never taken the time to gaze at them before. I laughed at myself for trying to figure out the constellations, knowing fully well I was getting it all wrong. I wonder what people would say about a grown lady on a swing at this time of the day. Who cares what they have to say! I had never been this peaceful before. I recounted the whole day in my head and it all just seemed to come to me. I'd had everything that gives me peace right by my side all along: the bicycle, the café, food, my crochet, the bookstore, the rocking chair, old and new books, the Papeterie owners, the stars right then in the park, and lastly...me. They had all been waiting for me to make the choice to find them, to know them. I had been to this park before, but never in my wildest dreams had I tried the swing or looked above my head to search for constellations. How amazing to realize that such a luxurious life already existed, and that happiness was in the most unexpected place.

I opened my bag and tried to choose a book from my new purchase. I picked the one about the girl who found peace. I stayed in the park for some time. I called it a night picnic even though I had no food with me. I hadn't used any electronics all day, but it seemed like the right time to put on my headphones. With the music dancing in my ears and the stars gazing from above, I opened the first page and dove into the world of the girl who found peace.

Idiakhosa Onaiwu-Osayi is a sixteen-year-old high school student at St. Mother Teresa Catholic Academy. She has a passion for writing, reading, crocheting, and cooking. Idiakhosa believes food brings people together, mental health isn't a topic to be scared of, and taking time to heal is very important. She appreciates taking time to reflect and destress as this helps her write better stories, and also volunteers in her spare time with organizations that work to protect and validate the voices of the youth. Idiakhosa hopes her writing can encourage people to keep pushing on and see the beauty in the world.

Email: pearlzcraft@gmail.com

Instagram handle: pearlzcraft

Conclusion

How do you deal with the conflicts that are directly related to the emotions you felt from your trust that has been broken? Your past can influence you in various ways as you journey into your future with the brokenness of your yesterdays. Sometimes, because trust has been shattered, people are afraid and often feel guilty and ashamed of their circumstances. They can become withdrawn and often closed-minded. They can even fall out of love with themselves and with others around them. Their choices become limited as they slowly lose their voices and eventually themselves to a bleeding world of brokenness, pain, heartaches, and depression. The year 2020 has been a very challenging time with a worldwide pandemic. We were all forced into transformation. For some individuals, it was great liberation, but for others, it was nothing but devastation. Either way, it created changes in us.

It is very important to change your world from the inside out, bring an end to all that has been broken in your life. Thriving to overcome the disbeliefs you have can be hard, but you can find your peace through persistence and self-reliance. As mentioned in the chapter entitled *"There is Purpose in Your Pain,"* although our society might be broken, you can indeed become unbroken within yourself spiritually. Yes, silence can be golden, but never be afraid to speak up about the things that matter in life. Sometimes, "Enough, is just Enough." As you begin to live your truth, everything will fall into place.

However, to fix your broken pieces, you first have to know what has been broken, whether it is in an entangled relationship, financial affairs, or in your wellness. At times, it could even be in your environmental elements like that of Covid-19, the worldwide pandemic, where we all masked and locked ourselves away from others to keep safe. Regardless, it's also important to understand that not everything in our lives needs fixing. Permit yourself to observe and embrace the beauty of your authentic self. Feel free to be that Purple Warrior or the brave soldier that you are.

Release your mind to focus on healing and have that sense of peace in your heart. Trust yourself and remember that your courage will turn your dreams into reality. As for me, I told myself I will...and I did.

Believe in yourself and focus on the positive things that are present in your life. Do not attach yourself to the negative emotional feelings. Never break your own trust. Follow your mind. I believe that the first thoughts that come to mind are usually the right ones. Believe what you are feeling and what your body is trying to tell you. Your spiritual vibration will always guide you. Become aware of your vibrations by knowing yourself.

Now that you have finished reading this anthology, it is my wish that you will use this book as a reference or a friendly companion whenever you need encouragement. I am hoping that it will help you to focus on that positive aspect and the healing part of your life. I trust that each chapter will help you to regain control and to take charge of your overall well-being. Just like each of my co-authors and myself, I do hope you will be able to position yourself to be the voice of the voiceless and for others who have been lost in the darkness and the brokenness of this universe.

The contents of this book have been a blessing to me, and I trust that they have touched you in a special way as you have read it.

Remember that sometimes life happens, and when it does, we all need a bit of inspiration and motivation to help us move forward. You are not alone. Now that you have read each chapter, if you have resonated with any of these stories, feel free to revisit the chapters. If you know of an individual who might benefit from reading this anthology, invite them to get a copy as well.

You can also look out for my next upcoming anthology, as well as my solo book entitled *Broken & Empowered – How I Found My Wings*.

You may contact me by email at rmarie1695@gmail.com, Facebook messenger, or on Instagram@ rose.marie.young

You can also contact my publisher, Anita Sechesky, at LWL Publishing House via her email: lwlclienthelp@gmail.com

Let's Stay Connected.

WRITE YOUR BOOK WITH US!

www.lwlpublishinghouse.com

lwlclienthelp@gmail.com

Manufactured by Amazon.ca
Bolton, ON

17799560R00149